FOLLOW THE LIVING PROPHETS

FOLLOW THE LIVING PROPHETS

BRENT L. TOP
LARRY E. DAHL
WALTER D. BOWEN

BOOKCRAFT
SALT LAKE CITY, UTAH

Library of Congress Catalog Card Number: 92-76025
ISBN 0-88494-869-2

First Printing, 1993

Printed in the United States of America

Believe in the Lord your God,
so shall ye be established;
believe his prophets,
so shall ye prosper.

—2 Chronicles 20:20

Contents

Appendixes

Preface

The scriptures are replete with warnings and admonitions to the Saints of the last days about the need not only to know and understand the revealed roles of the prophets but also, and even more important, to increase our responsiveness to them.

Over the past several years, while we have taught a religion course at Brigham Young University entitled "Teachings of the Living Prophets," we have witnessed lives changed, hearts softened, and personal faithfulness and obedience increased through the concepts and doctrines taught in the course. And we have felt an increasing need for these teachings to be made available to the broader Church audience.

In this book we have attempted to teach those principles that will inform and inspire the reader. We desire to increase doctrinal knowledge and faith in and loyalty to those whom the Lord has called and authorized to lead his church. In organizing the ideas contained herein we have selected many quotations from the Brethren that teach and testify of these principles of salvation, for it is more important to us that the reader know what *they* teach and feel than what *we* think about the matter. In addition to the many scripture references and quotations from General Authorities, we have included an appendix containing the entire text of several classic addresses by leaders of the Church that teach the role of living prophets and the relationship and responsibilities the Latter-day Saints have to them.

We wish to extend our appreciation to our many colleagues at BYU who have shared ideas with us and provided valuable feedback in the preparation of this book. We also appreciate the thousands of students who have enriched our lives and who through their lives and experiences continually teach us of the great blessings that come to those who earnestly seek to faithfully follow the living prophets.

It is the hope of our hearts that this book will increase each reader's appreciation for the inspired guidance of the living Church by living prophets and instill a renewed determination to be faithful to the covenant to sustain and uphold the Lord's appointed servants. There can be no exaltation without accepting the Lord and surrendering our hearts and souls to him and to his will. In turn, there can be no total surrender to the Lord without accepting and following his prophets. "For he that receiveth my servants," declared the Lord "receiveth me" (D&C 84:36). To the fulfillment of that ultimate objective this book is directed.

We do not lack a prophet; what we lack is a listening ear by the people and a determination to live as God has commanded. That is all we need.

—J. Reuben Clark, Jr., general conference, October 1948

CHAPTER 1

A Listening Ear

Following living prophets is a critical factor in nurturing our current spiritual health and in attaining exaltation. To hearken to them is to hearken to the Lord; to ignore or reject them is to reject the Lord. To the infant restored Church in November 1831 the Lord revealed: "What I the Lord have spoken, I have spoken, and I excuse not myself; and though the heavens and the earth pass away, my word shall not pass away, but shall all be fulfilled, whether by mine own voice or by the voice of my servants, it is the same" (D&C 1:38).

Earlier in the same revelation the Lord lamented the attitude of spiritual self-sufficiency of many in the world and declared the sad consequence of their stubborn determination to go their own way.

> And the arm of the Lord shall be revealed; and the day cometh that they who will not hear the voice of the Lord, neither the voice of his servants, neither give heed to the words of the prophets and apostles, shall be cut off from among the people;
>
> For they have strayed from mine ordinances, and have broken mine everlasting covenant;

They seek not the Lord to establish his righteousness, but every man walketh in his own way, and after the image of his own god, whose image is in the likeness of the world, and whose substance is that of an idol, which waxeth old and shall perish in Babylon, even Babylon the great, which shall fall (D&C 1:14–16; see also D&C 84:87–97; 124:46).

In contrast to being "cut off from among the people" for not giving heed to the Lord's servants there are promised blessings to those who "receive" them. During his personal ministry to the Nephites the Lord said, "Blessed are ye if ye shall give heed unto the words of these twelve whom I have chosen from among you to minister unto you, and to be your servants; and unto them I have given power" (3 Nephi 12:1). In our own dispensation, on the day the Church was organized, the Lord instructed the Saints to "give heed unto all (the) words and commandments" which the Prophet Joseph Smith would give, as if those words came from the Lord's own mouth. The promised blessing for so doing was that "the gates of hell shall not prevail against you; yea, and the Lord God will disperse the powers of darkness from before you, and cause the heavens to shake for your good" (see D&C 21:4–6). And as part of the blessings associated with "the oath and covenant which belongeth to the priesthood" the Lord declared, "For he that receiveth my servants receiveth me; and he that receiveth me receiveth my Father; and he that receiveth my Father receiveth my Father's kingdom; therefore all that my Father hath shall be given unto him" (D&C 84:36–38).

Learning How to Be Governed

With such great blessings promised the obedient, why would anyone resist following those the Lord has appointed to represent him and speak his mind and will? The Prophet Joseph Smith said, "But alas, it is in vain to warn and give precepts, for all men are naturally disposed to walk in their own paths as they are pointed out by their own fingers, and are not willing to consider and walk in the path which is pointed out by another, saying, This is the way, walk ye in it, although he should be an unerring director, and the Lord his God sent him" (*Teachings of the Prophet Joseph Smith*, pp. 26–27, hereafter cited as *Teachings*). Overcoming this natural tendency to resist counsel, even God's counsel, is admittedly a challenge. "It is also necessary," taught President John Taylor, "that we should learn the principles of order and government, but we must first learn how to govern ourselves, then how to govern our families, and lastly, learn how to be governed, which is the most difficult lesson that can be set us—it is infinitely worse than governing others" (*The Gospel Kingdom*, pp. 17–18).

The truth is, we need help in learning how to be governed. We must experience "a mighty change of heart." We must be "changed from [our] carnal and fallen state, to a state of righteousness," becoming "new creatures." We must be "born again"—"spiritually . . . born of God." (See Mosiah 27:25–26; Alma 5:12–26.) The agent of that change is the Holy Ghost. And we must "yield" to the enticings of the Holy Ghost if we are to "put off the natural man," who is an "enemy to God," and willingly respond to the governance of God (see Mosiah 3:19). Unless we enjoy the Spirit of God we cannot understand the things of God; in fact, the things of God will appear foolish to us (see 1 Corinthians 2:11–16).

Part of this conversion from a "natural" to a "spiritual" perspective consists in knowing by revelation to our own minds and hearts that the leaders of the Church are truly God's appointed spokesmen, and that the Lord expects us to give careful heed to their teachings. President Harold B. Lee spoke of the importance of obtaining such a testimony.

Now I want to impress this upon you. Someone has said it this way, and I believe it to be absolutely true: "That person is not truly converted until he sees the power of God resting upon the leaders of this church, and until it goes down into his heart like fire." Until the members of this church have that conviction that they are being led in the right way, and they have a conviction that these men of God are men who are inspired and have been properly appointed by the hand of God, they are not truly converted. (In Conference Report, April 1972, p. 118.)

Blind Obedience or Faith Obedience?

Does the Lord expect us to render blind obedience to the leaders of the Church? No. He expects enlightened or faith obedience. There is a world of difference between the two. The essence of the difference and what is required of us in order to achieve the proper obedience is captured in the following prophetic statements:

> Were your faith concentrated upon the proper object, your confidence unshaken, your lives pure and holy, every one fulfilling the duty of his or her calling according to the priesthood and capacity bestowed upon you, you would be filled with the Holy Ghost, and it would be as impossible for any man to deceive and to lead you to destruction as for a feather to remain unconsumed in the midst of intense heat.
>
> I am more afraid that this people have so much confidence in their leaders that they will not inquire for themselves of God whether they are being led by him. I am fearful they settle down in a state of blind security, trusting their eternal destiny in the hands of their leaders with a reckless confidence that in itself would thwart the purposes of God in their salvation, and weaken that influence they could give their leaders if they know for themselves by the revelations of Jesus Christ that they are led in the right way. Let every man and woman know by the whisperings of the Spirit of God to themselves whether their leaders are walking in the way the Lord dictates or not. (Harold B. Lee, quoting Brigham Young, in Conference Report, October 1950, p. 130.)

> To obey! To hearken! What a difficult requirement! Often we hear: "Nobody can tell me what clothes to wear, what I shall eat or drink. No one can outline my Sabbaths, appropriate my earnings, nor in any way limit my personal freedoms! I do as I please! I give no *blind obedience!*"
>
> Blind obedience! How little they understand! The Lord said through Joseph Smith: "Whatever God requires is right, no matter what it is, although we may not see the reason thereof until long after the events transpire." (*Scrapbook of Mormon Literature*, vol. 2, p. 173.)

When men obey commands of a creator, it is not blind obedience. How different is the cowering of a subject to his totalitarian monarch and the dignified, willing obedience one gives to his God. The dictator is ambitious, selfish, and has ulterior motives. God's every command is righteous, every directive purposeful, and all for the good of the governed. The first may be blind obedience, but the latter is certainly faith obedience. (Spencer W. Kimball, in Conference Report, October 1954, pp. 51–52.)

The difference between blind obedience and faith obedience, then, is knowing for oneself that the instruction is from God, and that God will not give any directives that are not right, that are not designed to bless our lives. That is not to say that all such instruction is easy to obey, or even that it will always appear "reasonable" to us, given our current level of understanding. Part of the business of this mortal life is to "prove" us—to see if we will "do all things whatsoever the Lord [our] God shall command [us]" (Abraham 3:25). This testing period involves seeming contradictions which truly challenge the depth of our faith in and commitment to the Savior and our Father in Heaven. Knowing that, and also knowing that God speaks through his appointed servants to guide his children safely through this mortal maze, it makes abundant sense to follow those servants. That course is not blind obedience but faith obedience.

Admittedly, all instruction, counsel, commandments, even from God, require a certain amount of sorting out as they are applied to our individual circumstances. And common sense as well as a committed heart is an important factor in that enterprise. The use of this reality to rationalize ignoring or rejecting living prophets is not uncommon, however. We know and God knows when we are thus engaged. Ultimately all will be held strictly accountable for their decisions, interpretations, and applications regarding the teachings of the Lord's servants.

The Lord desires our faithful obedience—obeying because we have a trust in his purposes and a testimony that we are led by living prophets. There is, however, an even higher form of obedience which, though it is spiritually strenuous, yields greater blessings and personal freedom. "It is not alone sufficient for us as Latter-day Saints to follow our leaders and to accept their counsel," President Harold B. Lee counseled, "but we have the greater obligation to gain for ourselves the unshakable testimony of the divine appointment of these men and the witness that what they have told us is the will of our Heavenly Father" (in Conference Report, October 1950, p. 130).

Rendering intelligent obedience to living prophets requires us to study and struggle, ponder and pray concerning the counsels and teachings that proceed from them. It is no easy task, and in large measure it rightfully shifts the responsibility from them to us. Prayerfully pleading with the Lord to bless us with a witness of the Spirit concerning their counsel yields a blessing of *knowing* the will of God for us individually. This knowledge makes easier our obedience to even difficult requirements. Without such a liberating witness one may be left to "kick against the pricks"—to either reject the prophetic words outright or obey them grudgingly and with a critical and murmuring heart.

Blind obedience is constrictive; but enlightened, faithful, intelligent obedience liberates the soul and brings abundant blessings. An experience in the life of President Marion G. Romney illustrates this principle. While serving earlier in a political office, he was faced with a painful, personal dilemma when the leaders of the Church in a tersely worded editorial denounced the trends of the political administration then in power. "When I read that editorial," Brother Romney said, "I knew what I should do—but that wasn't enough. I knew that I must feel right about following the counsel of the Church leaders and know that they were right. That took a whole night on my knees to accomplish." (*Improvement Era*, October 1962, p. 742.) On other occasions, President Romney gave this powerful testimony that serves as a guide for each of us as we seek to "intelligently obey" the Lord's anointed today:

> Those, and I testify to this out of my own experience, who will through mighty prayer and earnest study inform themselves as to what these living prophets say, and act upon it, will be visited by the Spirit of the Lord and know by the spirit of revelation that they speak the mind and will of the Father (in Conference Report, April 1945, p. 90).

It has been the rule of my life to find out if I could, by listening closely to what they said and by asking the Lord to help me interpret it, what they had in mind for the Latter-day Saints to do and then do it. I am happy to say, not boastfully but gratefully, that I have never hesitated to follow the counsel of the Authorities of the Church even though it crossed my social, professional or political life. (In Conference Report, April 1941, p. 123.)

A Listening Ear

In the October 1948 general conference President J. Reuben Clark, Jr., reminded the Saints and the world that the real lack in the world and in the Church is not a shortage of prophets and prophetic counsel; it is the lack of listening ears on the part of the people.

Some time ago a pamphlet came across my desk which unfortunately I threw away. On the outside page it was stated, "We need a prophet," and as I read it then, and as I think of it now, I think how blind the world is. We have had a prophet, an American prophet, one who spoke our language, one who was imbued with Christian ideals, and that prophet gave us the great righteous principles of which we know and of which the world partly knows; he gave them in our own language over a hundred years ago. These may all be read; we have been teaching them for a century. The trouble with the world is they do not want a prophet teaching righteousness. They want a prophet that will tell them that what they are doing is right, no matter how wrong it may be. . . .

Now our Prophet, Joseph Smith, and the prophets since his time—and there has always been a prophet in this Church, and prophets, and you sustain the brethren here, conference after conference, as prophets, seers, and revelators—the Prophet himself, through the Lord by revelation, gave certain great principles that would save the world if the world would but listen. We do not lack a prophet; what we lack is a listening ear by the people and a determination to live as God has commanded. That is all we need. The way has been made perfectly clear. (In Conference Report, October 1948, pp. 79–80.)

What is true of the world in this regard is true of some in the Church. Even for some who hear the teachings of the prophets there is a tendency to disregard or be selective in applying those teachings. It appears this is not a new posture. Ezekiel, millennia ago, decried the propensity of the people to gather, even excitedly, to hear the word of the Lord, then refuse to obey what was given them.

> Also, thou son of man, the children of thy people still are talking against thee by the walls and in the doors of the houses, and speak one to another, every one to his brother, saying, Come, I pray you, and hear what is the word that cometh forth from the Lord.
>
> And they come unto thee as the people cometh, and they sit before thee as my people, and they hear thy words, but they will not do them: for with their mouth they shew much love, but their heart goeth after their covetousness.
>
> And lo, thou art unto them as a very lovely song of one that hath a pleasant voice, and can play well on an instrument: for they hear thy words, but they do them not.
>
> And when this cometh to pass, (lo, it will come,) then shall they know that a prophet hath been among them. (Ezekiel 33:30–33.)

Of those who follow this pattern it may be said that they are not so much *hard of hearing* as they are *hard of hearkening*. Whether we refuse to hear the teachings of the prophets or we hear but refuse to obey, the result is the same. Great blessings are lost, both now and in eternity. The Lord commissions his prophets to teach his word to the Church and to the world; and he will hold members of the Church and the world accountable for how they respond to that word. In fact, as Moroni testifies, the Lord himself will remind us at the judgment bar that he did indeed proclaim his word to us through prophets:

> And I exhort you to remember these things; for the time

speedily cometh that ye shall know that I lie not, for ye shall see me at the bar of God; and the Lord God will say unto you: Did I not declare my words unto you, which were written by this man . . . ?

I declare these things unto the fulfilling of the prophecies. And behold, they shall proceed forth out of the mouth of the everlasting God; and his word shall hiss forth from generation to generation.

And God shall show unto you, that that which I have written is true. (Moroni 10:27–29.)

Moroni then exhorts his readers to "come unto Christ, and lay hold upon every good gift" (10:30). One of the critical good gifts we have access to is living in a day when prophets and Apostles walk the earth. Our challenge and opportunity is to lend a listening ear to their words and then "do them." As we study and learn what the Lord has stated as the role and responsibilities of the prophets and our relationship to them, our understanding will increase. As our *understanding* of the doctrines increases, so should our *desire* to do the will of the Lord. Understanding coupled with desire empowered by the Spirit of the Lord will enable us to have listening ears and hearkening hearts.

CHAPTER 2

A Living Fountain

The prophet Abraham was privileged to see in vision some of the events of the premortal world. In that vision he learned significant lessons concerning not only the premortal existence but also the fundamental objective for man's mortal existence. He recorded: "And there stood one among them that was like unto God, and he said unto those that were with him: We will go down for there is space there, and we will take of these materials, and we will make an earth whereon these may dwell; and we will prove them herewith, to see if they will do all things whatsoever the Lord their God shall command them" (Abraham 3:24–25).

The Lord has continued to remind his children of this primary purpose of life through the teachings and testimonies of his chosen witnesses—the prophets. From the time of Adam to the present day the message has remained constant: in order to return to our Heavenly Father and partake of eternal life with him we must learn his will and live it. To the Prophet Joseph Smith, the Lord said:

And I give unto you a commandment, that ye shall forsake all evil and cleave unto all good, that ye shall live by every word which proceedeth forth out of the mouth of God.

For he will give unto the faithful line upon line, precept upon precept; and I will try you and prove you herewith.

And whoso layeth down his life in my cause, for my name's sake, shall find it again, even life eternal.

Therefore, be not afraid of your enemies, for I have decreed in my heart, saith the Lord, that I will prove you in all things, whether you will abide in my covenant, even unto death, that you may be found worthy.

For if ye will not abide in my covenant ye are not worthy of me. (D&C 98:11–15.)

Learning and living "by every word which proceedeth forth out of the mouth of God" is a test of our obedience and loyalty to God, because it goes against the mortal tendencies of the natural man. The scriptures and history of the restored Church contain innumerable examples of men and women who were put through a variety of tests of obedience—"to see if they [would] do all things which the Lord their God [should] command them." Many failed because of the severity of the test, its seeming inconsistency, or even its simpleness. In resolving life's difficulties the natural man relies upon human reasoning and is rarely willing to submit to an unseen power. He denies himself the guidance of the Spirit of God (see Alma 41:11; 1 Corinthians 2:14). President Joseph F. Smith taught: "It is not easy for men to give up their vanities, to overcome their preconceived notions, and surrender themselves heart and soul to the will of God which is always higher than their own" (*Gospel Doctrine*, p. 9). President N. Eldon Tanner spoke of the plight of those who will neither seek nor submit to the wisdom and will of God, but rely instead on the arm of flesh to solve life's difficult problems. "Men are stumbling and groping for answers to their own and world problems and finding *their* attempts at solution to be totally inadequate, and indeed they are only getting more and more deeply into situations from which they are unable to extricate themselves" (*Ensign*, March 1975, p. 2).

The Nephite prophet-king Benjamin taught his people that to overcome the natural man one must yield his own will to the will of God. His counsel is as applicable to us today and the challenges of the modern world as it was in ancient times: "For the natural man is an enemy to God, and has been from the fall of Adam, and will be, forever and ever, unless he yields to the enticings of the Holy Spirit, and putteth off the natural man and becometh a saint through the atonement of Christ the Lord, and becometh as a child, submissive, meek, humble, patient, full of love, willing to submit to all things which the Lord seeth fit to inflict upon him, even as a child doth submit to his father" (Mosiah 3:19).

Yielding one's will to the will of God is not only a test of loyalty and faithfulness but is also the only sure way whereby we can receive spiritual guidance and protection in mortality, becoming sanctified from sin and prepared to receive exaltation in the world to come. The blessings resulting from submission to the will of God can be clearly seen in the example of the Church that was under the spiritual leadership of Nephi, son of Helaman. "They did fast and pray oft, and did wax stronger and stronger in their humility, and firmer and firmer in the faith of Christ, unto the filling their souls with joy and consolation, yea, even to the purifying and the sanctification of their hearts, which sanctification cometh because of their yielding their hearts unto God" (Helaman 3:35).

Difficult as it may be, it is imperative that we overcome the powerful mortal tendency to resist counsel and walk stubbornly in our own ways. As we strive to understand God's words and bring our hearts into harmony with his will we can look to the Savior as the perfect Exemplar. "I seek not my own will," he testified, "but the will of the Father which hath sent me" (John 5:30; see also John 6:38; Matthew 26:38–44). Through complete obedience he achieved total unity with the Father, and earnestly prayed that his apostles and those who believed on him through their words would similarly become one with him and his father (see John 17:1–26).

God's Will Made Known Through Living Prophets

There are those who agree that we must do the will of God yet insist that no mortal man can authoritatively represent the will of the Lord to them. Many even accept the Bible as scripture and profess belief in the ancient prophets, but think it absurd that God would continue to reveal his will to modern prophets. In a general conference address President Hugh B. Brown told of a conversation he had had many years earlier with a prominent British jurist who questioned the need for continuing revelation and modern prophets and challenged President Brown to defend his position. The conversation went as follows:

"May I proceed, sir, on the assumption that you are a Christian?"

"I am."

"I assume that you believe in the Bible—the Old and New Testaments?"

"I do!"

"Do you believe in prayer?"

"I do!"

"You say that my belief that God spoke to a man in this age is fantastic and absurd?"

"To me it is."

"Do you believe that God ever did speak to anyone?"

"Certainly, all through the Bible we have evidence of that."

"Did he speak to Adam?"

"Yes."

"To Enoch, Noah, Abraham, Moses, Jacob, and to others of the prophets?"

"I believe he spoke to each of them."

"Do you believe that contact between God and man ceased when Jesus appeared on the earth?"

"Certainly not. Such communication reached its climax, its apex at that time."

"Do you believe that Jesus of Nazareth was the Son of God?"

"He was."

"Do you believe, sir, that after the resurrection of Christ, God ever spoke to any man?"

He thought for a moment and then said, "I remember one Saul of Tarsus who was going down to Damascus to persecute the saints and who had a vision, was stricken blind, in fact, and heard a voice."

"Whose voice did he hear?"

"Well," he said, "the voice said 'I am Jesus whom thou persecutest: it is hard for thee to kick against the pricks.'"

"Do you believe that actually took place?"

"I do."

"Then, my Lord"—that is the way we address judges in the British commonwealth—"my Lord, I am submitting to you in all seriousness that it was standard procedure in Bible times for God to talk to men."

"I think I will admit that, but it stopped shortly after the first century of the Christian era."

"Why do you think it stopped?"

"I can't say."

"You think that God hasn't spoken since then?"

"Not to my knowledge."

"May I suggest some possible reasons why he has not spoken. Perhaps it is because he cannot. He has lost the power."

He said, "Of course that would be blasphemous."

"Well, then, if you don't accept that, perhaps he doesn't speak to men because he doesn't love us anymore. He is no longer interested in the affairs of men."

"No," he said, "God loves all men, and he is no respecter of persons."

"Well, then, if he can speak, and if he loves us, then the only other possible answer as I see it is that we don't need him. We have made such rapid strides in education and science that we don't need God any more."

And then he said, and his voice trembled as he thought of impending war, "Mr. Brown, there never was a time in the history of the world when the voice of God was needed as it is needed now." (*Improvement Era*, December 1967, pp. 36–37.)

Rejection of living prophets and of continuing revelation manifests itself in a variety of ways. Some of the arguments are openly humanistic, rejecting not only the need for revelation but even the need for God. Of this form of rejection, Jacob declared: "O that cunning plan of the evil one! O the vainness, and the frailties, and the foolishness of men! When they are learned they think they are wise, and they hearken not unto the counsel of God, for they set it aside, supposing they know of themselves, wherefore, their wisdom is foolishness and it profiteth them not." (2 Nephi 9:28.)

A more subtle yet just as real rejection of modern prophets and revelation comes in religious guise. These critics would never openly declare, "We do not need God," but the logic of their rejection of prophets would seem to say, "We don't need God (i.e., living prophets) because we have God's word." It is not uncommon to hear some say that everything that God would say or that we would need to hear from him is found in the Bible. To them, there is nothing more for God to say than what has already been said to the ancient prophets as recorded in the Bible. No doubt Nephi foresaw this modern rejection when he declared: "Wo be unto him that shall say: We have received the word of God, and we need no more of the word of God, for we have enough" (2 Nephi 28:29). The Book of Mormon prophet Moroni also added his warning to those who in the last days would reject revelations and miracles.

> And again I speak unto you who deny the revelations of God, and say that they are done away, that there are no revelations, nor prophecies, nor gifts, nor healing, nor speaking with tongues, and the interpretation of tongues;
>
> Behold I say unto you, he that denieth these things knoweth not the gospel of Christ; yea, he has not read the scriptures; if so, he does not understand them.
>
> For do we not read that God is the same yesterday, today, and forever, and in him there is no variableness neither shadow of changing.
>
> . . . Behold I say unto you . . . God has not ceased to be a God of miracles. . . .
>
> And who shall say that Jesus Christ did not do many mighty miracles? And there were many mighty miracles wrought by the hands of the apostles.
>
> And if there were miracles wrought then, why has God ceased to be a God of miracles and yet be an unchangeable Being? And behold, I say unto you he changeth not; if so he would cease to be God; and he ceaseth not to be God, and is a God of miracles. (Mormon 7:7–9, 15, 18, 19.)

There can be no true religion—no true worship of a living God—without continuing communication with the heavens, the living fountain of truth and light. "Whoever heard of true religion without communication with God?" asked President John Taylor.

> A good many people, and those professing Christians, will sneer a good deal at the idea of present revelation. Whoever heard of true religion without communication with God? To me the thing is the most absurd that the human mind can conceive. I do not wonder, when the people generally reject the principle of present revelation, that skepticism and infidelity prevail to such an alarming extent. I do not wonder that so many men treat religion with contempt, and regard it as something not worth the attention of intelligent beings, for without revelation religion is a mockery and a farce. If I can not have a religion that will lead me to God, and place me *en rapport* with him, and unfold to my mind the principles of eternal life, I want nothing to do with it. (In *Journal of Discourses* 16:371.)

The scriptures, both ancient and modern, confirm that God has revealed, does reveal, and will continue to reveal his will to man through his servants the prophets. The Old Testament prophet Amos testified, "Surely the Lord God will do nothing, until he revealeth the secret unto his servants the prophets" (JST, Amos 3:7). Nephi was taught by the Lord himself of the continual need for revelation and additional scripture, and of the last days, when many of the Gentiles would reject and revile the Book of Mormon and other modern revelation. Nephi recorded the Lord's own chastisement of those who would reject such revelations.

> And because my words shall hiss forth—many of the Gentiles shall say: A Bible! A Bible! We have got a Bible, and there cannot be any more Bible. . . .
>
> Thou fool, that shall say: A Bible, we have got a Bible, and we need no more Bible. Have ye obtained a Bible save it were by the Jews?
>
> Know ye not that there are more nations than one?

Know ye not that I, the Lord your God, have created all men, and that I remember those who are upon the isles of the sea; and that I rule in the heavens above and in the earth beneath; and I bring forth my word unto the children of men, yea, even upon all the nations of the earth?

Wherefore murmur ye, because that ye shall receive more of the word? Know ye not that the testimony of two nations is a witness unto you that I am God, that I remember one nation like unto another? Wherefore, I speak the same words unto one nation like unto another. And when the two nations shall run together the testimony of the two nations shall run together also.

And I do this that I may prove unto many that I am the same yesterday, today, and forever; and that I speak forth my words according to mine own pleasure. And because that I have spoken one word ye need not suppose that I cannot speak another; for my work is not yet finished; neither shall it be until the end of man, neither from that time henceforth and forever.

Wherefore, because that ye have a Bible ye need not suppose that it contains all my words; neither need ye suppose that I have not caused more to be written.

For I command all men, both in the east and in the west, and in the north, and in the south, and in the islands of the sea, that they shall write the words which I speak unto them; for out of the books which shall be written I will judge the world, every man according to their works, according to that which is written. (2 Nephi 29:3, 6–10.)

From the time of Adam, the Ancient of Days, to the present, God has continued to dispense his word and will to the world through mortal men inspired and empowered of God to be his prophet-spokesmen. Just as he spoke to prophets from Moses to Malachi (and beyond), he spoke to the Prophet Joseph Smith and declared anew the divine role of continuing revelation. As the heavens opened in the nineteenth century with the restoration of priesthood keys and the kingdom of God on earth, so came the doctrinal restoration confirming what Amos anciently declared—that God will always reveal his "secret" to his servants the prophets. "Wherefore, I the Lord, knowing the calamity which should come upon the inhabitants of the earth, called upon my servant Joseph Smith, Jun., and spake unto him from heaven, and gave him commandments; and also gave commandments to others, that they should proclaim these things unto the world; and all this that it might be fulfilled, which was written by the prophets" (D&C 1:17–18).

Of this unbroken chain of revelation from God to man, President Spencer W. Kimball testified: "For thousands of years there have been constant broadcasts from heaven of vital messages of guidance and timely warnings, and there has been a certain constancy in the broadcasts from the most powerful station. Throughout all those centuries there have been times when there were prophets who tuned in and rebroadcasted to the people. The messages have never ceased." (In Conference Report, April 1970, p. 121.)

Continuing Revelation and Living Prophets Necessary Today

For some reason many find it easier to accept the words and revelations of dead prophets than of the living ones. "Even in the Church," observed Elder Spencer W. Kimball, "many are prone to garnish the sepulchers of yesterday's prophets and mentally stone the living ones" (*Instructor*, August 1960, p. 257). This attitude reflects a misunderstanding of or disregard for what is perhaps the most important principle associated with continuing revelation—that it is always, as the Prophet Joseph Smith taught, "adapted to the circumstances."

We are differently situated from any other people that ever existed upon this earth; consequently those former revelations cannot be suited to our conditions; they were given to other people, who were before us; but in the last days, God was to call a remnant, in which was to be deliverance, as well as in Jerusalem and Zion. Now if God should give no more revelations, where will we find Zion and this remnant? (*Teachings*, pp. 70–71.)

God said, "Thou shalt not kill"; at another time He said,

"Thou shalt utterly destroy." This is the principle on which the government of heaven is conducted—by revelation adapted to the circumstances in which the children of the kingdom are placed. Whatever God requires is right, no matter what it is, although we may not see the reason thereof till long after the events transpire. (*Teachings*, p. 256.)

Whether Church members or not, it is not uncommon for people to feel uncomfortable when changes occur. At such a time some members may become critical of those who have been called, sustained, and authorized to "build up the church and regulate all the affairs of the same in all nations" (D&C 107:33). They may question the inspiration of leaders or wonder whether the Lord is indeed still revealing his will to the earth today. But changes in the Church are not only inevitable; also, as Elder Boyd K. Packer testified, they "are a testimony that revelation is on-going."

The gospel plan was revealed line upon line, precept upon precept, here a little, and there a little. And it goes on: "We believe that he will yet reveal many great and important things pertaining to the Kingdom of God" (Articles of Faith 1:9).

There will be changes made in the future as in the past. Whether the Brethren make changes or resist them depends entirely upon the instructions they receive through the channels of revelation which were established in the beginning.

The doctrines will remain fixed, eternal; the organization, programs, and procedures will be altered as directed by Him whose church this is. (In Conference Report, October 1989, pp. 18–19.)

The Church of Jesus Christ of Latter-day Saints is a dynamic organization—ever growing, ever changing—in a world of ever-fluctuating conditions and circumstances. It is a *living* (i.e., alive, vigorous, vital, responsive) organism, mercifully and wisely adapting to the current concerns of its people. Of this President John Taylor taught:

We require a living tree—a living fountain—living intelligence, proceeding from the living priesthood in heaven, through the living priesthood on earth. . . . And from the time that Adam first received a communication from God, to the time that John, on the Isle of Patmos, received his communication, or Joseph Smith had the heavens opened to him, it always required new revelations, adapted to the peculiar circumstances in which the churches or individuals were placed. Adam's revelation did not instruct Noah to build his ark; nor did Noah's revelation tell Lot to forsake Sodom; nor did either of these speak of the departure of the children of Israel from Egypt. These all had revelations for themselves. . . . And so must we, or we shall make a shipwreck. (*The Gospel Kingdom*, p. 34.)

The gospel of Jesus Christ is comprised of eternal principles having universal relevance and application. These eternal principles, laws, and ordinances never change, and adherence to them is required of all Saints, regardless of generation, locality, or individual circumstance. "The gospel is the divine plan for personal, individual salvation and exaltation," Elder Ronald E. Poelman taught. "The Church is divinely commissioned to provide the means and resources that implement this plan in each individual's life."

Procedures, programs, and policies are developed within the Church to help us realize gospel blessings according to our individual capacity and circumstances. Under divine direction, these policies, programs, and procedures may be changed from time to time as necessary to fulfill gospel purposes. . . .

The eternal principles of the gospel implemented through the divinely inspired Church apply to a wide variety of individuals in diverse cultures. . . .

A necessary perspective is gained by studying and pondering the scriptures. Reading the scriptures, we learn the gospel as it is taught by various prophets in a variety of circumstances, times, and places. . . .

In the scriptures we discover that varying institutional forms, procedures, regulations, and ceremonies were utilized—

all divinely designed to implement eternal principles. The practices and procedures change; the principles do not. (In Conference Report, October 1984, p. 79.)

The scriptures themselves dramatically illustrate how revelation through living prophets is "adapted to the circumstances in which the children of the kingdom are placed." Numerous examples could be given. Caring for the poor was accomplished partly by allowing them to glean the corners of harvested fields in Old Testament times, and through "United Order" systems in early Latter-day Saint history; and it is done by the means of fast offerings and an integrated welfare system in our day. The Saints in Moses' day were given a strict code of conduct in the Mosaic laws and carnal commandments as a "schoolmaster" to lead them to Christ (see Galatians 3:24). The Savior, in his day, gave a higher law adapted to a different generation with different circumstances and capacities. The strict health code of Old Testament times has been replaced by a modern "word of wisdom, showing forth the order and will of God in the temporal salvation of all saints in the last days" (D&C 89:2). Plural marriage was commanded at some times and forbidden in others. In our own day, organizational and program changes have been made to meet the pressing demands of an ever-expanding church. Local and missionary funding policies have also been altered. All these examples and numerous others illustrate how the Lord continually makes his will known, guiding the Church as it moves from one stage of physical, numerical, and spiritual growth to another. The lives of individual members are thus blessed with inspired instruction for applying eternal gospel principles to their own unique situations.

Prophets: Watchmen to God's Covenant People

"Son of man, I have made thee a watchman unto the house of Israel," the Lord told the prophet Ezekiel, "therefore hear the word at my mouth, and give them warning" (Ezekiel 3:17). Just as a watchman, from his vantage point high above the ground, is able to see potential dangers far in the distance and thus warn the inhabitants below, so does the prophet of God sound a warning. His singular entitlement to inspiration from the Almighty, coupled with his experience of living and leading *in* the world, allows him to perceive and then warn us of dangers that may threaten our happiness, stifle our spiritual progress, and veer us away from the "strait and narrow path which leads to eternal life" (2 Nephi 31:18).

In this dispensation the Lord has reiterated what he declared to Ezekiel (Ezekiel 33:17) and Jeremiah (Jeremiah 6:17) in Old Testament times and to the Book of Mormon prophet Alma the Younger (Alma 6:1): that the prophets serve as God's watchmen, not only to his church but also to the world. In a richly symbolic parable (see D&C 101:43–65) the Lord taught Joseph Smith the role of the latter-day prophet as a "watchman upon the tower" in the building and directing of the kingdom of God and the redemption of Zion. In the parable the lord of the vineyard tells his slothful servants, "And behold, the watchman upon the tower would have seen the enemy while he was yet afar off; and then ye could have made ready and kept the enemy from breaking down the hedge thereof, and saved my vineyard from the hands of the destroyer" (D&C 101:54).

The Lord has lovingly established his anointed prophets as watchmen not only to protect us and the Church from danger but also to enrich our lives with guidance and counsel. These watchmen are like vigilant shepherds to the flock. Declared President George Q. Cannon:

> Great responsibilities rest upon the officers of The Church of Jesus Christ of Latter-day Saints. The souls of the children of men are entrusted to their care. They are called shepherds of the flock of Christ, and if the sheep of the flock are injured or destroyed, the blame rests upon the shepherds. They are also called watchmen. They must stand and give warning of the approach of danger. They tell the people to prepare to escape threatened evil. If they are not watchful and vigilant, trouble may fall upon those whom they are appointed to guard and care for.
>
> . . . God has placed us as shepherds over His flock, and if we do not look out for the flock, He will smite us and remove us. We are placed as watchmen upon the walls of Zion, and if we do not give warning when we see danger,

then we are culpable and will be condemned of God. (*Gospel Truth*, p. 210.)

The kingdom of God—the earthly Church led by living prophets—can be the place where, as the Lord said, we "may contemplate the glory of Zion" and "receive . . . counsel from those whom I have set to be as plants of renown [i.e., "trees of righteousness," anointed leaders who have been "planted" by the Lord in the midst of the people—see also Ezekiel 34:29] and as watchmen upon her walls" (D&C 124:60–61). Elder John H. Groberg has shared the following personal experience from his missionary service in the South Pacific. It portrays this principle through an unforgettable image that will help us better visualize the prophets as our watchmen.

On one occasion we received word that a missionary was very ill on a somewhat distant island. The weather was threatening, but feeling responsible, and after prayer, we left to investigate the situation. Extra heavy seas slowed our progress, and it was late afternoon before we arrived. The missionary was indeed very ill. Fervent prayer was followed by administration, during which the impression came very strongly to get him back to the hospital on the main island and to do it now!

The weather had deteriorated to the point of a small gale. The seas were heavy, the clouds were thick, the wind was fierce, the hour was late, and the sun was sinking rapidly, betokening a long black night ahead. But the impression was strong—"Get back now"—and one learns to obey the all-important promptings of the Spirit.

There was much concern expressed and much talk about the darkness, the storm, and the formidable reef with its extremely narrow openings to the harbor we were attempting to gain. Some found reason to stay behind; but soon eight persons, including an ill missionary, a very experienced captain, and a somewhat concerned district president, boarded the boat, and the spiritually prompted voyage to home base began.

No sooner had we made our commitment to the open seas than the intensity of the storm seemed to increase sevenfold. The small gale now became a major storm. As the sun sank below the horizon, bringing with it darkness and gloom, so also did my spirit seem to sink into the darkness of doubt and apprehension. The thick clouds and driving rain increased the blackness of our already dark universe— no stars, no moon, no rest, only turmoil of sea and body and mind and spirit. And as we toiled on through that fearsome night, I found my spirit communing with the spirit of the father of an afflicted child in the New Testament, as he exclaimed, "Lord, I believe; help thou mine unbelief." (Mark 9:24.) And He did, and He does, and He will. That I know.

As we rolled and tossed closer and closer to the reef, all eyes searched for the light that marked the opening—the only entry to our home. Where was it? The blackness of the night seemed to increase; the fierceness of the raging elements seemed to know no bounds. The rain slashed at our faces and tore at our eyes—eyes vainly searching for that life-giving light.

Then I heard the chilling sound of the waves crashing and chewing against the reef! It was close—too close. Where was that light? Unless we hit the opening exactly, we would be smashed against the reef and ripped and torn by that thousand-toothed monster. It seemed that all the elements were savagely bent on our total destruction. Our eyes strained against the blackness, but we could not see the light.

Some began to whimper, others to moan and cry, and one or two even to scream in hysteria. At the height of this panic, when many were pleading to turn to the left or to the right, when the tumultuous elements all but forced us to abandon life and hope, I looked at the captain—and there I saw the face of calmness, the ageless face of wisdom and experience, as his eyes penetrated the darkness ahead. Quietly his weather-roughened lips parted, and without moving his fixed gaze and just perceptibly shifting the wheel, he breathed those life-giving words, "Ko e Maama e!" ("There is the light!")

I could not see the light, but the captain could see it. And I knew he could see it. Those eyes long experienced in ocean travel were not fooled by the madness of the storm nor were they influenced by the pleadings of those of lesser experience to turn to the left or to the right. And so with one last great swell we hurtled through the opening and into calmer waters.

The roaring of the reef was now behind us. Its infamous plan of destruction had been foiled. We were in the protected harbor. We were home. Then and only then did we see through the darkness that one small light—exactly where the captain had said it was. Had we waited until we ourselves could see the light, we would have been dashed to pieces, shredded on the reef of unbelief. But trusting in those experienced eyes, we lived.

And so the great lesson: There are those who, through years of experience and training, and by virtue of special divine callings, can see farther and better and more clearly—and can and will save us in those situations where serious injury or death, both spiritual and physical, would be upon us before we ourselves could see.

I sense in the world today an almost exact duplication of that voyage of nearly 20 years ago. We are in the midst of a major storm over moral values that will get worse before we arrive home. . . .

I thank the Lord for our great prophet-leader of today. In our moment of great need the Lord has provided one tested and molded and trained and instructed and clothed with divine authority, who in addition to the total of all his experience, which is great, draws upon the strength and power of not only generations of faithful leaders but also of angels and of gods.

I bear testimony that I know that God lives. I know that our Father in Heaven loves us. I know that Jesus is the Christ, the Savior of the world. I know that he is our personal Savior, that he is our Friend—and I know he is our Helper; he will help us each personally and individually as we merit that help.

I know that Joseph Smith is a prophet of God. I testify that in our day [the living prophet] is the man whose eyes see the light that can and will save us and the world. When all about us are sinking in darkness and fear and despair, when destruction seems close and the raging fury of men and demons ensnares us in seemingly insoluble problems, listen as he calmly says, "There is the light. This is the way." (*New Era*, March 1977, pp. 45–46.)

A seer is a revelator and a prophet also; and a gift which is greater can no man have, except he should possess the power of God, which no man can; yet a man may have great power given him from God.

—Mosiah 8:16

CHAPTER 3

The Living Oracles:
Prophets, Seers, and Revelators

The word *prophet* brings many images to people's minds. Some may think of the ancient biblical prophets—with long white beards and flowing robes, prophesying impending doom to ancient peoples. Still others may have a negative image of some cultic leader or religious charlatan who appropriates the title to himself for purposes of priestcraft, to manipulate and prey upon those who would follow him. Even among Church members there are many ideas and images of the prophetic role, the most common image springing to mind from the title *prophet* being that of the President of the Church. While it is true that *prophet* applies to the President, it is not the only way in which the term can or should be used.

In the parable of the nobleman cited in the previous chapter (see D&C 101:43–62), the Lord uses two similar yet distinct symbols to teach us a valuable lesson on the role of prophets. The first symbol is the "watch*man* upon the *tower*" and the second is the "watch*men* upon the *walls*." In referring to the watch*man*, the Lord declared that "*one* may overlook the land round about, to be a watchman upon the tower" (verse 45). In addition, others were "set [as] watchmen upon the walls" (verse 53) to assist the one watchman on the tower in his responsibilities

of discovering the enemy "while yet afar off," warning the inhabitants, and protecting the vineyard (Church) "from the hands of
the destroyer" (verse 54). To covenant Israel today, the one
"watchman on the tower" is the prophet-president of the
Church. Just as there were watchmen to assist in conveying the
messages and warnings of the watchman, so are there in the restored Church "prophets, seers, and revelators" and others with
varying prophetic responsibilities who are called and anointed
to assist in all parts of the vineyard—that is, in "building up and
regulating all the affairs of the [Church] in all nations" (D&C
107:34). Understanding the scriptural meaning of the terms
prophet, *seer*, and *revelator* not only will help us to see better the
role and responsibilities of the "Lord's anointed" but also, most
important, will help us to more clearly perceive our relationship
and responsibility to them.

Prophet: A Teacher of Known Truth

"Would God that all the Lord's people were prophets,"
Moses prayed, "and that the Lord would put his spirit upon
them!" (Numbers 11:29.) The term *prophet*, as used here by
Moses, can have both a general definition with a broad application to all faithful followers of God and a specific meaning with
a very narrow application to those who have been ordained to
that calling. This is manifest in the ancient usage of the term. In
Greek the word for *prophet* is *prophetes*—"one who speaks on be-
half of the gods." Its primary meaning was one of being a
"spokesman" or "announcer." The Old Testament usage of the
word *prophet* came from the Hebrew word *nabi*, which conveyed
the idea that a prophet is one called of God "to announce," or
"to proclaim," the mind and will of God (see B. N. Napier,
"Prophet, Prophetism," *Interpreter's Dictionary of the Bible*
3:896–97; Joseph Fielding McConkie, *Prophets and Prophecy*,
pp. 5–10). In our day, prophets of the Restoration have likewise
testified of the role of prophets. President Harold B. Lee taught
that "in a broad sense, a prophet is one who speaks, who is inspired of God to speak in His name" (*Stand Ye in Holy Places*, p.
153).

While many think of a prophet in terms of receiving revelations that would predict or foretell future events, the ancient usage "was never laden with such connotations as 'one who predicts the future' (the prefix *pro-* meant 'forth,' not 'fore') or 'inspired spokesman'" (David E. Aune, *Prophecy in Early Christianity and the Ancient Mediterranean World*, p. 195). While prophecy is the primary function of a prophet, prophesying is not so much predicting as it is proclaiming—more teaching and testifying than foretelling. "A prophet is a teacher," explained Elder John A. Widtsoe. "That is the essential meaning of the word. He teaches the body of truth, the gospel, revealed by the Lord to man; and under inspiration explains it to the understanding of the people. He is an expounder of truth." (*Evidences and Reconciliations*, p. 257.) President Anthony W. Ivins, a Counselor in the First Presidency in President Heber J. Grant's administration, taught the same truth.

A careful study of the etymology of the word and of the lives, works and character of the prophets of old makes clear the fact that a prophet was, and is, one called to act as God's messenger. He is to teach men the character of God, and define and make known to the people, his will. He is to denounce sin, and declare the punishment of transgression. He is to be above all else a preacher of righteousness, and when the people depart from the path which he has marked out for them to follow, is to call them back to the true faith. He is an interpreter of the scripture, and declares its meaning and application. When future events are to be declared he predicts them, but his direct and most important calling is to be a forth-teller, or director of present policy, rather than a foreteller of that which is to come. (In Conference Report, October 1925, p. 20.)

In addition to the prophetic roles of preacher of righteousness, forthteller rather than foreteller, and expounder of the truth, we have the expressions of John the Apostle and the Prophet Joseph Smith expanding further the meaning of the words *prophecy* and *prophet*. John declared, "The testimony of Jesus is the spirit of prophecy" (Revelation 19:10). Explaining the nature of a prophet and commenting on John's words, Joseph Smith taught:

If any person should ask me if I were a prophet, I should not deny it, as that would give me the lie; for, according to John, the testimony of Jesus is the spirit of prophecy; therefore, if I profess to be a witness or teacher, and have not the spirit of prophecy, which is the testimony of Jesus, I must be a false witness; but if I be a true teacher and witness, I must possess the spirit of prophecy, and that constitutes a prophet; and any man who says he is a teacher or preacher of righteousness, and denies the spirit of prophecy, is a liar, and the truth is not in him; and by this key false teachers and imposters may be detected. (*History of the Church* 5:215–16; hereafter cited as *HC*.)

Faithful members of the Church can be prophets in that they may be preachers of righteousness, forthtellers, or expounders of truth, but especially in that they can and should possess a testimony of Jesus. President Harold B. Lee said that "anyone who enjoys the gift by which he may have God revealed has the spirit of prophecy, the power of revelation, and, in a sense, is a prophet within the sphere of responsibility and authority given to him" (*Stand Ye in Holy Places*, p. 155). This is how the term *prophet* can be generally defined and applied.

Another, more specific, aspect of the word *prophet* must be examined and understood. It stems from the ancient Hebrew root of the word that is related to cognate Akkadian and Arabic words meaning "the called one" or "one who is anointed" (see Kittel & Friedrich, *Theological Dictionary of the Bible*, 6:796–97). This implies a more restricted usage of the term *prophet*, referring to those who have been given a particular calling or office with specialized responsibilities above and beyond teaching or testifying in general. This more lofty view of the prophetic role is evident in the following statement by Elder Bruce R. McConkie:

A true prophet is one who has the testimony of Jesus; one who knows by personal revelation that Jesus Christ is the Son of the living God, and that he was to be—or has been—crucified for the sins of the world; one to whom God speaks and who recognizes the still small voice of the Spirit. A true prophet is one who holds the holy priesthood; who is a legal administrator; who has power and authority from God to represent him on earth. A true prophet is a teacher of righteousness to whom the truths of the gospel have been revealed and who presents them to his fellowmen so they can become heirs of salvation in the highest heaven. A true prophet is a witness, a living witness, one who knows, and one who testifies. Such a one, if need be, foretells the future and reveals to men what the Lord reveals to him. (*The Mortal Messiah* 2:169.)

This definition of a prophet as "a called one" or "a legal administrator" differentiates between all faithful Saints, who can be filled with the spirit of prophecy, and those who are additionally called, sustained, and set apart as prophets to the people. Even though Moses prayed that all the Lord's people could be prophets, there was still a fundamental difference between what *they* could be as prophets and what *he* was as *the* prophet.

Seer: A Perceiver of Hidden Truth

The Old Testament Hebrew word for *seer* is *ro'eh* which means "one who sees" or "one who looks." The ancient usage of the term also designated seers as a distinct class of prophets (see Brown, Driver, & Driggs, *A Hebrew and English Lexicon of the Old Testament*, p. 909). It is clear from the ancient usage of the word that while there is a very close relationship in function, seers were in some special way different from a prophet as a proclaimer or teacher of truth. This distinction is clearly seen in Book of Mormon teachings. When King Limhi asked Ammon whether he could translate the twenty-four plates that contained Jaredite records Ammon told him no, but that Mosiah could because he was a seer (see Mosiah 8:5–12).

Now Ammon said unto him: I can assuredly tell thee, O king, of a man that can translate the records; for he has wherewith that he can look, and translate all records that are of ancient date; and it is a gift from God. And the things are called interpreters, and no man can look in them except he be commanded, lest he should look for that he ought not and he should perish. And whosoever is commanded to look in them, the same is called seer.

And behold, the king of the people who are in the land of Zarahemla [Mosiah II] is the man that is commanded to do these things, and who has the high gift from God.

And the king said that a seer is greater than a prophet.

And Ammon said that a seer is a revelator and a prophet also; and a gift which is greater can no man have, except he should possess the power of God, which no man can; yet a man may have great power given him from God. (Mosiah 8:13–16.)

The seeric gift goes beyond receiving the mind and will of God and proclaiming it to the world. It is a deeply spiritual responsibility to "see" or perceive the things of God in a more profound way than other people—even others who have "the spirit of prophecy," or the testimony of Jesus. "A seer is one who sees with spiritual eyes," declared Elder John A. Widtsoe. "He perceives the meaning of that which seems obscure to others; therefore he is an interpreter and clarifier of eternal truth. . . . In short, he is one who sees, who walks in the Lord's light with open eyes." (*Evidences and Reconciliations*, p. 258.) As Ammon taught, a seer is a prophet in that he is a proclaimer of truth and a forthteller, but a seer is a predictor or foreteller as well. Ammon taught: "But a seer can know of things which are past, and also of things which are to come, and by them shall all things be revealed, or, rather, shall secret things be made manifest, and hidden things shall come to light, and things which are not known shall be made known by them, and also things shall be made known by them which otherwise could not be known" (Mosiah 8:17).

The seeric responsibility and gift to see with "spiritual eyes" (Moses 1:11) things that cannot be "visible to the natural eye" (Moses 6:36), is no ordinary ecclesiastical duty within the Church but rather is a "supernatural endowment" belonging to those who have been sustained as seers and who hold those seeric keys (see Elder Orson F. Whitney, *Saturday Night Thoughts*, pp. 39–40). Functions of the seers are many and appear throughout the scriptures and the history of the Church, both ancient and modern. One of the most apparent, as seen in the seeric ministry of the Prophet Joseph Smith, was that of translating ancient records. Ammon taught that the seer can look into the "interpreters" and translate if he is commanded of the Lord to do so (Mosiah 8:13; see also Mosiah 28:13–16). In the Doctrine and Covenants we read that Joseph Smith was called and sustained not only as a prophet and seer but also as a "translator" (see D&C 21:1). In sustaining the prophet in general conference, "In current practice, the word 'translator' is omitted," wrote Elder Widtsoe, "since should records appear needing translation, the President of the Church may at any time be called, through revelation, to the special labor of translation" (*Evidences and Reconciliations*, p. 256).

Using the Urim and Thummin to translate records is one of the roles of a seer, but that role has been relatively rare and limited throughout history. The larger and more common function of a true seer, as a perceiver of truth, is that of being "a pillar of truth and righteousness" possessing "great spiritual strength and insight and wisdom, and whose knowledge and understanding of the Church and its needs is not surpassed" (Joseph Fielding Smith, *Improvement Era*, June 1970, p. 27).

Revelator: A Bearer of New Truth

It would seem logical to assume that a revelator is anyone who receives revelations. There are many statements to indicate that each of us as *general* prophets can receive revelation in our own personal lives and inspiration to guide us in our own stewardships. "There are, of course, ranks and grades of prophetic responsibility and authority," wrote Elder Bruce R. McConkie. "Every member of the Church should be a prophet as pertaining to his own affairs." (*Mormon Doctrine*, p. 606.) Just because we may be prophets in that we can receive revelation, that does not mean that we are revelators even in the general sense. Elder John A. Widtsoe taught that a revelator is "a bearer of *new* truth." "A revelator makes known, with the Lord's help, something before unknown. It may be new or forgotten truth, or a new or forgotten application of known truth to man's need. Always, the revelator deals with truth, certain truth (D&C 100:11) and always it comes with the divine stamp of approval. Revelation may be received in various ways, but it always presupposes that the revelator has so lived and conducted himself as to be in tune or harmony with the divine spirit of revelation, the spirit of truth, and therefore capable of receiving divine messages." (*Evidences and Reconciliations*, p. 258.)

With this definition as the foundation, we recognize that although individual members can receive and teach revelations that are in the body of already revealed truth, they cannot receive and declare as revelation truths and doctrines that have never previously been revealed. That is the sacred responsibility of the revelator. That is one of those important roles that separates a revelator from a prophet. Just as *seer* is a different class of "anointed" prophet or an enlargement of the prophetic mantle, so is *revelator*. Speaking of Joseph Smith as the "revelator" for the Church (and by implication all those revelators that have succeeded him), the Lord declared: "For behold, verily, verily, I say unto you, that ye have received a commandment for a law unto my church, through him whom I have appointed unto you to receive commandments and revelations from my hand. And this ye shall know assuredly—that there is none other appointed unto you to receive commandments and revelations until he be taken, if he abide in me." (D&C 43:2–3.)

Prophets, Seers, and Revelators

The Church as the kingdom of God on earth is governed and directed at the various levels by men and women who are entitled to the spirit of prophecy and to be guided by inspiration in their service. While this means that there may be many prophets within the Church, at any given time there are only fifteen men at a time whom the Lord has designated to be "prophets, seers, and revelators." These fifteen have been given what President J. Reuben Clark, Jr., characterized as "a special spiritual endowment" different from all others.

It should be in mind that some of the General Authorities have had assigned to them a special calling; they possess a special gift; they are sustained as prophets, seers, and revelators, which gives them a special spiritual endowment in connection with their teaching of the people. They have the right, the power, and authority to declare the mind and will of God to his people, subject to the over-all power and authority of the President of the Church.] Others of the General Authorities are not given this special spiritual endowment and authority covering their teaching; they have a resulting limitation, and the resulting limitation upon their power and authority in teaching applies to every other officer and member of the Church, for none of them is spiritually endowed as a prophet, seer, and revelator. ("When Are Church Leaders' Words Entitled to Claim of Scripture?" pp. 9–10.)

Those fifteen prophet-leaders who are endowed with special gifts and authority, and to whom we must look as the Lord's watchmen, are the President of the Church, the Counselors in the First Presidency, and the members of the Quorum of the Twelve.

The President of the Church

The President of the Church is uniquely different from all of the other prophets, seers, and revelators in that he "has a further and special spiritual endowment in this respect, for he is *the* Prophet, Seer, and Revelator for the entire Church" (J. Reuben Clark, Jr., "When Are Church Leaders' Words Entitled to Claim of Scripture?" p. 10). Speaking of the President of the Church as the "Presiding High Priest," the Lord declared: "Wherefore, it must needs be that one be appointed of the High Priesthood to preside over the priesthood, and he shall be called President of the High Priesthood of the Church; or, in other words, the Presiding High Priest over the High Priesthood of the Church" (D&C 107:65–66).

Elder Bruce R. McConkie explained what is meant by the term *Presiding High Priest*: "God's chief representative on earth, the one who holds the highest spiritual position in his kingdom in any age, is called *the high priest*. This special designation of the chief spiritual officer of the Church has reference to the administrative position which he holds rather than to the office to which he is ordained in the priesthood." (*Mormon Doctrine*, pp. 355–56.) The revelation further explains how the Presiding High Priest is the chief spiritual officer of the Church. "And

again, the duty of the President of the office of the High Priesthood is to preside over the whole church and to be like unto
Moses—behold, here is wisdom; yea, to be a seer, a revelator, a
translator, and a prophet, having all the gifts of God which he
bestows upon the head of the Church" (D&C 107:91–92).

Two phrases from the previous passage highlight the two dis-
tinctive administrative roles of the prophet, seer, and revelator—
"to preside over the whole church" and "to be like unto Moses."
Understanding the doctrinal meaning of these phrases illumi-
nates the uniqueness of the roles of the President of the
Church.

"To Preside over the Whole Church"

The word *preside*, the root word in *president* and *presidency*,
comes from the Latin *praesidere*, which literally means to "sit in
front of." The dictionary definition of the word is "to hold the
position of authority" and "to possess or exercise control or authority." In modern revelation the Lord has spoken of the authority and sealing power of the Prophet Joseph Smith (and his
successors) as the President of the Church:

> And verily I say unto you, that the conditions of this law
> are these: All covenants, contracts, bonds, obligations, oaths,
> vows, performances, connections, associations, or expecta-
> tions, that are not made and entered into and sealed by the
> Holy Spirit of promise, of him who is anointed, both as well
> for time and for all eternity, and that too most holy, by reve-
> lation and commandment through the medium of mine
> anointed, whom I have appointed on the earth to hold this
> power (and I have appointed my servant Joseph to hold this
> power in the last days, and there is never but one on the
> earth at a time on whom this power and the keys of the
> priesthood are conferred), are of no efficacy, virtue, or force
> in and after the resurrection from the dead; for all contracts
> that are not made unto this end have an end when men are
> dead (D&C 132:7).

What is this "power and the keys of the priesthood" that belong to one man only upon the earth—the Lord's anointed? The
answer begins to emerge in the scriptural account of the Savior's

meridian ministry with his twelve Apostles. Shortly after Jesus called the Twelve to be "fishers of men" (Matthew 4:19), he gave them "power against unclean spirits, to cast them out, and to heal all manner of sickness and all manner of disease" (Matthew 10:1). Though Peter, along with the other Apostles, had received the priesthood earlier, the Lord promised him additional authority. "And I will give unto thee the keys of the kingdom of heaven: and whatsoever thou shalt bind on earth shall be bound in heaven: and whatsoever thou shalt loose on earth shall be loosed in heaven" (Matthew 16:19).

President Joseph F. Smith explained the distinction between priesthood and the keys of the Priesthood.

> The Priesthood in general is the authority given to man to act for God. Every man ordained to any degree of the Priesthood has this authority delegated to him.
>
> But it is necessary that every act performed under this authority shall be done at the proper time and place, in the proper way, and after the proper order. The power of directing these labors constitutes the keys of the Priesthood. In their fulness, the keys are held by only one person at a time, the prophet and president of the Church. He may delegate any portion of this power to another, in which case that person holds the keys of that particular labor. Thus, the president of a temple, the president of a stake, the bishop of a ward, the president of a mission, the president of a quorum, each holds the keys of the labors performed in that particular body or locality. His Priesthood is not increased by this special appointment. . . . The president of an elders' quorum, for example, has no more Priesthood than any member of that quorum. But he holds the power of directing the official labors performed in the . . . quorum, or in other words, the keys of that division of that work. (*Gospel Doctrine*, p. 136.)

Elder Bruce R. McConkie explained this concept further.

> As pertaining to this mortal sphere, priesthood is the power and authority of God, delegated to men on earth, to act in all things for the salvation of men. It is the same power held by the noble and great spirits before the foundations of

this world were laid. It is the same power carried into the spirit world by the faithful elders when they depart this life. It is the same power the redeemed of the Lord will possess when they rise in glorious immortality and enter into their exaltation, when, reigning from eternal thrones, they will exercise this supreme power forever.

The keys of the priesthood are the right and power of presidency. They are the directing, controlling, and governing power. Those who hold them are empowered to direct the manner in which others use their priesthood. Every ministerial act performed by a priesthood holder must be done at the proper time and place and in the proper way. The power of directing these labors constitutes the keys of the priesthood. Every elder, for instance, has the power to baptize, but no elder can use this power unless he is authorized to do so by someone holding the keys.

The keys of the kingdom are the power, right, and authority to preside over the kingdom of God on earth, which is the Church, and to direct all of its affairs. (*A New Witness for the Articles of Faith*, p. 309.)

The President of the Church holds and exercises all of the keys of the priesthood that are necessary to "govern and direct all of the Lord's affairs on earth" (Joseph Fielding Smith, *Ensign*, July 1972, p. 87). All others who labor in the Church under the direction of the priesthood are empowered to do so by the authority of the President of the Church. It is through the keys of the priesthood which he holds that he governs, directs, and authorizes the use of priesthood on earth. "He is the one man on earth at a time who can both hold and exercise the keys of the kingdom in their fulness," wrote Elder Bruce R. McConkie. "By the authority vested in him, all ordinances of the gospel are performed, all teaching of the truths of salvation is authorized, and through the keys which he holds, salvation itself is made available to men of his day." (*Mormon Doctrine*, pp. 591–92.) In this way, the President of the Church—*the* prophet, seer, and revelator—presides over the whole Church. "He alone can give direction to all others, direction from which none is exempt" (Bruce R. McConkie, *Ensign*, May 1983, p. 23).

"To Be Like unto Moses"

Of Moses, Jehovah declared: "With him will I speak mouth to mouth, even apparently, and not in dark speeches; and the similitude of the Lord shall he behold" (Numbers 12:8). Moses was the prototype prophet "whom the Lord knew face to face" (Deuteronomy 34:10). In our day, as anciently, the President of the Church is "like unto Moses" in that he is God's sole mouthpiece. To him comes the word of the Lord. As the presiding high priest, the prophet is the only one empowered to receive revelations for the entire Church.

In the early days of this dispensation the importance of this lofty right of the Prophet Joseph Smith (and his successors) became apparent when some claimed to have received revelations for the Church. Several months after the Church was organized, Hiram Page (one of the eight witnesses of the Book of Mormon) maintained that he was receiving such revelations through a certain stone in his possession. Some members, including Oliver Cowdery, believed him. In a revelation given through Joseph Smith, speaking to Oliver specifically and the entire Church generally, the Lord instructed his Church regarding the principle of revelation: "But, behold, verily, verily, I say unto thee, no one shall be appointed to receive commandments and revelations in this church excepting my servant Joseph Smith, Jun., for he receiveth them even as Moses. And thou shalt be obedient unto the things which I shall give unto him. . . . And thou shalt not command him who is at thy head, and at the head of the church; for I have given him the keys of the mysteries, and the revelations which are sealed, until I shall appoint unto them another in his stead." (D&C 28:2–3, 6–7.)

Less than six months later this principle of revelation was again tested when a woman named Hubble "professed to be a prophetess of the Lord, and professed to have many revelations." She claimed "she should become a teacher in the Church." Appearing very sanctimonious, she "deceived some who were not able to detect her in her hypocrisy." (See *HC* 1:154, footnote.) The Lord then gave a revelation to Joseph Smith that clarified and further established the "law of revelation" by which the kingdom of God is governed.

For behold, verily, verily, I say unto you, that ye have received a commandment for a law unto my church, through him whom I have appointed unto you to receive commandments and revelations from my hand.

And this ye shall know assuredly—that there is none other [besides the Prophet] appointed unto you [the Church members] to receive commandments and revelations until he be taken, if he abide in me.

But verily, verily, I say unto you, that none else shall be appointed unto this gift except it be through him; for if it be taken from him he shall not have power except to appoint another in this stead.

And this shall be a law unto you, that ye receive not the teachings of any [other than the Prophet] that shall come before you as revelations or commandments;

And this I give unto you that you may not be deceived, that you may know they are not of me. (D&C 43:2–6.)

These revelations emphatically declare that revelation for the entire Church comes only through one person—the prophet, the presiding high priest. Several of the Lord's anointed leaders who have served as prophets, seers, and revelators have left their testimonies of this vital principle. President George Q. Cannon stated:

Now, there is only one way in which the commandments of God can be revealed unto us. God has not left this in doubt. He has not left us to grope in the dark respecting His methods of revealing His mind and will unto His children. In the very beginning of the work of God in these last days, to remove all doubt upon this subject, God gave revelations unto this Church in exceeding great plainness, and there was one principle that was emphatically dwelt upon and enforced, namely, that there was but one channel, one channel alone, through which the word of God and the commandments of God should come to this people. The word of God was not to come from the people up. It was not *vox populi, vox dei*, but it was to be *vox dei, vox populi*—that is, the voice of God and then the voice of the people—from God downward through the channel that He should appoint; by the means that He should institute. (In *Journal of Discourses* 24:362–63.)

Commenting on the "law of revelation" as declared by the Lord in sections 28 and 43 of the Doctrine and Covenants, Elder Joseph Fielding Smith wrote:

> There is order in the kingdom of God. There could not be order if every man was privileged to give commandments and claim the right to direct by revelation the members of the Church.
>
> This law is given for our government for all time. It is the one who holds the keys and who stands as the Presiding High Priest and President of the Church, who is the spokesman of the Lord for the members of the Church. Individual members may receive the inspiration and revelation for their own guidance, but not for the Church. Moreover, no member of the Church will profess to receive a revelation for his own guidance, that is contradictory of any revelation coming from the President of the Church. (*Church History and Modern Revelation* 1:172.)

President J. Reuben Clark, Jr., also taught that neither the Counselors in the First Presidency, members of the Quorum of the Twelve, nor any person in any position in the Church can receive revelations for the entire Church, declare doctrine, or speak as the Lord's representative without the authorization of the President.

> Here we must have in mind—must know—that only the President of the Church, the Presiding High Priest, is sustained as Prophet, Seer, and Revelator for the Church, and he alone has the right to receive revelations for the Church, either new or amendatory, or to give authoritative interpretations of scriptures that shall be binding on the Church, or change in any way the existing doctrines of the Church. He is God's sole mouthpiece on earth for The Church of Jesus Christ of Latter-day Saints, the only true church. He alone may declare the mind and will of God to his people. No officer of any other church in the world has this high right and lofty prerogative.

So when any other person, irrespective of who he is, undertakes to do any of these things, you may know he is not "moved upon by the Holy Ghost" in so speaking unless he has special authorization from the President of the Church. ("When Are Church Leaders' Words Entitled to Claim of Scripture?" p. 10.)

A Unique Promise

Some may suggest that, since prophets are mortal men with mortal frailties, it is potentially dangerous to "give heed unto all his words and commandments . . . as if from [God's] own mouth" (D&C 21:4–5). Therefore, how can we be sure the prophets speak for heaven? How can we be sure that they will not lead us astray?

While we do not claim infallibility for the prophet-president of the Church, we do have claim upon special promises and assurances about his prophetic ministry and counsel. Several men who have served as Presidents of the Church have left their solemn testimonies concerning this unique promise.

President Brigham Young:

The Lord Almighty leads this Church, and he will never suffer you to be led astray if you are found doing your duty. You may go home and sleep as sweetly as a babe in its mother's arms, as to any danger of your leaders leading you astray, for if they should try to do so the Lord would quickly sweep them from the earth. (In *Journal of Discourses* 9:289.)

President Wilford Woodruff:

I say to Israel, the Lord will never permit me or any other man who stands as president of the Church to lead you astray. It is not in the program. It is not in the mind of God. If I were to attempt that the Lord would remove me out of my place, and so he will any other man who attempts to lead the children of men astray from the oracles of God and from their duty. (*Discourses of Wilford Woodruff,* pp. 212–13.)

President Joseph F. Smith:

I testify in the name of Israel's God that He will not suffer the head of the Church, him whom He has chosen to stand at the head, to transgress His laws and apostatize; the moment he should take a course that would in time lead to it, God would take him away. Why? Because to suffer a wicked man to occupy that position, would be to allow, as it were, the fountain to become corrupted, which is something He will never permit. (In *Journal of Discourses* 24:192.)

President Heber J. Grant (as quoted by Elder Marion G. Romney):

Now . . . if we will keep these things in mind, we shall not be deceived by false teachings. I remember years ago when I was a bishop I had President [Heber J.] Grant talk to our ward. . . . Standing by me, he put his arm over my shoulder and said: "My boy, you always keep your eye on the President of the Church, and if he ever tells you to do anything, and it is wrong, and you do it, the Lord will bless you for it." Then with a twinkle in his eye, he said, "But you don't need to worry. The Lord will never let his mouthpiece lead the people astray." (In Conference Report, October 1960, p. 78.)

President Joseph Fielding Smith:

Now, brethren, I think there is one thing which we should have exceedingly clear in our minds. Neither the President of the Church, nor the First Presidency, nor the united voice of the First Presidency and the Twelve will ever lead the Saints astray or send forth counsel to the world that is contrary to the mind and will of the Lord. (In Conference Report, April 1972, p. 99.)

President Harold B. Lee:

Yes, we believe in a living prophet, seer, and revelator, and I bear you my solemn witness that we have a living prophet, seer, and revelator. We are not dependent only upon the revelations given in the past as contained in our standard works—as wonderful as they are—but we have a mouthpiece to whom God does reveal and is revealing His mind and will. God will never permit him to lead us astray. As has been said, God would remove him out of his place if he should attempt to do it. You have no concern. Let the management and government of God, then, be with the Lord. Do not try to find fault with the management and affairs that pertain to Him alone and by revelation through His prophet—His living prophet, His seer, and His revelator. (*Stand Ye in Holy Places*, p. 164.)

President Ezra Taft Benson:

Christ has provided us the gift of a prophet. Of all mortal men, we should keep our eyes most firmly fixed on the captain—the prophet, seer, and revelator, and President of The Church of Jesus Christ of Latter-day Saints. This is the man who stands closest to the fountain of living waters (Jeremiah 2:13; 1 Nephi 11:25). There are some heavenly instructions for us that we can only receive through the prophet. A good way to measure your standing with the Lord is to see how you feel about, and act upon, the inspired words of His earthly representative, the prophet-president. . . .

All men are entitled to inspiration, but only one man is the Lord's mouthpiece. Some lesser men have in the past, and will in the future, use their office unrighteously. Some will use it to lead the unwary astray; some will use it to persuade us that all is well in Zion; some will use it to cover and excuse their ignorance. Keep your eye on the prophet—for the Lord will never permit His prophet to lead this Church astray. (*The Teachings of Ezra Taft Benson*, pp. 140, 142.)

These testimonies assure us that we can have confidence in the living prophet. If we will faithfully obey him and "give heed unto all his words" as if from the Lord, we have been promised that "the gates of hell shall not prevail against you; yea, and the Lord God will disperse the powers of darkness before you" (see D&C 21:4–6). That is a marvelous promise in a world that is increasingly threatened with more and more darkness and confusion.

The First Presidency

When the Church was officially organized on April 6, 1830, in Fayette, New York, there was no First Presidency as we know it today. Joseph Smith was identified in the revelation as "an apostle of Jesus Christ, to be the first elder of this church" (D&C 20:2). Oliver Cowdery, who had assisted the Prophet with the work of the Restoration and had been at his side when the priesthood was restored by John the Baptist and later by Peter, James, and John, was "also called of God, an apostle of Jesus Christ, to be the second elder of this church" (D&C 20:3). It is interesting to note that Oliver was not called a counselor to Joseph, but rather the "second elder." In the earliest days and months of the Church's existence there was little reference to Joseph as "President of the Church." This changed, however, with the sustaining of Joseph as the "President of the High Priesthood" at a conference of the priesthood and membership of the Church in Amherst, Ohio, on January 25, 1832. Several weeks later, in March 1832, the Prophet received the revelation calling Counselors into the "Presidency of the High Priesthood" (see historical headings to D&C sections 75, 81–82). In fulfillment of this earlier revelation, Sidney Rigdon and Frederick G. Williams were ordained on March 18, 1833, by Joseph Smith as Counselors in the First Presidency. Of this important historical event, Joseph said: "Accordingly I laid my hands on Brothers Sidney and Frederick, and ordained them to take part with me in holding the keys of this last kingdom, and to assist in the Presidency of the High Priesthood, as my Counselors" (*HC* 1:334).

The Prophet's statement about the Counselors taking part in holding the keys of the kingdom reflect the words he had previously received by revelation concerning the responsibilities and authority of the Counselors. "The keys of the kingdom," declared the Lord, "belong always unto the Presidency of the High Priesthood" (D&C 81:2). Nearly a year later, the Lord further revealed:

> Thus saith the Lord, verily, verily I say unto you my son [Joseph Smith], thy sins are forgiven thee, according to thy petitions, for thy prayers and the prayers of thy brethren have come up into my ears.

Therefore, thou art blessed from henceforth that bear the keys of the kingdom given unto you; which kingdom is coming forth for the last time.

Verily I say unto you, the keys of this kingdom shall never be taken from you, while thou art in the world, neither in the world to come;

Nevertheless, through you shall the oracles [revelations] be given to another, yea, even unto the church.

And all they who receive the oracles of God [i.e., revelations and the prophets who give revelations], let them beware how they hold them lest they are accounted as a light thing, and are brought under condemnation thereby, and stumble and fall when the storms descend, and the winds blow, and the rains descend, and beat upon their house.

And again, verily I say unto thy brethren, Sidney Rigdon and Frederick G. Williams, their sins are forgiven them also, and they are accounted as equal with thee in holding the keys of this last kingdom. (D&C 90:1–6.)

How do the keys of the kingdom belong to the First Presidency, and in what way are the Counselors "equal" to the President? Commenting on the previously cited revelation Elder John A. Widtsoe addressed these pertinent questions and explained the proper relationship of the Counselors to the President.

Joseph Smith was given two Counsellors, the three forming the First Presidency of the Church (March 18, 1833). This was preceded on March 8, 1833, by a revelation declaring that "Through you [Joseph Smith] shall the oracles be given to another, even unto the Church." The pre-eminence of the President of the Church was maintained. The question as to whether the Counsellors held the same power as the President was soon debated among the people. What could the Counsellors do without direct appointment from the President? These questions were answered in a meeting on January 26, 1836. The Prophet there said, "The Twelve are not subject to any other than the First Presidency . . . *and where I am not, there is no First Presidency over the Twelve.*" In other words were the President taken, the Counsellors would have no authority. The Counsellors do not possess the power of the President and cannot act in Church matters without direction and consent of the President. (In Roy W. Doxey, comp., *Latter-day Prophets and the Doctrine and Covenants* 3:247. For a discussion concerning the controversy surrounding this statement see the note on page 81 of this book.)

In 1835, the revelation contained in Doctrine and Covenants section 107 was received. In this section, which deals with priesthood and Church government matters, the Lord further identified the responsibilities of the First Presidency.

> Of the Melchizedek Priesthood, three Presiding High Priests, chosen by the body, appointed and ordained to that office, and upheld by the confidence, faith, and prayer of the church, form a quorum of the Presidency of the Church. . . .
>
> Again, verily, I say unto you, the most important business of the church, and the most difficult cases of the church, inasmuch as there is not satisfaction upon the decisions of the bishop or judges, it shall be handed over and carried up unto the council of the church, before the Presidency of the High Priesthood.
>
> And the Presidency of the council of the High Priesthood shall have power to call other high priests, even twelve, to assist as counselors; and thus the Presidency of the High Priesthood and its counselors shall have power to decide upon testimony according to the laws of the church.
>
> And after this decision it shall be had in remembrance no more before the Lord; for this is the highest council of the church of God, and a final decision upon controversies in spiritual matters.
>
> There is not any person belonging to the church who is exempt from this council of the church. (D&C 107:22, 78–81.)

As the "highest council of the church," the First Presidency is responsible to administer both spiritually and temporally "the most important business of the church" and to make inspired judgments regarding "the most difficult cases of the church."

President Joseph Fielding Smith explained that the First Presidency is "the supreme governing power of the Church."

> The First Presidency preside over all councils, all quorums, and all organizations of the Church, with supreme appointing power and power of nomination. These powers of appointment, nomination, and presiding may be delegated by the First Presidency to others whom they may choose and whom the people sustain to represent the presidency in the government of the Church.
>
> The First Presidency are the living oracles of God and the supreme adjudicators and interpreters of the law of the Church. They supervise the work of the entire Church in all matters of policy, organization, and administration. No part of the work of the Church is beyond their authority. (*Improvement Era*, November 1966, p. 978.)

President N. Eldon Tanner, who served as a Counselor to four Presidents of the Church and was intimately familiar with the workings of the First Presidency, described how the principles outlined in the revelations were put into daily practice in the administration of the Church in his day.

> Let me list some of the things administered directly by the First Presidency: . . . budgeting, educational, historical, and personnel departments; temples; auditing; . . . and the welfare services. . . .
>
> In general, all these matters are under the direction of the First Presidency. Specifically, in regularly scheduled meetings, the First Presidency meet every Tuesday, Wednesday, Thursday, and Friday at 8 A.M. with a secretary who makes a complete record of all procedures. These discussions include the correspondence which has been addressed to the First Presidency—which contains almost everything from questions about pierced ears to appeals from decisions of excommunication by the stake presidency and high council. There are questions about dress and grooming standards, hypnotism, Sabbath observance, scripture interpretation, sensitivity training, sealings, complaints against local officers, reincarnation, donation of body parts to science or to others, cremation, transplants, legal matters, ad infinitum.

Their decisions also involve the selection of new temple presidencies, when and where new temples should be built, and other matters to be discussed when meeting with the Council of the Twelve Apostles and with the Presiding Bishopric. . . .

Tuesday morning at 10 A.M. they meet with the Expenditures Committee, which is made up of the First Presidency, four members of the Twelve, and the Presiding Bishopric. This is where heads of different departments present their expenditure requirements for consideration, and allocations are made. Examples include requests by the Physical Facilities Department for acquisition of lands and of buildings such as stake or ward houses, mission homes, visitors centers, and so on, and discussions of the costs of maintenance. Also, the Presiding Bishopric presents requests for expenditures involving welfare projects.

Wednesday First Presidency meetings are used for hearing reports from heads of different departments that come directly under the First Presidency, such as the Historical, Personnel, and Public Communications departments. Appointments for important visitors are also scheduled for Wednesday mornings where possible. I am always impressed by the influence the President of the Church has on these visitors as we receive direct and indirect feedback through correspondence or verbal reports.

Once a month on Wednesdays the First Presidency meets with the Combined Church Board of Education and Board of Trustees to deal with all matters affecting universities and colleges, institutes and seminaries, and other Church schools. Also, on one Wednesday each month they meet with . . . the Welfare Services Committee, as mentioned previously.

On Thursday mornings at 10 A.M. they join with the Council of the Twelve in the upper room of the temple, where the Twelve have been convened since 8 A.M. It is in this room that the leadership of the Church has been directed by the Lord since the temple was completed. Here one experiences a special spiritual feeling, and at times senses the presence of some of these great leaders who have gone on before. Portraits of the twelve Presidents of the Church, and also of Hyrum, the Patriarch, hang on the walls. There are also paintings of the Savior at the Sea of Galilee where he called some of his apostles, and others portraying his crucifixion and his ascension. Here we are reminded of the many great leaders who have sat in this council room, and under the direction of the Lord great decisions were made.

As the First Presidency enters this room at ten o'clock on Thursday mornings, we shake hands with all members of the Twelve, then change to our temple robes. We sing, kneel in prayer, and then join in a prayer circle at the altar, after which we change to our street clothes.

After discussing the minutes of the previous meeting, we consider such matters as the following: approval of changes in bishoprics as recommended by stake presidents—previously discussed in the meeting of the Twelve (you might be interested in knowing that during 1977 we approved an average of twenty-five to thirty new bishops every week); changes in stake, ward, mission, and temple organizations throughout the Church, including boundaries and officers; officers and administration of auxiliary organizations; matters brought in by the heads of different departments; and our reports of stake conferences and other activities during the week, such as funerals, speaking engagements, and so forth. It is in this body that any change in administration or policy is considered and approved, and it then becomes the official policy of the Church. . . .

On the first Thursday of every month the First Presidency meets with all the General Authorities—the members of the Twelve, the Seventy, and the Presiding Bishopric. In this meeting all are advised of any changes in programs or procedures and instructed in their duties or responsibilities. The President calls on members to bear their testimonies, after which we all dress in our temple clothes, partake of the sacrament, and have a prayer circle with all members present participating. At the conclusion of the prayer all, other than the First Presidency and Quorum of the Twelve, are dismissed, and those remaining change to their street clothes and carry on with the regular business of the Thursday meetings. A recording secretary makes a report of all that is said and done.

Following each Thursday meeting the First Presidency and Quorum of the Twelve have lunch in a room assigned for that purpose. In this room we have a lovely picture of the Last Supper. This is a period of relaxation, and in conversation we exchange experiences and discuss matters of common interest. I could tell you some interesting discussions if I had time. Friday at 9 A.M. the Presiding Bishopric meets with the First Presidency to give reports and discuss matters affecting the administration. (In Conference Report, October 1979, pp. 64, 67–69; also *Ensign*, November 1979, pp. 45–48.)

The Quorum of the Twelve Apostles

Even before the Church was officially organized, the Lord told Joseph Smith through revelation that there were to be "others who are called to declare my gospel, both unto Gentile and unto Jew; yea, even twelve; and the Twelve shall be my disciples" (D&C 18:26–27). The word *apostle* literally means "one who is sent forth," with an added emphasis on the "commission or authority to represent another." Revelations received from 1829 to 1835 contain several references to apostles. However, an expanded understanding of the unique meaning of the word as an ecclesiastical calling in a presiding quorum of the Church did not come until what is now section 107 of the Doctrine and Covenants was revealed in 1835.

The twelve traveling councilors are called to be the Twelve Apostles, or special witnesses of the name of Christ in all the world—thus differing from other officers in the church in the duties of their calling.

And they form a quorum equal in authority and power to the three presidents previously mentioned. . . .

The Twelve are a Traveling Presiding High Council, to officiate in the name of the Lord, under the direction of the Presidency of the Church, agreeable to the institution of heaven; to build up the church, and regulate all the affairs of the same in all nations, first unto the Gentiles and secondly unto the Jews. . . .

> The Twelve [are] sent out, holding the keys, to open the
> door by the proclamation of the gospel of Jesus Christ . . .
> first unto the Gentiles and then unto the Jews. . . .
>
> It is the duty of the Twelve, in all large branches of the
> church, to ordain evangelical ministers, as they shall be desig-
> nated unto them by revelation. (D&C 107:23–24, 33, 35, 39.)

These verses highlight five important duties of the Quorum
of the Twelve. Each is unique, yet is interrelated with the others
and is essential in the overall administration of the Church and
the fulfillment of the Savior's charge to the Apostles, "Go ye
into all the world, and preach the gospel to every creature"
(Mark 16:15).

"Special Witnesses of the Name of Christ in All the World"

Prior to his ascension to heaven, the resurrected Christ
commissioned his Apostles to proclaim the gospel throughout
the world. He taught them that "it behoved Christ to suffer, and
to rise from the dead the third day: and that repentance and remission of sins should be preached in his name among all nations, beginning at Jerusalem. And ye are witnesses of these
things." (Luke 24:46–48.) The charge is the same today: "The
foremost responsibility of the Twelve Apostles," declared President Ezra Taft Benson, "is to bear witness to the divinity of
Jesus Christ and to the restoration of His gospel in these latter
days to all the world" ("150th Year for Twelve: 'Witnesses to All
World,'" p. 3).

What does it mean to be a special witness of the name of
Christ? President Joseph F. Smith said:

> All these, your brethren, that are called to the apostleship
> . . . are endowed, or ought to be endowed, richly with the
> spirit of their calling. For instance these twelve disciples of
> Christ are supposed to be eye and ear witnesses of the di-
> vine mission of Jesus Christ. It is not permissible for them to
> say, I believe, simply; I have accepted it simply because I be-
> lieve it. Read the revelation (D&C 18:26–33); the Lord in-
> forms us they must *know*, they must get the knowledge for

themselves, it must be with them as though they had seen with their eyes and heard with their ears and they know the truth. That is their mission, to testify of Jesus Christ and Him crucified and risen from the dead and clothed now with almighty power at the right hand of God, the Savior of the world. That is their mission, and their duty. (In Conference Report, April 1916, p. 6.)

President Smith's use of the phrase, "as though they had seen with their eyes and heard with their ears" implies a profound knowledge—a discerning, perceiving, or understanding—that comes by means beyond the auditory or visual senses. From the scriptures and statements of the prophets it is clear that Apostles, as special witnesses of the name of Christ, must know that he lives and must know him, but that special knowledge comes from an even greater witness than sight or hearing—the witness of the Holy Ghost. While serving as President of the Church, President Harold B. Lee told the students at Brigham Young University that there is a witness "more important than sight."

As I pray for the guidance of the Spirit, and seek to rise to the responsibility that has been given me, I don't ask for any special endowment. I ask only to go where the Lord would have me go, and only to receive what the Lord would have me receive, knowing that more important than sight is the witness that one may have by the witness of the Holy Ghost to his soul that things are so and that Jesus is the Christ, a living personage. It is that which guides me through many of the experiences of life. ("Be Loyal to the Royal Within You," p. 88.)

President Joseph Fielding Smith also testified that "impressions on the soul" are "far more significant than a vision." This important principle applies not only to the apostolic witness but also to the testimony of the risen Lord that each member of the Church should possess. President Smith taught:

They [the Twelve Apostles] are special witnesses for Jesus Christ. It is their right to know the truth and to have an abiding witness. This is an exacting duty upon them, to know that Jesus Christ is in very deed the Only Begotten Son of God, the Redeemer of the world, and the Savior of all those who will confess their sins, repent, and keep his commandments.

The question frequently arises: "Is it necessary for a member of the Council of the Twelve to see the Savior in order to be an apostle?" It is their privilege to see him if occasion requires, but the Lord has taught that there is a stronger witness than seeing a personage, even of seeing the Son of God in a vision. Impressions on the soul that come from the Holy Ghost are far more significant than a vision. When Spirit speaks to spirit, the imprint upon the soul is far more difficult to erase. Every member of the Church should have impressions that Jesus is the Son of God indelibly pictured on his soul through the witness of the Holy Ghost. (*Improvement Era*, November 1966, p. 979.)

Just as President Joseph Fielding Smith taught that every member of the Church can have a sure witness or knowledge of the reality of Christ, so also did the Prophet Joseph Smith. He stated: "God hath not revealed anything to Joseph, but what He will make known unto the Twelve, and even the least Saint may know all things as fast as he is able to bear them" (*HC* 3:380). By virtue of the baptismal covenant, all members of the Church also "stand as witnesses of God at all times and in all things, and in all places" (Mosiah 18:9). As witnesses it is also their privilege to obtain a perfect knowledge of the Savior's divinity, even to seeing him face to face (see D&C 67:10; 88:68; 93:1; see also Bruce R. McConkie, *The Promised Messiah*, pp. 592–95). What, then, is the difference between rank and file members of the Church who are "witnesses" of Christ and members of the Twelve who stand as "special witnesses" of His name? One difference can be found in the *scope* of the apostolic witness. While we can have the same knowledge revealed to us as the Twelve, we are not called as "special witnesses of the name of Christ in all the world." Also, we do not have the keys of authority they possess which endow their apostolic witness with saving power.

"Equal in Authority and Power to the Three Presidents"

At the time of their ordination, the members of the Twelve have conferred upon their heads all of the same keys as those resident in the prophet-president of the Church (see D&C 90:6). Although as a quorum they may be "equal in authority and power to the three presidents" (D&C 107:24) there is a difference in how they can exercise or act upon those given keys. President Joseph Fielding Smith wrote:

> Each of the apostles when he is ordained has conferred upon him all the keys and authorities which were given by Joseph Smith to the apostles before his death. These brethren, however cannot exercise these authorities except when the occasion arises that they come to the presidency. Before that time the powers lie dormant. This is one reason why they are sustained as prophets, seers, and revelators in the Church, but there can be but one revelator for the Church at a time. (*Church History and Modern Revelation* 2:151.)

Elder Bruce R. McConkie provides us with additional insight as to how the Twelve hold all the keys yet serve "under the direction of the Presidency of the Church" (see D&C 107:33).

> The keys of the kingdom of God—the right and power of eternal presidency by which the earthly kingdom is governed—these keys, having first been revealed from heaven, are given by the spirit of revelation to each man who is both ordained an Apostle and set apart as a member of the Council of the Twelve.
> But since keys are the right of presidency, they can only be exercised in their fulness by one man on earth at a time. He is always the senior Apostle, the presiding Apostle, the presiding high priest, the presiding elder. He alone can give direction to all others, direction from which none is exempt.
> Thus, the keys, though vested in all of the Twelve, are used by any one of them to a limited degree only, unless and

until one of them attains that seniority which makes him the Lord's anointed on earth. (*Ensign*, May 1983, pp. 22–23.)

Thus, although the scriptures speak of the Quorum of the Twelve as being "equal in authority and power" with the First Presidency, it does not mean that they can function or use their powers independent of the senior prophet, seer, and revelator. President Joseph Fielding Smith clarified the meaning of the phrase "equal in authority" as it applies to the Twelve and the First Presidency. "I think it must be said that the Apostles could not be equal in authority with the Presidency when the First Presidency is fully and properly organized," he wrote. "There could not be two heads—or three heads—of equal authority at the same time, for such a thing would lead to confusion." (*Improvement Era*, November 1966, p. 979.) As long as the First Presidency is functioning, neither the Quorum of the Twelve as a body nor individual Apostles are entitled to lead or direct the Church without the authorization and guidance of the First Presidency. Their labor is to direct the business of the Church that is delegated to them by the presiding quorum—the First Presidency. "It becomes our business when the President of the Church delegates to us some of the keys which he holds in fulness," Elder Harold B. Lee stated. "Until he gives us the authority, it is not our business and we do not have the right to take his place." (*Stand Ye in Holy Places*, p. 156.) The keys of the kingdom that are equally and fully conferred upon each member of the Council of the Twelve lie dormant in the individual Apostle until he becomes the senior Apostle. Meanwhile, any and all other exercising of keys and/or apostolic authority by individual members of the Twelve is by delegation from the President of the Church.

As a quorum, the Twelve become "equal in authority" and the presiding quorum of the Church only when there is no First Presidency. (This doctrine and its implications to succession in the Presidency will be discussed at length in the next chapter.) These important concepts concerning the authority of the Twelve and their relationship to the First Presidency and the President of the Church are summarized in the following statement of President George Q. Cannon:

Every man who is ordained to the fullness of the Apostleship has the power and authority to lead and guide the people of God whenever he is called upon to do it and the responsibility rests upon him. . . . And while it is the right of all the Twelve Apostles to receive revelation and for each one to be a Prophet, to be a Seer, to be a Revelator and to hold the keys in the fullness, it is only the right of one man at a time to exercise that power in relation to the whole people and to give revelation and counsel and direct the affairs of the Church—of course, always acting in conjunction with his fellow-servants.

And while we say that the Twelve Apostles have the right to govern, that the Twelve have the authority, that the Twelve Apostles are the men who preside, we do not mean that every one of the Twelve is going to give revelation to this great people, that every one of the Twelve has the right to counsel and dictate and regulate the affairs of the Church as emergencies may arise, independent of the rest. . . .

Any one of them, should an emergency arise, can act as President of the Church, with all the powers, with all the authority, with all the keys and with every endowment necessary to obtain revelation from God and to lead and guide this people in the path that leads to celestial glory; but there is only one man at a time who can hold the keys, who can dictate, who can guide, who can give revelation to the Church. The rest must acquiesce in his action; the rest must be governed by his counsels. (*Gospel Truth*, pp. 207–8.)

To Build Up and Regulate the Affairs of the Church in All Nations

Serving under the direction of and upon delegation from the First Presidency, the Twelve are commissioned to regulate, or "put in good order," the Church and to supervise the implementation of its mission—perfecting the Saints, proclaiming the gospel, and redeeming the dead—in all parts of the world. President Ezra Taft Benson, while serving as the President of the Quorum of the Twelve, explained how this is done in the Church today.

Each Thursday, the Quorum of the Twelve meets in council in an upper room in the Salt Lake Temple. Gold-gilded, framed paintings of each Church president grace the side and back walls of this room, reminding us that here the prophets of God have conducted the business of the Church. We meet from 8 to 10 A.M. to conduct the business of the council and approve matters for the consideration of the First Presidency. At 10 A.M. we join the First Presidency and decide in council the business before us. When the matters affect the entire Church, they are announced through letter, special statement, or the *Bulletin.*

President Spencer W. Kimball, while serving as an apostle, wrote the following words concerning the Thursday temple meeting, which we endorse today as applied to his administration as Church president:

"When in a Thursday temple meeting, after prayer and fasting, important decisions are made, new missions and new stakes are created, new patterns and policies initiated, the news is taken for granted and possibly thought of as mere human calculations. But to those who sit in the intimate circles and hear the prayers of the prophet and the testimony of the man of God; to those who see the astuteness of his deliberations and the sagacity of his decisions and pronouncements, to them he is verily a prophet." (*Instructor,* August 1960, pp. 256–57.)

The mission of the Church to preach the gospel, perfect the saints and redeem the dead is facilitated today by three executive councils.

The Missionary Executive Council considers all the policy matters relating to preaching the gospel throughout the world. The Priesthood Executive Council considers priesthood policies and programs (including the auxiliary organizations of the Church), and the Temple and Genealogy Executive Council considers matters pertaining to temples and genealogical work.

Additionally, each executive council has geographical jurisdiction for a major area of the world including one-third of the United States and Canada. Area presidencies report to a member of the Twelve on one of the three executive councils.

Through other committees of the Twelve, all training and curriculum materials are correlated and reviewed for appropriateness and doctrinal correctness.

Under the direction of the First Presidency, individual members of the Twelve may put in order matters of the Church. This includes doctrine, priesthood procedures, administration of Church funds, and restoration of blessings. (*Church News*, January 27, 1985, p. 3.)

To Open the Doors of Nations for the Proclamation of the Gospel

One of the first and most important functions of the Twelve in the last days was and is to travel to the ends of the earth opening the doors of nations for the teaching of the restored gospel and for the establishment of the Church there. In other words, they are to effect the gathering of Israel. "The Twelve . . . are not to serve tables," the Prophet Joseph Smith taught, "but to bear the keys of the Kingdom to all nations, and unlock the door of the Gospel to them" (*HC* 2:432). The Twelve, acting under the direction of the First Presidency, "unlock" these doors through negotiations with heads of state and through the priesthood ordinance of dedication or rededication. "Proselyting the gospel in nations of the world only occurs when a member of the Twelve dedicates the land for that purpose," President Ezra Taft Benson explained. "The Church works within the laws of each nation to ensure that Church practices do not conflict with the law or the customs of that nation. We do not proselyte where the laws of that country prohibit the practice." (*Church News*, January 27, 1985, p. 3.) Responsibility for geographical areas of the world, being divided among them, members of the Twelve not only regulate the affairs of the Church but also, through their faith, prayers, and apostolic ordination and keys, seek ways to break down cultural or political barriers and increase mutual understanding so that doors can be opened, nations dedicated, missionaries sent forth, and the gospel proclaimed "unto the ends of the earth."

"To Ordain Evangelical Ministers"

The Prophet Joseph Smith taught that "an Evangelist is a Patriarch" and that "wherever the Church of Christ is established in the earth, there should be a Patriarch for the benefit of the posterity of the Saints" (*HC* 3:381). The revelations outline the responsibility of the Twelve with regard to the calling and ordaining of patriarchs in the stakes of Zion. "It is the duty of the Twelve, in all large branches of the church [stakes], to ordain evangelical ministers, as they shall be designated unto them by revelation" (D&C 107:39). For many years in the Church, all patriarchs were approved by the Council of the Twelve and then called and ordained by one of its members. As the Church has become larger, the practice or administration has been modified, but it still remains one of the fundamental responsibilities of the Twelve to approve the names of those to be called as patriarchs and to authorize stake presidents to extend the call and ordain them. Of this duty of the Twelve, President Ezra Taft Benson said: "As defined by revelation, an evangelical minister is a patriarch. The Twelve have responsibility of approving all patriarchs in the world. Stake presidents may recommend calls and ordain a patriarch when approved by the Quorum of the Twelve. Approval of the calls of patriarchs rests with the Quorum of the Twelve." (*Church News*, January 27, 1985, pp. 3, 11.)

Unanimous Voice of the First Presidency and the Twelve

Just as the Lord has given a unique promise that the individual prophet-president of the Church will never lead us astray, he has given us the same promise concerning the collective prophets, seers, and revelators—the quorums of the First Presidency and the Twelve Apostles. As previously cited, President Joseph Fielding Smith taught that "the united voice of the First Presidency and the Twelve will [never] lead the Saints astray or send forth counsel to the world that is contrary to the mind and will of the Lord" (in Conference Report, April 1972, p. 99). That we can be secure in this assurance is clear from this revelation from the Lord:

Every decision made by either of these quorums [the First Presidency, the Twelve Apostles, and the Seventy] must be by the unanimous voice of the same; that is, every member in each quorum must be agreed to its decisions, in order to make their decisions of the same power or validity one with the other—

A majority may form a quorum when circumstances render it impossible to be otherwise—

Unless this is the case, their decisions are not entitled to the same blessings which the decisions of a quorum of the three presidents were anciently, who were ordained after the order of Melchizedek, and were righteous and holy men.

The decisions of these quorums, or either of them, are to be made in all righteousness, in holiness, and lowliness of heart, meekness and long suffering, and in faith, and virtue, and knowledge, temperance, patience, godliness, brotherly kindness and charity;

Because the promise is, if these things abound in them they shall not be unfruitful in the knowledge of the Lord. (D&C 107:27–31.)

This principle of unanimity is a profound blessing to the entire Church. As Elder James E. Faust said, it "provides a check on bias and personal idiosyncrasies. It ensures that God rules through the Spirit, not man through majority or compromise. It ensures that the best wisdom and experience is focused on an issue before the deep, unassailable impressions of revealed direction are received. It guards against the foibles of man." (In Conference Report, October 1989, p. 11.)

The First Presidency and the Quorum of the Twelve, working together, comprise the "constitutional body of the Church." Elder Stephen L Richards taught: "They [the First Presidency] are the supreme court here on earth in the interpretation of God's law. . . . In formulating their interpretations and decisions they always confer with the Council of the Twelve Apostles who by revelation are appointed to assist and act with them in the government of the Church. When, therefore, a judgment is reached and proclaimed by these officers it becomes binding upon all members of the Church, individual views to the contrary notwithstanding. God's Kingdom is a kingdom of law and order." (In Conference Report, October 1938, pp. 115–16.)

This inspired principle provides us with the assurance that the inadequacies and limitations that all mortal, individual leaders of the Church possess will not, indeed cannot, derail the Church or misdirect the Saints. Elder Boyd K. Packer so testified:

> We who have been called to lead the Church are ordinary men and women with ordinary capacities struggling to administer a church which grows at such a pace as to astound even those who watch it closely. Some are disposed to find fault with us; surely that is easy for them to do. But they do not examine us more searchingly than we examine ourselves. A call to lead is not an exemption from the challenges of life. . . .
>
> We are sorry for our inadequacies, sorry we are not better than we are. We can feel, as you can see, the effect of the aging process as it imposes limitations upon His leaders before your very eyes.
>
> But this we know. There are councils and counselors and quorums to counterbalance the foibles and frailties of man. The Lord organized His church to provide for mortal men to work as mortal men, and yet He assured that the spirit of revelation would guide in all that we do in His name. (In Conference Report, October 1989, p. 19.)

Speaking to the students of Brigham Young University, Elder Packer explained the principle of unanimity as it works in the presiding quorums of the Church. He not only spoke of the practical workings of councils and quorums but also testified of the resulting spiritual blessing that comes to the entire Church through the unified voice of the prophets, seers, and revelators.

> When a matter comes before the First Presidency and the Quorum of the Twelve Apostles in a temple meeting, one thing that is determined very quickly is whether it is of serious consequence or not. One or another of us will see in an apparently innocent proposal issues of great and lasting consequence.
>
> It is clear from the revelations that the decisions of the presiding quorums "must be by the unanimous voice of the

same. . . . Unless this is the case, their decisions are not entitled to the same blessings" (D&C 107:27, 29). In order to ensure that to be the case, matters of consequence are seldom decided in the meeting where they are proposed. And, if the proposal is a part of a larger issue, sufficient time is taken to "bring us all along" so that it is clear that each of us has either a clear *understanding* of the issue or, as is often the case, has a very clear *feeling* about it. . . .

It would be unthinkable to deliberately present an issue in such a way that approval depended upon how it was maneuvered through channels, who was presenting it, or who was present or absent when it was presented.

Often one or more of us is away during regular meetings. We all know that the work must proceed and will accept the judgment of our brethren. However, if a matter has been studied by one of the Quorum in more detail than by the others or he is more familiar with it either by assignment, experience, or personal interest, the matter is very often delayed until he can be in on the discussion.

And, always, if one of us cannot understand an issue or feels unsettled about it, it is held over for future discussion.

I remember occasions when a delegation was sent to the hospital to discuss with a member of the Council who was ill some urgent matter that could not be delayed but which needed that "unanimous consent." There are occasions, as well, when one of us will leave the meeting temporarily to call one of our number who is abroad to get his feelings on a matter under discussion.

There is a rule we follow: A matter is not settled until there is a *minute entry* to evidence that all of the Brethren in council assembled (not just one of us, not just a committee) have come to a unity of feeling. Approval of a matter in principle is not considered authority to act until a minute entry records the action taken—usually when the minutes are approved in the next meeting.

Sometimes an afterthought keeps one of us restless over a decision. That is never dismissed lightly. It cannot be assumed that that restless spirit is not in fact the Spirit of Revelation.

That is how we function—in council assembled. That

provides safety for the Church and a high comfort level for each of us who is personally accountable. Under the plan, men of ordinary capacity may be guided through counsel and inspiration to accomplish extraordinary things.

Even with the best of intentions, it does not always work the way it should. Human nature may express itself on occasion, but not to the permanent injury of the work. I have a deep, even sacred, regard for councils; inspiration is evident in them. If ever another course has been followed, trouble has followed as surely as night follows day. ("I Say Unto You, Be One," pp. 83–84.)

Even if the President of the Church may be slowed in his service or debilitated by age or illness, the principle allows for counselors and councils comprised of other prophets, seers, and revelators, endowed with the same keys, to ensure the continuance of the proper leadership and direction for the Lord's kingdom on earth. From the vantage point of his unique personal experience President Gordon B. Hinckley, in an address entitled "In . . . Counselors There Is Safety," testified of the roles of unanimity, keys, and councils in the administration of the Church.

No president in any organization in the Church is likely to go ahead without the assurance that his counselors feel good about the proposed program. A man or woman thinking alone, working alone, arriving at his or her own conclusions, can take action which might prove to be wrong. But when three kneel together in prayer, discuss every aspect of the problem which is before them, and under the impressions of the Spirit reach a united conclusion, then we may have the assurance that the decision is in harmony with the will of the Lord.

I can assure all members of this Church that in the First Presidency we follow such a procedure. Even the President of the Church, who is Prophet, Seer, and Revelator, and whose right and responsibility it is to make judgment and direct the course of the Church, invariably consults with his counselors to determine their feelings. If there is a lack of unity, there follows an absence of action. Two counselors, working with a president, preserve a wonderful system of checks and balances. They become a safeguard that is seldom, if ever, in error and affords great strength of leadership. . . .

In some circumstances, *a counselor may serve as a proxy for his president*. The power of proxy must be granted by the president, and it must never be abused by the counselor. . . .

It may not be easy to be a counselor. President J. Reuben Clark, Jr., who, as a counselor, had responsibility for the operation of the Church while President Heber J. Grant was ill, said to me on one occasion, "It is difficult to have responsibility without authority."

He was saying, in effect, that he had to move forward in handling those duties which ordinarily devolve upon the President, but while doing so, he did not have the authority of the President.

I came to understand that situation in a very real way. If I may share with you some personal feelings: During the time that President Kimball was ill, President Tanner's health failed and he passed away. President Romney was called as First Counselor, and I as Second Counselor to President Kimball. Then President Romney became ill, thus leaving to me an almost overwhelming burden of responsibility. I counseled frequently with my Brethren of the Twelve, and I cannot say enough of appreciation to them for their understanding and for the wisdom of their judgment. In matters where there was a well-established policy, we moved forward. But no new policy was announced or implemented, and no significant practice was altered without sitting down with President Kimball and laying the matter before him and receiving his full consent and full approval.

In such circumstances when I would go to visit him, I always took a secretary who kept a detailed record of the conversation. I can assure you . . . that I never knowingly moved ahead of my file leader, that I never had any desire to move out ahead of him in Church policy or instruction. I knew that he was the appointed Prophet of the Lord in that day. Even though I, too, had been sustained as a prophet, seer, and revelator, along with my Brethren of the Twelve, I knew also that none of us was the President of the Church. . . .

President Benson is now ninety-one years of age and does not have the strength or vitality he once possessed in abundance. Brother Monson and I, as his counselors, do as has been done before, and that is to move forward the work of the Church, while being very careful not to get ahead of the President nor to undertake any departure of any kind from long-established policy without his knowledge and full approval.

I am grateful for President Monson. We have known one another for a long time and have worked together in many responsibilities. We counsel together. We deliberate together. We pray together. We postpone action when we are not fully certain of our course and do not move forward until we have the blessing of our President and that assurance which comes from the Spirit of the Lord.

We pray for our President. We pray often and with great earnestness. We love him and know our proper relationship to him, as well as our responsibility to the entire Church. We counsel with the Twelve and partake of their judgment, which is a greater resource than I am able to describe.

Do not fear . . . there is a Presidency over this Church. (*Ensign*, November 1990, pp. 50–51.)

Other General Authorities of the Church

Although they are not sustained as prophets, seers, and revelators, and do not have the same keys of the kingdom conferred upon them as do the First Presidency and the Twelve, there are other "watchmen on the walls" who are sustained as General Authorities of the Church. "These brethren are all delegated *general administrative* authority by the President of the Church," Elder Bruce R. McConkie wrote concerning General Authorities. "That is, they are called to preach the gospel, direct church conferences, choose other church officers, perform ordinations and settings apart, and handle the properties and interests of the Church generally. The labors of their ministries are not confined to stake, ward, or regional areas, but they have general jurisdiction in all parts of the Church." (*Mormon Doctrine*, p. 309.)

The revelations identify the Seventy and the Presiding Bishopric as those other watchmen who serve under the direction of and in cooperation with the First Presidency and the Twelve in administering the worldwide Church and ministering to the Saints. While they are not prophets, seers, and revelators in the same sense as the Presidency and the Twelve, they are nonetheless prophets to the Church in the general sense—as forthtellers and preachers of righteousness. Each group has important duties that affect the Church and its members both spiritually and temporally.

The Seventy

The Prophet Joseph Smith taught that the Twelve are to "call upon the Seventies to follow after them, and assist them" (*HC* 2:432). The Lord revealed the duties of the Seventy and how they were to assist the Twelve. "The Seventy are also called to preach the gospel, and to be especial witnesses unto the Gentiles in all the world—thus differing from other officers in the church in the duties of their calling. And they form a quorum, equal in authority to that of the Twelve special witnesses or Apostles just named. . . . The Seventy are to act in the name of the Lord, under the direction of the Twelve or the traveling high council, in building up the church and regulating all the affairs of the same in all nations." (D&C 107:25–26, 34.)

During the administration of President Spencer W. Kimball, the First Quorum of the Seventy was reconstituted (1975–76) to better fulfill the divine charge found in the revelations. President Kimball said of this important development:

> With this move, the three governing quorums of the Church defined by the revelations—the First Presidency, the Quorum of the Twelve Apostles, and the First Quorum of the Seventy—have been set in their places as revealed by the Lord.
>
> This will make it possible to handle efficiently the present heavy workload and to prepare for the increasing expansion and acceleration of the work, anticipating the day when the Lord will return to take direct charge of His church and kingdom. (In Conference Report, October 1976, p. 10.)

We have seen in the last several years a more complete application of these revealed instructions [D&C 107:33–34]. Today we should even more clearly understand how they are to be applied in building up the Church in all nations. Events in the world may make this approach to managing the affairs of the kingdom not only practical but a necessity in the years ahead.

As the kingdom thus functions, these wonderful men of the Quorum of the Twelve can go about the Church and set things in order as is necessary, but be relieved of their assignments to manage programs and departments as they once did. The work of the managing and directing our various departments and programs is now the work of our General Authorities in the First Quorum of the Seventy, and they have the willing and capable support of the Presiding Bishopric and our temporal departments—all to the end that we can move forward in unity and at a pace never before known. (In Conference Report, April 1979, pp. 139–40.)

Since President Kimball made the latter statement in 1979, a Second Quorum of the Seventy has been created (April 1989) to meet the growing demands of a worldwide Church. This development is another step toward the fulfillment of the revelation on the Seventy that allows for the calling of additional Seventies even "until seven times seventy, if the labor in the vineyard of necessity requires it" (D&C 107:96). With the organization in place to accommodate almost unlimited growth, the Seventy are called upon to assist the Twelve in many ways. They have an apostolic calling to be "especial witnesses unto the Gentiles and in all the world" and to act "under the direction of the Twelve . . . in building up the church and regulating all the affairs of the same in all nations" (D&C 107:25, 34). Elder J. Thomas Fyans explained how the Seventy fulfill this divine mandate.

Assignments that the First Presidency and the Quorum of the Twelve have given to the First Quorum of the Seventy can be divided into two categories: headquarters assignments and field assignments.

Headquarters assignments include serving as directors of Church headquarters departments and organizations. At the head of a Church department is an executive director and two or more managing directors, all of whom are members of the First Quorum of the Seventy.

The quorum presidents serve as executive directors of the Correlation, Curriculum, Missionary, Priesthood, Genealogical and Historical departments. Other quorum members serve as executive director of the Temple Department and as managing directors in all of the departments. In addition, members of the quorum serve as the general presidency of the Sunday School and the Young Men, as presidents of several temples and as president of the International Mission.

The second category of assignments, field assignments, include serving in an area presidency. The First Presidency and Quorum of the Twelve organized the area presidencies to meet the needs of an expanding Church. Each area presidency reports to one of the three Church Executive Councils (Priesthood Executive Council, Missionary Executive Council, and Genealogy Executive Council). The area presidency structure provides a direct communication channel from Church headquarters to stakes and missions throughout the world and from the stakes and missions to Church headquarters.

Each area presidency, acting under the direction of the First Presidency and the Quorum of the Twelve, is responsible for the affairs of the Church in its assigned geographical area of the world. Some area presidencies live at Church headquarters and have domestic assignments (United States and Canada). Others live at headquarters and have overseas assignments. Still others live in the areas where they preside. . . .

Area presidencies are responsible for the supervision and leadership development of mission presidents, regional representatives and stake presidents. They also direct Church managers for real estate, construction, physical facilities, finances and budgets. The presidencies supervise, train, and direct in a variety of ways. They attend stake conferences nearly every weekend. They hold two mission president seminars each year. During a tour of each mission, they meet with all of the missionaries and mission leaders, hold mission firesides, and take care of the needs of mission districts. The presidencies also hold quarterly leadership meetings with Regional Representatives and stake and mission presidents to answer questions, solve problems and help plan the work.

Church headquarters organizations work with area presidencies instead of dealing directly with local officers, fostering cooperation and coordination between area leaders and headquarters offices. ("Seventies Began 150 Years Ago," p. 6.)

The Presiding Bishopric

Since the earliest days of the Church—when Edward Partridge and Newell K. Whitney served as bishops—the Presiding Bishopric has worked under the direction of the First Presidency in temporal matters, including the charge to search out and administer relief to the poor of the Church. The Lord specified in the revelations that the Bishopric is "set apart unto the ministering of temporal things, having a knowledge of them by the Spirit of truth" (D&C 107:71). While the basic responsibility to minister in temporal things will remain constant, the manner in which the Presiding Bishopric fulfills this charge has changed and will continue to change through the years as technologies and the needs of the Church change (see D&C 42:31–32; 51:5, 12–13). Many of the duties and challenges of the current Presiding Bishopric could not even be imagined in the early days of the Church. Yet each Bishopric, whatever the requirements of the times, was, is, and will be responsible for the temporal welfare of the Church.

Bishop Victor L. Brown, who served in the Presiding Bishopric for nearly a quarter of a century, explained the nature of the temporal work of the Presiding Bishopric: "The Presiding Bishopric, under the direction of the First Presidency, has the responsibility for administering many of the temporal affairs of the Church. These include physical facilities, finance, welfare services, materials management, and information systems. We administer this network of temporal functions to support and service priesthood needs and Church activities throughout the world." (In Conference Report, April 1979, p. 125.)

The temporal support services provided by the Presiding Bishopric, under the direction of the First Presidency and the Twelve, include things such as acquisition of lands, construction and maintenance of buildings, operation of Deseret Industries, storehouses, employment services, social services, and welfare production facilities. They work closely with area presidencies and bless the Saints "in the field" with important services such as translation and distribution of Church materials. One of the most important duties of the Presiding Bishopric is to work closely with the First Presidency and the Twelve on the disposition of tithes and offerings (see D&C 120; see also *Ensign*, April 1977, pp. 94–95). In addition to their temporal duties, they are also General Authorities with a spiritual ministry to travel around the Church testifying and teaching and "building up and regulating" the affairs of the Church.

All things—both temporal and spiritual—are done in "wisdom and order" through the unified service of and close cooperation with all of the General Authorities of the Church, under the delegation and direction of the senior prophet, seer, and revelator. As members of each quorum faithfully discharge their divine duties, individual members of the Church, as well as the institutional Church, are blessed and benefited by the living oracles of God. Our lives are enriched by better understanding the role and responsibilities of the living oracles and our relationship to them. Of this blessing, Elder Spencer W. Kimball testified: "The authorities which the Lord has placed in his Church constitute for the people of the Church a harbor, a place of refuge, a hitching post, as it were. No one in this Church will ever go far astray who ties himself securely to the Church Authorities whom the Lord has placed in his Church." (In Conference Report, April 1951, p. 104.)

Each President has been uniquely selected for the time and situation which the world and Church needed. All were "men of the hour". . . . Contemplate the miracle of that foreordination and preparation! Though called and given keys many years prior to the time that the mantle fell upon him, the President was always the right man in the right place for the times.

—Ezra Taft Benson
The Teachings of Ezra Taft Benson, p. 142

CHAPTER 4

Succession in the Presidency

When the Prophet Joseph Smith was martyred, there were many saints who died spiritually with Joseph," President Harold B. Lee declared. "So it was when Brigham Young died: so it was when John Taylor died. . . . Some Church members died spiritually with Wilford Woodruff, with Lorenzo Snow, with Joseph F. Smith, with Heber J. Grant, with George Albert Smith. We have some today willing to believe someone who is dead and gone and to accept his words as having more authority than the words of a living authority today." (*Stand Ye in Holy Places,* p. 153.)

There are several ways in which this spiritual demise of some Saints may occur with the passing of a prophet. Some "die spiritually" with the death of a President of the Church when they second-guess the Lord about who should be the new prophet and then become disgruntled when the Lord's choice does not correspond with their own short-sighted reasoning. Some fail to sustain the new President, to follow his counsel and leadership, because they feel he is in some way unqualified to be the prophet and President. They may point to his ill health, or his advanced age, or some of his teachings and writings. Whatever the issue, their failure to perceive and accept the Lord's hand in the choice evidences a lack of understanding of the principles involved in succession in the Presidency.

While there may even be some innocent speculation or "supposing" among many of the Saints concerning who will succeed the prophet when he dies, there is no doubt among the brethren of the Twelve, who are commissioned to ordain him. This sureness comes because they know the Master who makes that choice and are intimately familiar with the principles surrounding succession. Elder Harold B. Lee shared the following account from the life of President Heber J. Grant that illustrates this idea.

> The simple faith, to accept that which comes from the inspired utterances of those whom God has set to preside over his Church, is indicated in the simple pure faith of the late President Heber J. Grant who had been stricken, and in his advanced years it was thought that he would not be long upon the earth. As is frequently the case among the Saints there is a lot of supposing; supposing that the president should die, supposing that the next in the line of authority were not physically or mentally able to carry on his work. Some of you may live through such periods and you might be one to suppose. One of his own family approached him on such occasion and said, "Grandfather, suppose that the president of the Church should die, and suppose that the next in line of authority was not prepared to carry on after his death." The President impatiently said, "Stop that supposing; there is no supposing with the Lord; he knows who he wants to preside over his Church." ("Be Secure in the Gospel of Jesus Christ," p. 6.)

Perhaps the only time in the history of the Church at which such supposing and speculating was justifiable was at the death of the Prophet Joseph Smith. The early Saints had never experienced the death of a Church President, and though many of the principles of succession had been taught, they had not observed them in practice—no precedent had been set. As the Saints counseled together on how to proceed and who should lead them, they were blessed with a miraculous manifestation in the form of the "transfiguration" of Brigham Young. As President

Young spoke, to members of the congregation he looked and sounded like Joseph Smith. To them this was a sign that Brigham Young, not Sidney Rigdon, was the Lord's chosen, rightful successor to Joseph. (For an extensive discussion of the doctrinal significance of this historical event see B. H. Roberts's *Comprehensive History of the Church* 2:413–25; see also Wilford Woodruff's account of this event in *Journal of Discourses* 15:81; also Emmeline B. Wells's account cited in Preston Nibley's *Faith-Promoting Stories*, p. 138.)

For us today, however, there is need neither for wonder and worry nor for a dramatic sign from heaven, inasmuch as the pattern has already been laid, the precedents set, and the principles taught. "It [is] not required, nor [is] it requisite or needed, that the Lord give any revelation, that any special direction be given," Elder Bruce R. McConkie said of the pattern of succession. "The law [is] already ordained and established." ("Succession in the Presidency," p. 19.) Understanding those laws and principles and recognizing the divinely inspired pattern will open our eyes to the fact that God's house is a "house of order" (see D&C 132:8) and that his earthly kingdom is governed in an orderly and systematic way. Of this Elder Spencer W. Kimball testified:

> The work of the Lord is endless. Even when a powerful leader dies, not for a single instant is the Church without leadership, thanks to the kind Providence who gave his kingdom continuity and perpetuity. As it already has happened [several] times before in this dispensation, a people reverently close a grave, dry their tears, and turn their faces to the future.
>
> The moment life passes from a President of the Church, a body of men become the composite leader—these men already seasoned with experience and training. The appointments have long been made, the authority given, the keys delivered. For [a few] days, the kingdom moves forward under this already authorized council. No "running" for position, no electioneering, no stump speeches. What a divine plan! How wise our Lord, to organize so perfectly beyond the weakness of frail, grasping humans. (In Conference Report, April 1970, p. 118.)

Keys of the Kingdom Conferred on the Twelve

The Prophet Joseph began the pattern for succession during the months preceding his death. This he did by teaching the Twelve their roles and by conferring upon them all of the authority necessary to carry forth the kingdom after his death. Commanded by the Lord, Joseph conferred upon the Twelve, as he said, "every key, power, principle, that the God of heaven has revealed to me." After fulfilling that commandment, Joseph declared to the Twelve: "Now if they kill me you have got all the keys, and all the ordinances and you can confer them upon others, and the hosts of Satan will not be able to tear down the kingdom, as fast as you will be able to build it up; and . . . on your shoulders will the responsibility of leading this people rest" (*Times and Seasons* 5:651). President Wilford Woodruff, who received those keys from Joseph and heard with his own ears the teachings of the Prophet concerning the relationship of the keys held by the Twelve and the pattern of succession, testified:

> We had had our endowments; we had had all the blessings sealed upon our heads that were ever given to the apostles or prophets on the face of the earth. On that occasion the Prophet Joseph rose up and said to us: "Brethren, I have desired to live to see this temple built. I shall never live to see it, but you will. I have sealed upon your heads all of the keys of the kingdom of God. I have sealed upon you every key, power, principle that the God of heaven has revealed to me. Now, no matter where I may go or what I may do, the kingdom rests upon you."
>
> . . . "But," he said, after having done this, "ye apostles of the Lamb of God, my brethren, upon your shoulders this kingdom rests; now you have got to round up your shoulders and bear off the kingdom." . . .
>
> When the Lord gave the keys of the kingdom of God, the keys of the Melchizedek Priesthood, of the apostleship, and sealed them upon the head of Joseph Smith, he sealed them upon his head to stay here upon the earth until the coming of the Son of Man. Well might Brigham Young say, "The keys of the kingdom of God are here." They were with him to the day of his death. They then rested upon the head

of another man—President John Taylor. He held those keys to the hour of his death. They then fell by turn, or in the providence of God, upon Wilford Woodruff.

I say to the Latter-day Saints, the keys of the kingdom of God are here, and they are going to stay here, too, until the coming of the Son of Man. Let all Israel understand that. They may not rest upon my head but a short time, but they will then rest on the head of another apostle, and another after him, and so continue until the coming of the Lord Jesus Christ in the clouds of heaven to "reward every man according to the deeds done in the body." (*Discourses of Wilford Woodruff*, pp. 72–74.)

In our day, the established pattern is followed. "Succession in the presidency happens in an orderly and systemized way," Elder Bruce R. McConkie stated, "because the Lord has conferred upon the members of the Council of the Twelve all of the keys and powers and authorities that have ever been held in any dispensation or any age of the past. Each key is given to each apostle who is set apart a member of the Council of the Twelve." ("Succession in the Presidency," p. 25.) Hence, the first principle or step in succession is the conferral of the keys of the kingdom on every man who is ordained an Apostle and set apart as a member of the Quorum of the Twelve. President Harold B. Lee taught:

The beginning of the call of one to be President of the Church actually begins when he is called, ordained, and set apart to become a member of the Quorum of the Twelve Apostles. Such a call by prophecy, or in other words, by the inspiration of the Lord to the one holding the keys of presidency, and the subsequent ordination and setting apart by the laying on of hands by that same authority, places each apostle in a priesthood quorum of twelve men holding the apostleship.

Each apostle so ordained under the hands of the President of the Church, who holds the keys of the kingdom of God in concert with all other ordained apostles, has given to him the priesthood authority necessary to hold every position in the Church, even to a position of presidency over the

Church if he were called by the presiding authority and sustained by a vote of a constituent assembly of the membership of the Church. (In Conference Report, April 1970, p. 123.)

This foundational principle—that all the keys of the kingdom are conferred upon each member of the Twelve—ensures that the authority and power to administer the kingdom of God on earth are never lost. If they did not reside with each member of the Quorum, but only with the President, those keys and powers would need to be restored with every death of a prophet-president. However, these keys lie dormant, as it were, in all of the Apostles but one—the senior Apostle. For as the Lord stated, "there is never but one on the earth at a time on whom this power and the keys of this priesthood are conferred" (D&C 132:7).

Order of Seniority:
A Governing Principle of Presidency

The factor which determines who presides among the Twelve and who may actively exercise all of the keys of the kingdom at the death of the President of the Church is the principle of seniority. "The members of the Council of the Twelve are of equal priesthood authority," wrote Elder John A. Widtsoe. "Yet when they meet in their deliberations one is called to act as chairman or President."

Since these men are of equal priesthood authority, it might be thought that any one of them might be called to the presidential office. Under the practice of the Church, based upon the latter-day revelations of the Lord, this is not done. Instead, the senior member of the council, that is, the one who has held the apostleship the longest, is appointed and sustained as the President of the Council of the Twelve Apostles.

The members of the first apostolic quorum in this day, all called at the same time, were arranged according to their ages. Elder Thomas B. Marsh became the senior member and President of the Council, but apostatized and was excommunicated from the Church. That left Brigham Young the ranking Apostle. . . .

Since that time there has been no deviation from the rule that the senior member should preside over the Council. In the troublesome days following the death of the Prophet, Brigham Young became the President of the Council, which, until a new President was chosen, presided over the Church. When finally the Lord moved upon the Council to reorganize the First Presidency, Brigham Young, then President of the Council of the Twelve, was called to be President of the Church.

This order of succession to the presidency of the Council of Twelve, and to the presidency of the Church, has been followed, and will continue to be the rule of the Church until the Lord speaks and commands another procedure. (*Evidences and Reconciliations*, pp. 260–61.)

When a man is called, sustained, and ordained a member of the Twelve, he receives not only the keys of the kingdom but also his place of seniority. The seniority in the first Quorum of the Twelve in this dispensation was arranged by age. Since then, seniority has been determined by dates of ordination, the Apostle who has served the longest being the most senior. When two or more men are ordained on the same date, the one ordained first is the more senior. When this has happened in the past, the older man has generally been ordained first. Seniority determines who presides over the Quorum of the Twelve, and the Lord controls seniority and succession through the natural means of life and death. President Spencer W. Kimball testified concerning the principle of seniority and its importance in the selection of a new President of the Church.

Full provision has been made by our Lord for changes. Today there are fourteen apostles holding the keys in suspension, the twelve and the two counselors to the President, to be brought into use if and when circumstances allow, all ordained to leadership in their turn as they move forward in seniority.

There have been some eighty apostles so endowed since Joseph Smith, though only eleven have occupied the place of the President of the Church, death having intervened; and since the death of his servants is in the power and control of the Lord, he permits to come to the first place only the one who is destined to take that leadership. Death and life become the controlling factors. Each new apostle in turn is chosen by the Lord and revealed to the then living prophet who ordains him.

The matter of seniority is basic in the first quorums of the Church. All the apostles understand this perfectly, and all well-trained members of the Church are conversant with this perfect succession program. (In Conference Report, October 1972, p. 29.)

In addition to determining presidency, the principle of seniority provides rich, practical blessings in Church administration—wisdom, knowledge, and inspiration that have been acquired and tempered through plentiful experience. "Through long years of dedicated service," stated Elder Gordon B. Hinckley concerning all those prophet-presidents who have followed Joseph Smith, "they have been refined and winnowed and chastened and molded for the purposes of the Almighty. . . . The Lord subdued their hearts and refined their natures to prepare them for the great and sacred responsibility later thrust upon them." (In Conference Report, October 1973, p. 164.) The wisdom of the Lord is always manifest in the preparation of his chosen prophets through their many assignments and responsibilities in the Twelve. "This is a wise procedure," Elder Widtsoe testified. "It places at the head of the Church the apostle who has been longest in service. He is known well to the people and trusted by them. He himself knows the procedure of Church affairs. He is no novice to be trained for the position. . . . It eliminates the shadow of politics from the operations of the Council." (*Evidences and Reconciliations*, p. 264.)

At President's Death
There Is No First Presidency

The Prophet Joseph Smith declared in a special meeting with the Twelve Apostles in 1836 that the Twelve were not subject to any other than the First Presidency, namely, "myself, Sidney Rigdon, and Frederick G. Williams, who are now my Coun-selors, and where I am not, there is no First Presidency over the Twelve" (*Teachings*, pp. 105–6).[1] This concept became a founda-tional factor in Brigham Young's ascent to the Presidency fol-lowing the death of Joseph. It set the precedent and became the pattern in subsequent successions. President Harold B. Lee ex-plained: "Immediately following the death of a President, the next ranking body, the Quorum of the Twelve Apostles, be-comes the presiding authority, with the President of the Twelve automatically becoming the acting President of the Church until a President of the Church is officially ordained and sus-tained in his office" (in Conference Report, April 1970, p. 123).

As President Lee pointed out, at the death of the President the quorum of the First Presidency is automatically dissolved, the two Counselors return to their respective places of seniority in the Twelve (if they came from the Twelve), and the Quorum of the Twelve becomes, as it were, the Presidency of the Church. It is at this moment in time that the Twelve truly be-come "equal in authority and power to the three presidents" (D&C 107:24). President N. Eldon Tanner explained how this principle operated at the death of President Harold B. Lee.

> I would like to explain to you exactly what took place fol-lowing the unexpected death of President Harold B. Lee on 26 December 1973. I was in Phoenix, Arizona, to spend Christmas with my daughter and her family, when a call came to me from Arthur Haycock, secretary to President Lee. He said that President Lee was seriously ill, and he

---

1. In "The Mormon Succession Crisis of 1844," *BYU Studies* 16 (Winter 1976), page 189, D. Michael Quinn states that the phrase "Where I am not, there is no First Presidency over the Twelve" was not in the original minutes of the 1834 meeting. Even so, the insertion in the Joseph Smith History in the 1850s can still be accepted as valid, for as Wilford Woodruff and George A. Smith wrote upon the publication of that history, its compilers, contempo-raries of the Prophet, "were eye and ear witnesses of nearly all the transactions recorded . . . and, where they were not personally present, they have had ac-cess to those who were" (quoted in Dean C. Jesse, "The Writing of Joseph Smith's History," *BYU Studies* [Summer 1971], 11:4, p. 473). In any event, Brigham Young certainly understood and taught the concept, as have later Church Presidents and other Apostles who have authoritatively used the ex-pression in question as a key principle in succession to the Presidency.

thought that I should plan to return home as soon as possible. A half-hour later he called and said: "The Lord has spoken. President Lee has been called home."

President Romney, Second Counselor, in my absence was directing the affairs of the Church, and was at the hospital with Spencer W. Kimball, President of the Council of the Twelve. Immediately upon the death of President Lee, President Romney turned to President Kimball and said, "You are in charge." Remember, the Prophet Joseph Smith had said that without the President there was no First Presidency over the Twelve.

Not one minute passed between the time President Lee died and the Twelve took over as the presiding authority of the Church. (In Conference Report, October 1979, p. 62.)

Reorganization of the First Presidency

With the First Presidency dissolved at the death of the President the Quorum of the Twelve becomes the Presidency of the Church, and the senior Apostle or President of the Twelve automatically, by virtue of seniority, becomes the presiding high priest. At that point, instead of "three presiding high priests"—a President and two Counselors—the Presidency of the Church is comprised of fourteen "presiding high priests"—a President plus thirteen apostles who act as counselors. The President of the Twelve, as the presiding officer of the presiding quorum, actively holds and exercises all the keys of the kingdom and "presides over the whole church." He is not only the acting president of the Church; he is in very deed, by virtue of those keys and as the presiding high priest, the prophet and President of the Church. "There is no mystery about the choosing of the successor to the President of the Church," President Joseph Fielding Smith confirmed. "The Lord settled this a long time ago, and the *senior apostle automatically becomes the presiding officer of the Church*, and he is so sustained by the Council of the Twelve which becomes the presiding body of the Church when there is no First Presidency." (*Doctrines of Salvation* 3:156.)

This presiding quorum is as much a Presidency of the Church and as "equal in authority" as the First Presidency is when it is fully organized and operative. Likewise the President of the Twelve at that time is also as much the President of the Church in function and authority as when he becomes ordained as such and the First Presidency is reorganized. As the presiding high priest he also holds the keys to receive revelations, "even as Moses," for the Church. President Brigham Young received revelations while the Twelve presided over the Church prior to his being sustained as the President of the Church in a newly organized First Presidency (see D&C section 136). There have been three times when the President of the Twelve, along with the Quorum acting as counselors, has presided over the Church for extended periods of time—Brigham Young for three and one-half years (June 1844–December 1847), John Taylor for just over three years (August 1877–October 1880), and Wilford Woodruff for just less than two years (July 1887–April 1889). Not long before his death, President Wilford Woodruff instructed the Twelve that it was not the will of the Lord that there be a lengthy delay in future in reorganizing the First Presidency after the death of the President. Since that time, the Council of the Twelve has presided over the Church for only a matter of days before the President has been officially ordained and the First Presidency reorganized.

As the presiding officer, it becomes the prerogative of the President of the Twelve to receive revelation from the Lord regarding when to reorganize the First Presidency and, theoretically, who shall be ordained as the President of the Church. Elder Bruce R. McConkie explained how this pattern was followed and how the principles were put into operation at the death of President Harold B. Lee.

> When the President of the Church passes on, the First Presidency is disorganized, and the mantle of leadership—the reins of presidency—go to the senior man left and to the Council of the Twelve as a body; in effect the Council of the Twelve then becomes the First Presidency of the Church and so continues unless and until a formal reorganization takes place. These words I read to you from President Joseph F. Smith:
>
> "There is always a head in the Church, and if the presidency of the Church are removed by death or other cause,

then the next head of the Church is the Twelve Apostles, until a presidency is again organized of three presiding high priests who have the right to hold the office of First Presidency over the Church; and, according to the doctrine laid down by President Wilford Woodruff, who saw the necessity for it, and that of President Lorenzo Snow, if the President should die, his counselors are then released from that presidency, and it is the duty of the Twelve Apostles to proceed at once, in the manner that has been pointed out, to see that the First Presidency is reorganized, so that there may be no deficiency in the working and order of the priesthood in the Church of God" (Conference Report, April 1913, pp. 4–5).

Harmonious with that policy, that counsel, and that instruction—which has been followed in previous instances—the Council of the Twelve met in the upper room of the Salt Lake Temple on Sunday, December 30 [1973], at 3:00 P.M. for the purpose of reorganizing the First Presidency of the Church. Normally in that upper room there are three chairs occupied by the First Presidency and twelve chairs in a semicircle in front of them occupied by the members of the Council of the Twelve. On this occasion, however, there were fourteen chairs in the semicircle, because there were fourteen Brethren present who had been sustained and ordained and set apart as members of the Council of the Twelve.

We took our places in those chairs, and President Kimball presided in the meeting, which lasted for about 3 1/2 hours. In the course of this meeting President Kimball explained the business to be transacted, the things that might be done if the Brethren felt so guided and led. . . .

He expressed himself as to what should be done, and he said that the proposition to be first considered was whether the First Presidency should then be reorganized or whether the Church should continue to function with the Council of the Twelve as its presiding officers. He then invited each member of the Twelve, commencing with Elder Ezra Taft Benson and continuing around the circle to me, to arise in turn and express himself frankly and fully and freely as to what ought to be done. . . .

. . . Each member of the Council in turn, specifically and pointedly, expressed himself to the effect that now was the time to reorganize the First Presidency of the Church, that there should not be further delay, that the effective and proper operation of this great organization that we have from the Lord needed this administrative arrangement. Each one in turn expressed himself that President Spencer W. Kimball was the man whom the Lord wanted to preside over the Church; there was no question whatever about that. There was total and complete unity and harmony. ("Succession in the Presidency," pp. 19–22.)

President N. Eldon Tanner, who had returned to his place of seniority in the Twelve, also attended this meeting. He reported that President Kimball said "he had spent Friday in the temple talking to the Lord, and had shed many tears as he prayed for guidance in assuming his new responsibilities, and in choosing his counselors" (in Conference Report, October 1979, p. 62). It is interesting to note that, according to Elder McConkie and implicit in President Kimball's statement, there was no asking the Lord for a special revelation as to who should be the President of the Church. When the Lord's will was made known with the last heartbeat of President Lee, President Kimball knew, as did each of the Twelve, whom the Lord had selected. It is significant that President Kimball prayed for inspiration and guidance in assuming the position of President, which was his by seniority, and in choosing his counselors.

Despite this established pattern and the revealed principles evident in its practice, some wonder whether someone other than the President of the Quorum of the Twelve could be called to the position of Church President. President Harold B. Lee explained: "Some thought on this matter would suggest that any other than the senior member could become President of the Church only if the Lord reveals to that President of the Twelve that someone other than himself could be selected" (in Conference Report, April 1970, p. 123). This authoritative explanation is based on the Lord's statement concerning his revelator—the President of the Church—coming to his ordained place through the appointed "gate" or established order: "For verily I say unto you, that he that is ordained of me shall come in at the gate and be ordained as I have told you before, to teach those revelations which you have received and shall receive through him whom I have appointed" (D&C 43:7). Commenting on this passage and the meaning of "the gate," Elder Joseph Fielding Smith stated:

> This commandment [D&C 43:7] is the key by which the members of the Church are to be governed and protected from all those who profess to be appointed and empowered to guide the Church. . . .
>
> We frequently hear discussions in our classes and between brethren to the effect that any man could be called, if the authorities should choose him, to preside over the Church and that it is not the fixed order to take the senior apostle to preside, and any member of the quorum could be appointed. The fact is that the senior apostle automatically becomes the presiding officer of the Church on the death of the President. If some other man were to be chosen, then the senior would have to receive the revelation setting himself aside. (*Church History and Modern Revelation* 1:172–73.)

Although it is theoretically possible, as indicated in the foregoing statements, for the President of the Twelve as the presiding high priest and the Lord's mouthpiece to receive a revelation appointing someone else as President, it has never occurred, nor is it likely to happen in the future. President Wilford Woodruff stated that it was very unlikely that the President of the Council of the Twelve would ever be set aside for someone else in the appointment of a new Church President. He felt that if a man was worthy and able to serve as the President of the Twelve, the same man would be "fit to preside over the Church," since the Lord had allowed him to come to the senior position. (See *Discourses of Wilford Woodruff*, pp. 91–92.)

Church President Ordained by Twelve and First Presidency Reorganized

When it is determined that the time has arrived to reorganize the First Presidency, the new President is ordained and set apart as the President of the Church by the members of the Quorum of the Twelve, who hold the keys and authority to fulfill this important function. President N. Eldon Tanner recounted for the Church how this was done with the ordination of President Spencer W. Kimball.

> Dressed in the robes of the holy priesthood, we held a prayer circle; President Kimball asked me to conduct it and Elder Thomas S. Monson to offer the prayer. Following this, President Kimball explained the purpose of the meeting and called on each member of the quorum in order of seniority, starting with Elder Ezra Taft Benson, to express his feelings as to whether the First Presidency should be organized that day or whether we should carry on as the Council of the Twelve. Each said, "We should organize now," and many complimentary things were spoken about President Kimball and his work with the Twelve.
>
> Then Elder Ezra Taft Benson nominated Spencer W. Kimball to be the President of the Church. This was seconded by Elder Mark E. Petersen and unanimously approved. President Kimball then nominated N. Eldon Tanner as First Counselor and Marion G. Romney as Second Counselor, each of whom expressed a willingness to accept the position and devote his whole time and energy in serving in that capacity.
>
> They were unanimously approved. Then Elder Mark E. Petersen, second in seniority in the Twelve, nominated Elder Ezra Taft Benson, the senior member of the Twelve, as President of the Quorum of the Twelve. This was unanimously approved.
>
> At this point all the members present laid their hands upon the head of Spencer W. Kimball, and President Ezra Taft Benson was voice in blessing, ordaining, and setting apart Spencer W. Kimball as the twelfth President of The Church of Jesus Christ of Latter-day Saints.
>
> Then, with President Kimball as voice, N. Eldon Tanner was set apart as First Counselor and Marion G. Romney as Second Counselor in the First Presidency of the Church. Following the same procedure, he pronounced the blessing and setting apart of Ezra Taft Benson as President of the Quorum of the Twelve. (In Conference Report, October 1979, p. 63.)

"The Twelve," declared President Joseph Fielding Smith,"

in the setting apart of the President do not give him any additional priesthood, but *confirm* upon him that which he has *already* received; they *set him apart* to the office, which it is their right to do" (*Doctrines of Salvation* 3:155). As President, he is then the only man on earth authorized to exercise the keys of the kingdom in their fulness.

When the First Presidency is reorganized it again assumes its revealed role as the "highest council of the Church." The Twelve return to their roles as councilors serving under the direction of the First Presidency. The second senior Apostle (assuming the most senior Apostle is set apart as the President of the Church) is always sustained as the President of the Quorum of the Twelve. If he is called as counselor in the First Presidency, or if he is unable by reason of illness to carry out those responsibilities, then the next senior member of the Quorum of the Twelve is sustained as the Acting President of the Quorum of the Twelve Apostles.

With these actions completed, the pattern and precedent followed, the leading quorums of the Church are again fully organized and operative. The membership of the Church is given the opportunity at the next general conference of the Church to formally sustain the action and to commit themselves to follow the newly ordained prophet-president of the Church, the newly reorganized First Presidency, and the Quorum of the Twelve. Each member of these quorums is also sustained as a prophet, seer, and revelator.

The Solemn Assembly

Solemn assemblies in ancient biblical times were held in conjunction with religious feasts, festivals, and sacrifices and were times of solemn worship of the Lord. In this dispensation the Lord commanded Joseph Smith to hold solemn assemblies for the purpose of instructing and spiritually edifying the Saints (see D&C 88:117; 95:7; 109:6–10; 124:39). Elder Bruce R. McConkie wrote: "In modern Israel *solemn assemblies* have been called in temples from time to time as the Lord has revealed or as his Spirit has indicated. As of old, their purpose is one of solemn worship, when by fasting, prayer, and faith the saints can draw near to the Lord and receive an outpouring of his Spirit. They are not held for the world or before the world, but are for those who have sanctified and purified themselves before the Lord. . . . Dedicatory services for temples have always been solemn assemblies." (*Mormon Doctrine*, p. 739.)

There are several spiritually significant meetings, held under the direction of the prophets, that could be characterized as solemn assemblies, including formal meetings called by the First Presidency and the Twelve to instruct, inspire, and train invited and worthy priesthood leaders in important issues affecting the Church.

The solemn assembly that is held in conjunction with the sustaining of a new President of the Church is somewhat different from these other types. It is held at general conference and affords the entire Church the blessing and opportunity of sustaining the new Prophet. It also is a meeting of worship, of remembering the Lord, of individual and institutional rededication to the building of the kingdom of God, a time of spiritual outpouring from the Lord.

At the solemn assembly where President Ezra Taft Benson was sustained as the thirteenth President of The Church of Jesus Christ of Latter-day Saints, President Gordon B. Hinckley indicated how this voting traditionally had been conducted and explained the modifications necessitated by the numerical growth and geographical expansion of the modern Church.

Dating from October 10, 1880, when John Taylor was sustained to succeed Brigham Young as prophet, seer, revelator, and President of the Church, each such occasion has been designated a formal Solemn Assembly of the body of the Church to express the voice of the Church. There have been ten such in the past. In each case, holders of the various offices of the priesthood were assembled in this Tabernacle and seated by quorums or groups in various areas of the building, each voting as a quorum or group on the officers of the Church as they were presented.

We have now reached a point where many times the number seated in the Tabernacle are assembled in other church halls across the United States and Canada, as well as in other parts of the world. Furthermore, many are seated in their homes, listening to the conference. All of you, wherever you may be, are invited to participate in this solemn and sacred undertaking when we sustain a new President of the Church together with other officers. In these present circumstances, it is considered unfeasible to seat by quorums those assembled in the Tabernacle and the many other halls. We shall, however, vote by quorums and groups. Wherever you are, you are invited to stand when requested and express by your uplifted hands whether you choose to sustain those whose names will be put before you. (In Conference Report, April 1986, p. 93.)

At the solemn assembly, the body of the Church sees the new prophet-president set before the people as the Lord's chosen and authorized earthly head of the Church, and binds itself by covenant to sustain and "uphold" him with its "confidence, faith, and prayers" (see D&C 107:22). The solemnization of his appointment blesses not only the prophet but also the entire Church. The windows of heaven can be opened, as it were, and a spiritual blessing and confirmation can be poured out upon the entire Church—not just upon those assembled in the Tabernacle. At the solemn assembly where he was sustained as the eleventh President of the Church, President Harold B. Lee spoke of the singular spiritual outpouring that is associated with this sacred gathering.

> Today, as never before, have I more fully realized the importance of that last requirement: that this presidency, in the Lord's language, must be upheld by the confidence, the faith, and the prayers of the Church—which means, of course, the entire membership of the Church. . . .
>
> Again, in the mighty demonstration of this solemn assembly, I am moved with emotions beyond expression as I have felt the true love and bonds of brotherhood. There has been here an overwhelming spiritual endowment, attesting, no doubt, that in all likelihood we are in the presence of personages, seen and unseen, who are in attendance. Who knows but that even our Lord and Master would be near us on such an occasion as this, for we, and the world, must never forget that this is his church, and under his almighty

direction we are to serve! (In Conference Report, October 1972, pp. 17–18.)

There has come to me in these last few days a deepening and reassuring faith. I can't leave this conference without saying to you that I have a conviction that the Master hasn't been absent from us on these occasions. This is his church. Where else would he rather be than right here at the head-quarters of his church? He isn't an absentee master; he is concerned about us. He wants us to follow where he leads. I know that he is a living reality, as is our Heavenly Father. I know it. I only hope that I can qualify for the high place to which he has called me and in which you have sustained me.

I know with all my soul that these sayings are true, and as a special witness I want you to know from the bottom of my heart that there is no shadow of doubt as to the genuine-ness of the work of the Lord in which we are engaged, the only name under heaven by which mankind can be saved. (In Conference Report, October 1972, pp. 176–77.)

All things shall be done by common consent in the church, by much prayer and faith, for all things you shall receive by faith.

—D&C 26:2

CHAPTER 5

The Law of Common Consent: Sustaining the Lord's Anointed

In one of the earliest revelations to the restored Church the Lord instructed the Prophet Joseph that "no person is to be ordained to any office in this church, where there is a regularly organized branch of the same, without the vote of that church" (D&C 20:65). The usage of the word *vote* invokes the image of an election, such as in the political arena. Even in the Church, we use terms such as *nominate, vote,* and *elect* with regard to the procedure described by the Lord in the revelations. There is a fundamental difference, however, between what those terms mean in a theocratic or Church government setting and what they mean in a democratic or political setting. While "running" for office, giving campaign speeches, and soliciting the support of the electorate are all appropriate and important components in the political election process, they would be totally inappropriate and spiritually offensive in a Church context. The vote of the Church required by the Lord's law of common consent (see D&C 26:2) allows for a "sustaining vote," not a vote for or against a candidate nor a recall vote to remove a person from office. These differences in the meaning of the word *vote* as it applies to the "election" of the Lord's anointed servants are seen in the following explanation by President J. Reuben Clark, Jr.

In this Church all the General Authorities and other Church-wide officers are "sustained"—in a certain sense, "elected"—by the body of the Church in a General Conference, which is, speaking politically, a constituent assembly.

In this Church, the power of "nominating" or calling to office, is not in the body of the Church. This power is vested in the General Authorities of the Church, and in the final analysis in the President of the Church who comes to his place under the guidance of inspired revelation. As a matter of fact, as our Articles of Faith—more or less the equivalent of the creeds of other churches—declare:

"We believe that a man must be called of God, by prophecy, and by the laying on of hands, by those who are in authority to preach the Gospel and administer in the ordinances thereof."

When the presiding authority has so "nominated" or chosen, or called any man to office, that man is then presented to the body of the Church to be *sustained,* in political language "elected."

Thus the body of the Church has no *calling* or "nominating" power, but only the sustaining, or politically speaking, the "electing" power.

When the presiding authority presents any man to the body of the Church to be sustained, the only power which the assembly has is to vote, by uplifted hand, either to sustain or not to sustain.

Obviously, neither the body of the Church, nor any of its members, can propose that other men be called to office, for the calling of men is the sole power and function of the presiding authority.

Therefore all debate, all proposals of other names, all discussions of merit and worthiness, are wholly out of order in such an assemblage. Any person attempting so to interrupt the proceedings would be a disturber of the public peace, amenable to the ordinary peace officers of the law and would of course be so dealt with. (In Conference Report, October 1940, pp. 28–29.)

Thus, the vote of the Church or common consent is not a vote necessarily for or against a person who is called to be a leader, since it is not the prerogative of the people to select or install the Lord's chosen servants. Such a vote is also not a periodic election in which the "candidate" stands accountable to the people—as in a democratic system of government. In the theocratic system of calling leaders, the Lord, through inspiration to the presiding officer who holds the keys or authority, selects and calls whom He desires. Those leaders, also called and set apart by those with inspiration and authority, are accountable to the Lord directly and only indirectly to the people they serve. Why then does the Lord not only allow for but require a vote of common consent to "approve of those names" or "disapprove of them" (see D&C 124:44)?

Perhaps the answer can be seen in the example of the ordination and "sustaining" of Joseph Smith and Oliver Cowdery as the first and second elders of the Church. They had received their ordination to the higher priesthood under the hands of heavenly beings—Peter, James, and John (see *Ensign,* June 1979, pp. 5–10). There was no doubt in their minds as to the source of their calling and authority. The Prophet Joseph recorded the reason for waiting from June 1829 to April 6, 1830, to ordain each other to those positions of leadership.

> We had for some time made this matter a subject of humble prayer, and at length we got together . . . more particularly to seek of the Lord what we now so earnestly desired; and here, to our unspeakable satisfaction, did we realize the truth of the Savior's promise—"Ask, and it shall be given unto you" . . . for we had not long been engaged in solemn and fervent prayer, when the word of the Lord came unto us in the chamber [of father Whitmer in Fayette], commanding us that I should ordain Oliver Cowdery to be an Elder in the Church of Jesus Christ; and that he also should ordain me to the same office; and then to ordain others, as it should be made known unto us from time to time. We were, however, commanded to defer this ordination until such times as it should be practicable to have our brethren, who had been and who should be baptized, assembled together, when we must . . . have them decide by vote whether they were willing to accept us as spiritual teachers or not. (*HC* 1:60–61.)

From this statement we can see that, even in the case of the Prophet of the Restoration, the Lord does not impose his chosen leaders upon the Church against the will of the members. "We deny the existence of arbitrary power in the Church," declared the First Presidency in 1907, "and this because its government is moral government purely, and its forces are applied through kindness, reason, and persuasion. . . . The members are at the liberty to vote as they choose." (*Improvement Era,* May 1907 pp. 487–88.) Explaining why Joseph and Oliver were required to be sustained or accepted as the leaders of the Church, Elder Orson F. Whitney taught:

> Obedient to the divine mandate spoken to them in Father Whitmer's humble home, Joseph and Oliver took steps to ascertain whether or not their brethren would sanction their ordination as Elders of the Church and were willing to come under their spiritual tutelage.
>
> What!—exclaims one. After these men had communed with heavenly beings and received from them commandments for their guidance; after receiving divine authority to preach the Gospel, administer its ordinances, and establish once more on earth the long absent Church of Christ! After all this must they go before the people and ask their consent to organize them and preside over them as a religious body? Yes, that was precisely the situation. Notwithstanding all those glorious manifestations, they were not yet fully qualified to hold the high positions unto which they had been divinely called. One element was lacking—the consent of the people. Until that consent was given, there could be no church with these people as its members and those men as its presiding authorities. The Great Ruler of all never did and never will foist upon any of his people, in branch, ward, stake or Church capacity, a presiding officer whom they are not willing to accept and uphold. (In Conference Report, October 1930, p. 45.)

The sustaining vote required by the revelations has a two-fold blessing—it blesses the Church institutionally and the members individually. Common consent providentially provides the collective Church with a protection from the onslaught of false claims of authority and revelation by ensuring that there can be neither secret ordinations performed nor secret doctrines taught by a select few within the Church. Elder Boyd K. Packer explained how such a scenario is precluded by the principle of common consent.

> There are those who claim authority from some secret ordinations of the past. Even now some claim special revealed authority to lead or to teach the people. Occasionally they use the names of members of the First Presidency or of the Twelve or of the Seventy and imply some special approval of what they teach.
>
> There have been too many names presented, too many sustaining votes taken, too many ordinations and settings apart performed before too many witnesses; there have been too many records kept, too many certificates prepared, and too many pictures published in too many places for anyone to be deceived as to who holds proper authority. Claims of special revelation or secret authority from the Lord or from the Brethren are false on the face of them and really utter nonsense!
>
> The Lord never operated that way; these things were not done in a corner (see Acts 26:26); there is light on every official call and every authorized ordination, and it has always been that way. (In Conference Report, April 1985, p. 43.)

Those who have been selected, called, and authorized are thus publicly presented to the membership of the Church for approval as a way of acknowledging the Lord's selection, formally accepting it, and making it a matter of official record. The public witness and approval of these transactions safeguards the unity and integrity of the Church and ratifies the authority and inspiration of those who are called and empowered to receive such.

In addition, the Lord's revealed law of common consent safeguards individual agency. It allows for the agency and vote of the people to acknowledge the mind and will of God and to voluntarily approve or disapprove of his choices. Although the Church is not a democratic institution, this procedure nonetheless allows for the "voice of the people" to be heard. "No man can preside in this Church in any capacity without the consent of the people," Elder Joseph Fielding Smith wrote. . . . "No man, should the people decide to the contrary, could preside over any body of Latter-day Saints in this Church, and yet it is not the right of the people to nominate, to choose, for that is the right of the priesthood." (*Doctrines of Salvation* 3:123.) Such a rejection or vote of disapproval does not necessarily indicate that the call was uninspired or that the person would not or could not fulfill and magnify the calling. It means, however, that the people themselves have voluntarily chosen not to sustain the action and that they desire something different from what has been presented by those in authority.

This principle is seen in the scriptural example of the Israelites' request—"Give us a king to judge us. . . . that we also may be like all the nations." (1 Samuel 8:6, 20.) Although the prophet Samuel taught the people the pitfalls and evils of kingly rule, the Lord allowed their agency to operate even when it was contrary to his will. "But the thing displeased Samuel, when they said, Give us a king to judge us. And Samuel prayed unto the Lord. And the Lord said unto Samuel, Hearken unto the voice of the people in all that they say unto thee: for they have not rejected thee, but they have rejected me, that I should not reign over them." (1 Samuel 8:6–7.)

In a similar way today, if without proper cause (as discussed later in this chapter) we refuse to vote to approve or sustain an action or the name of a leader presented to the Church for a vote of common consent, we are not really rejecting the person presented or "voting against" him or his "record." Rather, we are rejecting the Lord and repudiating the inspiration and authority of those whose right it is to call and set apart leaders in the kingdom. Even then, the Lord still recognizes our agency. If the people are unwilling to sustain those whom he has called to lead, the Lord may then grant them their desire and someone else may be chosen that the people will sustain, though it may well be to their detriment, or at least of lesser advantage. President Ezra Taft Benson called this the "Samuel principle."

> God has to work through mortals of varying degrees of spiritual progress. Sometimes he temporarily grants to men their unwise requests in order that they might learn from

their own sad experiences. Some refer to this as the "Samuel principle." The children of Israel wanted a king like all the other nations. The prophet Samuel was displeased and prayed to the Lord about it. . . . The Lord told Samuel to warn the people of the consequences if they had a king. Samuel gave them the warning. But they still insisted on their king. So God gave them a king and let them suffer. They learned the hard way. God wanted it to be otherwise, but within certain bounds He grants unto men according to their desires (see Alma 41:5). Bad experiences are an expensive school that only fools keep going to. (*The Teachings of Ezra Taft Benson,* p. 84.)

Common Consent: An Individual Covenant

The act of common consent in the Church should be much more than rote ritual or a tradition devoid of personal thought and introspection. It is a sacred and solemn responsibility with accompanying spiritual blessings. "It may seem rather a dry and formal matter to some of the people to come together and lift up their hands to sustain the authorities of the Church," observed Elder Charles W. Penrose, "but it is a necessary duty and, if we look at it properly, we shall take pleasure therein" (in *Journal of Discourses* 21:45). When we "look at it properly" we see that the practice of common consent—the sustaining of Church officers—is a time of making and renewing covenants. "When you vote affirmatively you make a solemn covenant with the Lord," President Harold B. Lee taught (in Conference Report, April 1970, p. 103). The actual practice of raising one's hand in a sustaining vote is an outward symbol or token of a significant covenant to which we are agreeing and binding ourselves.

Elder Loren C. Dunn spoke of the symbolism associated with this important concept. "When we sustain officers, we are given the opportunity of sustaining those whom the Lord has already called by revelation. . . . The Lord, then, gives us the opportunity to sustain the action of a divine calling and in effect express ourselves if for any reason we may feel otherwise. To sustain is to make the action binding on ourselves and to commit ourselves to support those people whom we have sustained. When a person goes through the sacred act of raising his arm to the square, he should remember, with soberness, that which he has done and commence to act in harmony with his sustaining vote both in public and in private." (In Conference Report, April 1972, p. 19.)

Common Consent:
Personal Responsibilities and Blessings

We can no more look at the sustaining of officers in the Church as an insignificant practice than we can view the sacrament as nothing more than a mid-meeting snack. This "vote of the Church" is an act of entering into individual covenants— covenants involving obligations on our part and promised blessings from the Lord. This vote is more than approval—it is a personal promise to "give full loyalty and support, without equivocation or reservation, to the officer for whom you vote" (Harold B. Lee, in Conference Report, April 1970, p. 103). When we perceive common consent as a personal covenant, we focus no longer on the person for whom we are "voting" but, rather, on ourselves. More than a mere judgment of others' abilities to serve in various callings, it requires an examination of our own ability and willingness to fulfill the covenant we are being asked to make. When we "sustain" officers in the Church, whether they be Apostles, bishops, or Primary teachers, we promise to be loyal to them, support them in their assignments, and strengthen them in our conversations, with our prayers, and in all our doings (see D&C 108:7), both publicly and privately. Concerning how we can better sustain those who have been called to preside over and counsel us, Elder Boyd K. Packer taught: "There are some specific things that you can do. Search your soul. How do you regard the leadership of the Church? Do you sustain your bishop? Do you sustain your stake president and the General Authorities of the Church? Or are you among those who are neutral, or critical, who speak evilly, or who refuse calls? Better ask, 'Lord, is it I?' Avoid being critical of those serving in responsible priesthood callings. Show yourself to be loyal. Cultivate the disposition to sustain and to bless. Pray. Pray continually for your leaders." (*That All May Be Edified,* p. 243.)

Further, our covenant to sustain the living oracles—those General Authorities who have been empowered with a "special spiritual endowment" to teach the people and be "watchmen" to the Church—goes beyond support, loyalty and the avoidance of criticism. It includes the promise to hearken to and heed their counsel and teachings. With regard to our covenant to sustain the living prophet, as well as those others who are prophets, seers, and revelators, we note the Lord's words respecting the first prophet of this dispensation: "Wherefore, meaning the church, thou shalt give heed unto all his words and commandments which he shall give unto you as he receiveth them, walking in all holiness before me; for his word ye shall receive, as if from my own mouth, in all patience and faith" (D&C 21:4–5). Elder James E. Talmage testified:

> Do you ever think of the inconsistency of raising your right hand in solemn witness before God that you will sustain certain men who have been called and ordained, in the manner appointed of God, as your leaders, as prophets unto the people, verily as revelators, and then, though perchance you come together and hear their words, going away and pay no attention to them? . . .
>
> You cannot, we cannot, pass by lightly the words that come by way of counsel and instruction from the ordained servants of God, and escape the inevitable penalty of that neglect. Nevertheless, we have our agency; we may choose to disobey, but we must take the consequences of that choice. (In Conference Report, October 1921, pp. 187–88.)

Faithfulness to our covenant means to sustain, support, and be loyal to the General Authorities but is also linked to our willingness to uphold local leaders and officers. "A man who says he will sustain the President of the Church or the General Authorities, but cannot sustain his own bishop is deceiving himself," Elder Boyd K. Packer taught. "The man who will not sustain the bishop of his ward and president of his stake will not sustain the President of the Church." (That All May Be Edified, p. 239.) The reverse order is also true—a person who fails to sustain the prophet, his Counselors, the Twelve, and the other General Authorities cannot and does not sustain the local leaders. Rather than just an *action* of raising one's arm to "vote," sustaining is more an *attitude* of commitment to the gospel, a conviction of the guiding influence of the Spirit in Church administration, and a desire to support and strengthen.

Whatever the level, whoever the leader, understanding the principles associated with inspired callings and the divine administration of the Lord's earthly kingdom causes us to look beyond the ordinary nature of the men who are called to preside in the wards and stakes and whom we sustain. "There is something extraordinary about them," Elder Packer observed. "It is the mantle of priesthood authority and the inspiration of the call which they have received." (*That All May Be Edified*, p. 240.) Raising our arms, we acknowledge that mantle and authority. What we do *after* we raise our arms to the square in the vote of common consent is an indicator of our willingness to follow and serve the Lord. "For he that receiveth my servants receiveth me," the Lord declared, "and he that receiveth me receiveth my Father; and he that receiveth my Father receiveth my Father's kingdom; therefore all that my Father hath shall be given unto him" (D&C 84:36–38).

As with any covenant, blessings are predicated upon obedience (see D&C 130:20–21), and rejection of the covenant results in the withholding of blessings (see D&C 58:32). Failing to sustain the prophet with our loyalty, prayers of faith, and obedience is not only a rejection of the covenant of common consent but is also, as President Gordon B. Hinckley said, a "repudiation" of the prophet's sacred calling (see *Ensign*, January 1974, p. 125). Those who reject the covenant of common consent—either by a formal vote of disapproval or by the unwillingness to faithfully live up to the commitments they have made—need to be reminded of the Lord's words given in the context of building the Nauvoo Temple. "But if they will not hearken to my voice, nor unto the voice of these men whom I have appointed, they shall not be blest. . . . And . . . if you build a house unto my name, and do not do the things that I say, I will not perform the oath which I make unto you, neither fulfill the promises which ye expect at my hands, saith the Lord. For instead of blessings, ye, by your own works, bring cursings, wrath, indignation, and judgments upon your own heads." (D&C 124:46–48.) The temporal and spiritual blessings that come from being true and faithful to our covenant to sustain are real—as are the consequences that result from a rejection of that covenant. (For an in-depth discussion of the specific consequences associated with accepting or rejecting the Lord's anointed servants see chapters 8 and 9.)

Is a Disapproving Vote Ever Appropriate?

Understanding that the sustaining vote is not a democratic vote for a person but rather an individual covenant, and that the Church is a theocratic or God-governed institution, some may assume that it is never appropriate to vote contrary to the action being presented. The Lord has given us the right to vote our conscience, but we must recognize that it is the Lord who directs calls to service and leadership in the Church. Because of that fundamental principle, the parameters in which a vote of disapproval would be appropriate are indeed narrow. Elder Joseph Fielding Smith stated:

> The priesthood selects, under the inspiration of our Father in heaven, and then it is the duty of the Latter-day Saints, as they are assembled in conference, or other capacity, by the uplifted hand, to sustain or to reject; and I take it that no man has the right to raise his hand in opposition, or with contrary vote, *unless he has a reason for doing so that would be valid if presented before those who stand at the head.* In other words, I have no right to raise my hand in opposition to a man who is appointed to any position in this Church, simply because I may not like him, or because of some personal disagreement or feeling I may have, but *only on the grounds that he is guilty of wrong doing, of transgression of the laws of the Church which would disqualify him for the position which he is called to hold.* (*Doctrines of Salvation* 3:123–24.)

As seen from the previous statement, the only justification for voting to oppose a particular calling is that we know of unworthiness that "would disqualify [the person] for the position which he is called to hold." Believing that the person is not competent, or that others are more qualified, and/or having personal feelings of dislike for the person are irrelevant in a theocratic system and cannot be grounds for withholding our support in either symbolic vote or actual practice.

If we have knowledge of serious transgression on the part of the person being sustained, it becomes our right to vote to oppose the proposed action and still be faithful to the covenant of common consent. If we choose to do so, we will be given the opportunity to voice our concerns to the presiding officer, who will then determine whether the person in question can or should still be called to the position concerned. The presiding officer, as a judge in Israel and by virtue of his keys, makes the final decision. If he decides, after prayerful consideration, that the person who was called should still be sustained, then we must either accept or reject the covenant of common consent and recognize that we will reap the consequences of our choice.

There is another approach that may also be appropriate when we have knowledge of what seems to us to be disqualifying unworthiness. We can still vote to sustain the action of the presiding officer—signifying our support for him and our understanding that it is according to his right and authority to call whomsoever the Lord desires. To ensure our feeling right and good about our sustaining covenant, we could then seek an opportunity to express our concerns to the presiding officer privately, allowing him to make the judgment and decision that belong to him by virtue of his authority. In such cases, frequently the presiding officer was already aware of the circumstances in question and still felt impressed to proceed with the call. If in this instance he was not aware of the transgression, however, we will have still done our duty, and it will now become the province of the presiding officer to resolve the matter and either revoke the call or allow the person to serve in the position to which he or she was called and sustained. Pursuing such a course will help the concerned member to purge ill-feelings from his soul, feel good about his covenant, and demonstrate his willingness to follow and sustain those whose right it is, under the influence of revelation, to extend calls to lead and serve in the Church.

When we understand that we are not really voting for the person but are acknowledging the theocratic authority of those who preside and are making an individual covenant, we can always cast a vote of approval—a symbol of our commitment to the kingdom of God and our willingness to faithfully support and sustain those called to serve therein. "This church is run by revelation," Elder Boyd K. Packer testified. "It comes to those who have the responsibility to preside. I am not sure you could get me to vote against a proposition presented by my presiding authority." (*New Era*, June 1977, p. 52.)

The Lord administers His earthly kingdom through the use of mortal and imperfect servants, yet he expects us to see beyond their mortal imperfections and sustain them in their divinely inspired callings. Elder Boyd K. Packer recounted a story from the life of Karl G. Maeser, one of the most influential educators in the early development of Brigham Young University, that illustrates this concept:

> On one occasion he was going with a group of young missionaries across the Alps. They were crossing a high mountain pass on foot. There were long sticks stuck into the snow of the glacier to mark the path so that travelers could find their way safely across the glacier and down the mountain on the other side.
>
> When they reached the summit, Brother Maeser wanted to teach the young elders a lesson. He stopped at the pinnacle of the mountain and pointed to those sticks that they had followed. And he said, "Brethren, behold the priesthood of God. They are just common old sticks, but it's the position that counts. Follow them and you will surely be safe. Stray from them and you will surely be lost." And so it is in the Church. We are called to leadership positions and given the power of the priesthood. And we are just common old sticks, but the position we are given counts. It is separate and apart from us, but while we hold it, we hold it.
>
> Now in our wards and in our branches and in our stakes, the Lord calls to positions of leadership the brethren who are there. None of them is perfect. But they hold the office, and we are to be obedient to them. . . . [They] might just be a common old stick, but it would be the position that counts. (*New Era*, June 1977, p. 51.)

These mortal leaders of God's earthly kingdom may be "common old sticks" with idiosyncrasies and imperfections, but each becomes magnified beyond his natural abilities not only through the power of the Spirit but also by the sustaining of the people—through their support, loyalty, faith, and prayers. Being faithful to our covenant of common consent allows us to see beyond the mortal nature of these men we have sustained and to perceive "the power of God resting upon the leaders of this Church" (Harold B. Lee, *Ensign,* July 1972, p. 103). Such a conviction, stemming from our faithful adherence to the covenant of common consent, "goes down into [our] heart like fire" and becomes to us a sustaining influence, a blessing of peace, and a promise of guidance as we seek to heed the words of the prophets.

And whatsoever they shall speak when moved upon by the Holy Ghost shall be scripture, shall be the will of the Lord, shall be the mind of the Lord, shall be the word of the Lord, shall be the voice of the Lord, and the power of God unto salvation.

—D&C 68:4

CHAPTER 6

Living Oracles and the Standard Works

The dictionary defines scripture as "the sacred writings of a religion" and "a body of writings considered as authoritative" (*Webster's New Collegiate Dictionary*). The word itself is derived from the Latin *scriptus,* which literally means "an act of writing" or "something written." In a theological sense, scripture has come to mean the body of writings espoused, revered, and utilized in worship by a particular religion. These writings are often referred to as the *canon* of a given religion or denomination. For example, to Christians the Bible—both Old Testament and New Testament—is canon; to the Jews the Old Testament is canon, with the Torah (or first five books of the Old Testament) holding special significance; the Koran is canon to Muslims. In each of these cases (Restoration-based Christians excepted) the writings referred to comprise the total scriptural canon, which is viewed as closed—nothing is to be added to it (see "Scripture: Scriptures" by W. D. Davies and Truman G. Madsen in *Encyclopedia of Mormonism* 3:1277–80). Even within the major religions of the world, different denominations may have a different canon or version of a given scripture.

Latter-day Saints define scripture differently. In 1831 the Lord declared: "And this is the ensample unto them, that they shall speak as they are moved upon by the Holy Ghost. And whatsoever they shall speak when moved upon by the Holy Ghost shall be scripture, shall be the will of the Lord, shall be the mind of the Lord, shall be the word of the Lord, shall be the voice of the Lord, and the power of God unto salvation." (D&C 68:3–4.)

Thus scripture is more broadly defined for Latter-day Saints because it denotes not only written documents but also the spoken word of inspired servants of the Lord. "Any message, whether written or spoken," wrote Elder Bruce R. McConkie, "that comes from God to man by the power of the Holy Ghost is *scripture*" (*Mormon Doctrine,* p. 682). Because of this more comprehensive view of what constitutes scripture, the corpus of LDS scripture is substantially larger than that of the traditional Christian canon. "We of the Latter-day Saints have our own scriptures," President J. Reuben Clark, Jr., declared. "We have the scriptures which other Christian sects use, namely, the Bible, including the Old and New Testaments, but we also have the Book of Mormon, the Doctrine and Covenants, the Pearl of Great Price, and the Living Oracles of the Church." (*Church News,* 17 December 1960, p. 14.) This inclusion of the living oracles and the myriad other inspired messages makes our body of scripture ever-expanding and never-ending.

Thus there are two different yet complementary categories of scripture in the Church—the standard works, which are canonized, and the inspired messages of living and now-deceased oracles that are not canonized but are authoritative nonetheless.

Canonized Scripture: The Standard Works

There are in the Church four volumes of canonized scripture—the Bible, the Book of Mormon, the Doctrine and Covenants, and the Pearl of Great Price. As Latter-day Saints we seldom speak of them as "canonized scripture," since the word *canon* in the traditional religious vernacular often carries a connotation of finality and closure. We refer to these volumes more often as the standard works. An inspired message or document becomes canonized, and thus included in the body of the standard works, by a dual process. First, it is presented to the

Church by the President of the Church with the unanimous consent of the First Presidency and the Twelve, who hold the keys of declaring doctrine and establishing scripture for the Church. Second, it must be accepted by the vote of the Church according to the law of common consent. By this vote of acceptance the members of the Church bind themselves by covenant to uphold it as scripture.

Canonized scripture—the standard works: those fundamental revelations, doctrines, and principles that are universally applicable and binding upon the entire Church. "It fixes permanently the *general truths* which God has revealed," wrote Elder B. H. Roberts.

> It preserves, for all time and for all generations of men, the great framework of the plan of salvation—the Gospel. There are certain truths that are not affected by ever-changing circumstances; truths which are always the same, no matter how often they must be revealed; truths which are elementary, permanent, fixed; from which there must not be, and cannot be, any departure without condemnation. The written word of God preserves the people of God from vain and foolish traditions, which, as they float down the stream of time, are subject to changes by distortion, by addition or subtraction, or by the fitful play of fancy in fantastic and unreliable minds. It forms a standard by which even the living oracles of God may instruct themselves, measure themselves, and correct themselves. It places within the reach of the people, the power to confirm the oral words, and the ministry of the living oracles, and thus to add faith to faith, and knowledge to knowledge. (*Improvement Era*, May 1900, pp. 576–77.)

The word *canon* derives from a Greek word which originally meant "a rod for testing straightness" (see LDS Bible Dictionary, p. 630). As seen in the above statement by Elder B. H. Roberts, canonized scripture is the norm or standard against which all other teachings are to be measured. This principle is treated later in this chapter.

The standard works themselves testify that the written word of God, although canonized and universally binding upon the

Church, is insufficient and incomplete in conveying to man the mind and will of the Lord to all generations of his children on earth. One of the first principles taught to Joseph Smith and the early Saints was the need for continual revelation—living scripture through living prophets. In the first revelation received after the organization of the restored Church, before the Doctrine and Covenants was accepted by the Church as canon, the Lord taught the Saints that they were to "give heed unto all his [Joseph Smith's] words and commandments which he shall give unto you as he receiveth them, walking in all holiness before me; for his word ye shall receive as if from mine own mouth, in all patience and faith" (D&C 21:4–5). Numerous other canonized scriptural statements also attest to the ongoing need for additional revelation, through living oracles, that may expand or constrict previously revealed principles and programs and provide interpretations and applications of canonized scriptures to modern-day needs and circumstances (see Amos 3:7, 2 Nephi 28:29–30; 29:3–13; 3 Nephi 12:1; 28:34–35; D&C 1:11–16, 38–39; 112:20; 124:45–46, 84; 133:65–72).

It is therefore foolish for someone to dismiss revelations or inspired teachings merely because they are not written, canonized, and leather-bound. "Sometimes we get the notion that if something is printed in a book, it is more authentic than if it was spoken in the last general conference," observed President Harold B. Lee. "Just because something is written in a book does not make it more of an authority to guide us." *(Stand Ye in Holy Places,* p. 157.) Elder Orson Pratt testified: "The very moment that we set aside the living oracles we set aside the revelations of God. Why? Because the revelations of God command us plainly that we shall hearken to the living oracles. Hence, if we undertake to follow the written word, and at the same time do not give heed to the living oracles of God, the written word will condemn us." (In *Journal of Discourses* 7:373.)

Uncanonized Scripture: Inspired Messages from Living Prophets

Scripture, as defined by the Lord (see D&C 68:2–4), comes to us not only through the medium of formally accepted, published revelations but also anytime the Holy Ghost is the bearer of the message. It is this continual communication from God to man that blesses us with current scripture adapted to our unique circumstances and modern challenges (see D&C 5:10). Such inspired instruction, whether canonized or not, flows freely and frequently, if unobtrusively, from God to his children through his anointed servants on earth by the power of the Holy Ghost. President Spencer W. Kimball so testified: "Expecting the spectacular, one may not be fully alerted to the constant flow of revealed communication. I say, in the deepest of humility, but also by the power and force of a burning testimony in my soul, that from the prophet of the Restoration to the prophet of our own year, the communication line is unbroken, the authority is continuous, and light, brilliant and penetrating, continues to shine. The sound of the voice of the Lord is a continuous melody and a thunderous appeal. For nearly a century and a half there has been no interruption." (In Conference Report, April 1977, p. 115.)

It is the uncanonized, inspired utterances of the Lord's servants that provide the continual nourishment needed for spiritually healthy souls. Feasting upon the words of Christ (see 2 Nephi 32:3) involves not only reading and pondering the standard works but also hearing and heeding the words of living prophets. Relying only upon canonized scriptures, observed President Wilford Woodruff, "would scarcely be sufficient to guide us twenty-four hours" (in *Journal of Discourses* 9:324). Whereas the canon of scripture serves as a foundational standard of judgment, living scripture given by living prophets serves as the dynamic and flexible framework of the "constitution of the Church of Christ." Elder Orson F. Whitney said:

> The Latter-day Saints do not do things because they happen to be printed in a book. They do not do things because God told the Jews to do them; nor do they do or leave undone anything because of the instructions that Christ gave to the Nephites. Whatever is done by this Church is because God, speaking from heaven in our day, has commanded this Church to do it. No book presides over this Church, and no book lies at its foundation. You cannot pile up books enough to take the place of God's priesthood.

inspired by the power of the Holy Ghost. That is the constitution of the Church of Christ. . . . Divine revelation adapts itself to the circumstances and conditions of men, and change upon change ensues as God's progressive work goes on to its destiny. There is no book big enough or good enough to preside over this Church. (In Conference Report, October 1916, p. 55.)

Clearly, pitting canonized scripture against those inspired teachings that have not been canonized is a false dichotomy. It is foolishness to reject the words of living oracles because of the feeble yet oft-used excuse, "It's not in the scriptures." Such attempts to minimize inspiration or to rationalize away the significance of current scripture, whatever its nature, expose a misunderstanding or a blatant rejection of the fundamental truth that scripture is whatever the Lord's servants speak "as they are moved upon by the Holy Ghost" (D&C 68:3). President Charles W. Penrose declared that it is a mistake to assume that the established canon is more valid or binding than the current revelation.

> We have some books which we recognize as containing the word of God: The Bible, composed of the Old and New Testaments, and the Book of Mormon, and the Doctrine and Covenants, and the Pearl of Great Price, which we recognize as the written standards of doctrine in the Church. These contain revelations given in the past; some of them in the very distant past. But it is a great consolation to me and must be to all Israel that we have the living word of God today, and that that which is spoken under the influence of the Holy Ghost is just as much the word of God, just as important and just as binding upon the people of God, as that which was given in former times. (In Conference Report, April 1915, p. 32.)

Some members of the Church wrest the words of the prophets and seek to place limitations on their prophetic declarations. In a quest to simplify the discernment of what is scripture and what is not, some would like readily recognizable labels attached to prophetic teachings. The Lord, in his infinite wisdom, has not made such easy, effortless perception possible. He has declared to us what constitutes scripture: it is that which is delivered to man, whether spoken or written, by the power of the Holy Ghost. It is not how it is said or where it is spoken or whether it is published that determines what is scripture. Neither is it determined by the position of the person who says it. There are no flashing lights in the Tabernacle that alert the Church as to when general conference speakers are giving us scripture. We only recognize scripture and ultimately receive it as such through the same power by which the revelation is given—"as moved upon by the Holy Ghost."

Knowing When Speakers Are Inspired

As part of the process of spiritual development, the Lord expects us to do all we can to learn for ourselves the mind and will of God and then do what he wishes. He does not force-feed us the things of the Spirit, nor does he imbue us with spiritual knowledge without any effort on our part. He expects us to avail ourselves of those resources that he has mercifully and abundantly provided for our personal growth and spiritual enlargement. So it is with learning to recognize spoken scripture—that is, discerning when the Lord's servants speak or write "as moved upon by the Holy Ghost" and knowing how to properly interpret and apply those inspired utterances in our own lives. Some desire knowledge via an approach devoid of personal thought and spiritual effort. They expect, even demand, that genuinely inspired declarations be prefaced by the phrase "Thus saith the Lord." To those who rigidly reject as uninspired any sermon or writing that does not possess the proper "label," President J. Reuben Clark, Jr., issued a warning. "There are those who insist that unless the Prophet of the Lord declares 'Thus saith the Lord,' the message may not be taken as a revelation. This is a false testing standard. For while many of our modern revelations as contained in the Doctrine and Covenants do contain these words, there are many that do not." ("When Are the Church Leaders' Words Entitled to Claim of Scripture?" p. 10.)

Spiritual self-reliance requires that, instead of expecting Church leaders to alert us to inspired statements by means of external labels or formal announcements, we take the responsibility upon ourselves to do all we can to ascertain the inspiration that accompanies prophetic teachings. The Lord has provided at least three basic means or tests whereby we can know for ourselves the inspiration (or lack thereof) of any teaching, publication, or declaration. The means are given to us to discern, but, like the Liahona in Lehi's day, these guides will only have power to direct us according to our own diligence and faith. Although not free from the requirement of personal study and effort, two of these "tests" of scripture are more external, whereas one is, and must be, internal and personal. Each of these three resources that the Lord has provided for our protection against deception (see Joseph Smith—Matthew 1:22, 37) is phrased below in the form of questions that may serve as "tests" of the validity and inspiration of "scripture."

1. Is It in Harmony with the Standard Works?

A major purpose for canonized scriptures, as previously discussed, is to serve as a measuring rod or standard against which all other teachings are to be judged. In a revelation "embracing the law of the Church" given to the Prophet Joseph Smith in 1831, the Lord declared: "Thou shalt take the things which thou hast received, which have been given unto thee in my scriptures for a law, to be my law to govern my church" (D&C 42:59). President Joseph Fielding Smith elaborated upon the role of canonized scripture as this governing law or standard. "It makes no difference what is written or what anyone has said, if what has been said is in conflict with what the Lord has revealed, we can set it aside. My words, and the teachings of any other member of the Church, high or low, if they do not square with the revelations, we need not accept them. Let us have this matter clear. We have accepted the four standard works as the measuring yardsticks, or balances, by which we measure every man's doctrine." (*Doctrines of Salvation* 3:203.)

Concerning this matter Elder Bruce R. McConkie also stated:

> The books, writings, explanations, expositions, views, and theories of even the wisest and greatest men, either in or out of the Church, do not rank with the standard works.

Even the writings, teachings, and opinions of the prophets of God are acceptable only to the extent they are in harmony with what God has revealed and what is recorded in the standard works. [When the living oracles speak in the name of the Lord or as moved upon by the Holy Ghost, however, their utterances are then binding upon all who hear, and whatever is said will without any exception be found to be in harmony with the standard works.] The Lord's house is a house of order, and one truth never contradicts another. (*Mormon Doctrine,* p. 765.)

From the earliest days of the Restoration the prophets and Apostles have taught that both types of scripture—the standard works *and* the inspired declarations of living prophets—are valid, authoritative, and absolutely essential for us to be able to "live by every word which proceedeth forth from the mouth of God" (D&C 84:44; see also Deuteronomy 8:3). They work in tandem for our salvation. However, while new revelation will always be anchored in the fundamentals laid down in the standard works, it is immeasurably more essential and pertinent to our salvation than those scriptures. President Wilford Woodruff recounted an event that occurred in the early days of the Church wherein the Prophet Joseph Smith taught the relationship of uncanonized scripture given through the living oracles to the written word of God found in the canonized scriptures.

I will refer to a certain meeting I attended in the town of Kirtland in my early days. At that meeting some remarks were made that have been made here today, with regard to the living oracles and with regard to the written word of God. The same principle was presented . . . when a leading man in the Church got up and talked upon the subject, and said: "You have got the word of God before you here in the Bible, Book of Mormon, and Doctrine and Covenants; you have the written word of God, and you who give revelation should give revelations according to those books, as what is written in those books is the word of God. We should confine ourselves to them."

When he concluded, Brother Joseph turned to Brother Brigham Young and said, "Brother Brigham, I want you to take the stand and tell us your views with regard to the living oracles and the written word of God.'(Brother Brigham took the stand, and he took the Bible, and laid it down; he took the Book of Mormon, and laid it down; and he took the Book of Doctrine and Covenants, and laid it down before him, and he said: "There is the written word of God to us, concerning the word of God from the beginning of the world, almost to our day." "And now," said he, "when compared with the living oracles those books are nothing to me; those books do not convey the word of God direct to us now, as do the words of a Prophet or a man bearing the Holy Priesthood in our day and generation. I would rather have the living oracles than all the writing in the books." That was the course he pursued. When he was through, Brother Joseph said to the congregation: "Brother Brigham has told you the word of the Lord, and he has told you the truth." (In Conference Report, October 1897, pp. 22–23.)

Testifying to that principle, taught by the Prophet Joseph, Brigham Young, and Wilford Woodruff, President Ezra Taft Benson has declared: "The most important prophet, so far as we are concerned, is the one who is living in our day and age. This is the prophet who has today's instructions from God to us today. God's revelation to Adam did not instruct Noah how to build the ark. Every generation has need of the ancient scripture plus the current scripture from the living prophet. Therefore, the most crucial reading and pondering which you should do is of the latest inspired words from the Lord's mouthpiece." (In Conference Report, Seoul Area Conference, 1975, p. 52.)

In these guidelines the standard of safety is established. However, while we may immediately reject and dismiss any alleged current revelation if it clearly *contradicts* the standard works, there may be times when a divergence is not clear. President Harold B. Lee has provided us with further valuable guidance in this matter.

It is not to be thought that every word spoken by the General Authorities is inspired, or that they are moved upon by the Holy Ghost in everything they write. I don't care what his position is, if he writes something or speaks something that goes beyond anything you can find in the standard church works, unless that one be the prophet, seer, and revelator—please note that one exception—you may immediately say, "Well, that is his own idea." And if he says something that contradicts what is found in the standard church works, you may know by the same token that it is false, regardless of the position of the man who says it. (*Stand Ye in Holy Places,* pp. 162–63.)

Thus there are really two ways whereby canon serves to verify genuine scripture and expose counterfeit claims of inspiration. President Lee here confirms that, as mentioned, any teaching that goes *contrary* to the fundamental principles of the gospel as established in the standard works can be immediately recognized as false and uninspired. Moreover, he explains that teachings that go *beyond* the standard works are solely the province of the Lord's anointed prophet. Only the President of the Church has the right under the direction of the Holy Ghost to officially amend, modify, and/or expand upon that which has been canonized. Anyone else who does so without his direct authorization is expressing his own views and opinions on the subject.

We note, however, that President Lee did not say we must reject such teachings as being false, but only that we recognize that they represent a personal opinion and are therefore not binding upon the Church. The teaching may in fact be true, but because it is expressed outside the established, prophetic parameters, it does not represent the official doctrine or position of the Church. "With all their inspiration and greatness, prophets are yet mortal men with imperfections common to mankind in general," explained Elder Bruce R. McConkie. "They have their opinions and prejudices and are left to work out their problems without inspiration in many instances."

Thus the opinions and views, even of a prophet, may contain error, unless those opinions and views were inspired by the Spirit. Inspired scripture or statements should be accepted as such. . . .

Well, the point of this is that prophets are men and that when they act by the spirit of inspiration, what they say is the voice of God; but still they are mortal and they are entitled to and do have private opinions. Unless these are inspired and unless they accord with the revelations, they are just as subject to being in a field by themselves, as anyone else in the Church. What I really ought to do is, not talk about General Authorities, but talk about bishops and elders, because the principle is precisely the same where everyone is concerned. ("Are the General Authorities Human?" p. 5.)

Resting upon each individual is the personal responsibility to search the scriptures and obtain an in-depth, sound understanding of the doctrines of the gospel as found in the standard works. Only when we have devoted ourselves to serious, extensive, and continual study of these scriptures (see Joseph Smith—Matthew 1:37) can they serve us as "measuring rods" in determining whether someone is moved upon by the Holy Ghost. This responsibility to know, teach, and judge truth by the scriptures is an individual as well as an institutional obligation and blessing.

2. *Is It in Harmony with the Teachings of the Living Prophet?*

In addition to the standard works, the Lord has provided another objective "test" or means whereby we can ascertain when the words of the Lord's servants are inspired and therefore binding upon us as individuals. The prophet, seer, revelator-president of the Church has been given the responsibility to receive and declare the mind and will of the Lord. As has been promised, he will never lead the Church astray, nor will his counsel go contrary to the desires and designs of God (see Chapter 3). Like the standard works, the prophet-president stands as an earthly safeguard against deception and false doctrine. That is to say, the inspiration and truth of others' teachings must not only harmonize with the standard works but must also conform to and be within the parameters established by the teachings and declarations of the living prophet. Addressing seminary and institute personnel at Brigham Young University on July 7, 1954, President J. Reuben Clark offered what he characterized as "elemental rules that, as to certain matters, will enable us to know when others than the Presiding High Priest, the Prophet, Seer, and Revelator, the President of the Church, will not be speaking as 'moved upon by the Holy Ghost.' "

Here we must have in mind—must know—that *only* the President of the Church, the Presiding High Priest, is sustained as Prophet, Seer, and Revelator for the Church, and he alone has the right to receive revelations for the Church, either new or amendatory, or to give authoritative interpretations of scriptures that shall be binding upon the Church, or change in any way the existing doctrines of the Church. He is God's sole mouthpiece on earth for The Church of Jesus Christ of Latter-day Saints, the only true Church. He alone may declare the mind and will of God to his people. No officer of any other church in the world has this high right and lofty prerogative.

So when any other person, irrespective of who he is, undertakes to do any of these things you may know he is not "moved upon by the Holy Ghost," in so speaking, unless he has special authorization from the President of the Church. (D&C 90:1–4, 9, 12–16; 107:8, 65–66, 91–92; 115:19; 124:125; *HC* 2:477; 6:363). . . .

When any one except the President of the Church undertakes to proclaim a revelation from God for the guidance of the Church, we may know that he is not "moved upon by the Holy Ghost."

When any one except the President of the Church undertakes to proclaim that any scripture of the Church has been modified, changed, or abrogated, we may know that he is not "moved upon by the Holy Ghost," unless he is acting under the direct authority and direction of the President.

When any one except the President of the Church undertakes to proclaim a new doctrine of the Church, we may know that he is not "moved upon by the Holy Ghost," unless he is acting under the direct authority and direction of the President.

When any one except the President of the Church undertakes to proclaim that any doctrine of the Church has been modified, changed, or abrogated, we may know that he is not "moved upon by the Holy Ghost," unless he is acting under the direction and by the authority of the President.

When any man, except the President of the Church, undertakes to proclaim one unsettled doctrine, as among two or more doctrines in dispute, as the settled doctrine of the Church, we may know that he is not "moved upon by the Holy Ghost," unless he is acting under the direction and by the authority of the President.

Of these things we may have a confident assurance without a chance for doubt or quibbling. ("When Are Church Leaders' Words Entitled to Claim of Scripture," pp. 10–11.)

The most essential of all the Lord's earthly servants is the President of the Church. He is the one to whom we should pay particular attention. All of the other living oracles can speak and write as "moved upon by the Holy Ghost," but their teachings cannot go beyond and do not supersede those of the Prophet. Our obligation, therefore, is to become thoroughly familiar with the inspired teachings of the President of the Church by carefully studying his words and recognizing them as an additional standard against which the counsel and teachings of others can be measured.

President Henry D. Moyle, who served in the First Presidency as a Counselor to President David O. McKay, observed the importance of carefully hearing and heeding the words of the prophet-president of the Church. "The older I get and the closer the contact I have with the President of the Church, the more I realize that the greatest of all scriptures which we have in the world today is current scripture. What the mouthpiece of God says to His children is scripture. It is intended for all the children of God upon the earth. It is His word and His will and His law made manifest through His ordained and anointed servant to the world. What the President says is scripture, and I love it more than all other. It applies to me today specifically, and to you all." ("Beware of Temptation," pp. 7–8.)

3. *Is It in Harmony with the Witness of the Holy Ghost?*

Though the first two criteria tend to be somewhat exoteric, they are both inextricably linked with the third, more esoteric, standard of analysis—the confirmation of the Holy Ghost. The Lord has promised this internal measuring rod whereby we can ultimately know whether someone is "moved upon by the Holy Ghost." It works in conjunction with the other two tests, guiding our study and understanding of the standard works, confirming the inspired words of the living prophets and their interpretations of the standard works, and finally, bearing witness of the veracity or falsity of a proposed principle. "There isn't any way in heaven or on earth for anyone to know of the truth and validity of a revelation," Elder Bruce R. McConkie declared, "except to have the same Spirit rest upon him that rested upon the revelator who received it" (*Ensign,* June 1980, p. 58). Thus it is only as we receive the witness of the Holy Ghost that we may know with surety that what someone has taught is inspired and is scripture for us. However, this internal test of scripture necessitates a commitment on our part to be in tune with the Spirit. Obtaining such a witness does not come without considerable effort. The Spirit gives us guidance in proportion to our individual faith, personal worthiness, and diligence in seeking the truth. It requires spiritual sensitivity gained through "the bending of the whole soul through worthy living" (President Harold B. Lee, in Conference Report, April 1971, p. 94).

Nevertheless it would be not only shortsighted but also spiritually perilous to reject prophetic guidance and counsel merely because one had not yet received a personal witness of its inspiration. Though we may not be "moved upon by the Holy Ghost," that does not negate or devalue the inspiration of the Lord's servants. There may be many reasons why we do not immediately receive a spiritual confirmation of the truth and inspiration of the words of the prophets. It may be that we have not yet paid the price necessary to receive such. It may be that the Lord is testing our faith and obedience. It may also be that our own pride and prejudices have stifled the workings of the Spirit. Whatever the reason, it is not the obligation of the prophets to declare to us when *they* are inspired; rather, it is our obligation to study, seek, and live in such a way that *we* will be "moved upon by the Holy Ghost" and recognize those inspired teachings as scripture that is personally binding upon us as the "voice of the Lord, and the power of God unto salvation" (D&C 68:4). "We can know . . . that they are speaking under inspiration," President Harold B. Lee taught, "if we so live that we can have a witness that what they are speaking is the word of the Lord. There is only one safety, and that is that we shall live to have the witness to know." (*Stand Ye in Holy Places,* p. 163.)

Conference time is a season of spiritual revival when knowledge and testimony are increased and solidified. . . .

—Howard W. Hunter, general conference, October 1981

CHAPTER 7

General Conference: A Season of Revelation and Renewal

In an April 1830 revelation the Lord said: "The several elders composing this church of Christ are to meet in conference once in three months, or from time to time as said conferences shall direct or appoint; and said conferences are to do whatever church business is necessary to be done at the time" (D&C 20:61–62). Since then, many church conferences have been held, both locally and for the general church. There we assemble, as President Spencer W. Kimball expressed it, "to worship the Lord, to feast upon the words of Christ, and to be built up in faith and testimony" (*Ensign*, May 1978, p. 45).

General conference is the Lord's conference—a conference wherein he instructs his people, as he himself stated at one such conference, "by mine own voice or by the voice of my servants, it is the same" (D&C 1:38). The Lord in fact refers to general conference as "my conference" (see D&C 124:88)—a conference at which the revealed will of the Lord is made manifest "by the voice of the conference" (D&C 73:2; see also 72:7).

General conference, as a season of revelation and renewal, is not unique to the Church in this last dispensation. Throughout time there have been many significant gatherings and conferences of the Lord's people in which the "voice of the Lord" was manifested through inspired instruction and profound spiritual outpourings. One of the earliest great conferences was the gathering of Adam, Eve, and their righteous posterity in the valley of Adam-ondi-Ahman (see D&C 107:53–57). Prior to the Savior's glorious second coming another momentous conference of the Lord's faithful Saints will be held in that same valley (see D&C 116; also Daniel 7:9–10, 13–14; *HC* 3:386–87). Throughout the scriptures we are able to catch glimpses of and teachings about other significant gatherings of God's people. Elder Alvin R. Dyer compared modern conferences of the restored Church to the feasts and festivals of ancient Israel.

> In ancient biblical times, "the feast" was a time of gathering, a time of harvest, a time of rejoicing, and what is more particularly significant, "the feast" was designated by the Lord as a time of remembrance. These observances were established among the people for various reasons. "Three times," said the Lord, "thou shalt keep a feast unto me in the year": the feast of the harvest, the feast of the weeks, the feast of tabernacles, and there were others (see Exodus 23:14, 16; 34:22; Leviticus 23:34; Deuteronomy 16:10, 16). But in all of these there seemed to be a central motive, a time of the renewal of spirit, of regeneration, that the people might continue with gratitude and sacrifice to fulfill the purposes of the Lord, which were intended for their good and blessing.
>
> There are "feasts" that we observe at which we also gather to rejoice and be renewed in spirit and in thought, and to which we too bring the harvest of our achievements to evaluate, and then, with renewed determination, go forward to do better. Here, as in all the "feasts" of ancient times, is to be found the need of the people themselves, seeking the strength and the fortitude to push on. From such occasions will come this strength, if our hearts and minds can be brought in tune with the Spirit of God. (In Conference Report, October 1966, p. 133.)

In the Book of Mormon we read of two such gatherings where souls were strengthened and renewed and where revelations were abundantly poured out upon the Saints as the "dews from heaven." King Benjamin gathered his people together to bless them as well as teach them. His inspired words were written down and distributed to those who could not hear them, so that they could be read, reread, pondered, and discussed (see Mosiah chapters 1–5). When the resurrected Christ appeared among the Nephites, he too gathered them together on more than one occasion to teach them, pray for them, and bless them (see 3 Nephi chapters 9–27). In each of these gatherings revelations of such overwhelming magnitude were communicated that the people were overcome with joy, and mortal words could not adequately record them. Souls were strengthened, covenants were renewed, sins were forgiven, hearts were changed, and personal resolves to be "steadfast and immovable, always abounding in good works" (Mosiah 5:15) were fortified.

For us today the purposes of the general conference and the blessings that flow therefrom are much the same. As we understand the value and objective of the Lord's conferences, prepare for them, and apply them to our lives, we too can experience a similar outpouring of the Spirit. The following counsel of King Benjamin to his people remains for us a clarion call to likewise gather and be nourished by the "bread of life" and the "living waters" that abound at general conferences: "My brethren, all ye that have assembled yourselves together, you that can hear my words which I shall speak unto you this day; for I have not commanded you to come up hither to trifle with the words which I shall speak, but that you should hearken unto me, and open your ears that ye may hear, and your hearts that ye may understand, and your minds that the mysteries of God may be unfolded to your view" (Mosiah 2:9).

Just as the presence of Jehovah attended the ancient camp of Israel and an angel instructed King Benjamin in what he should teach his people, so too are the Lord's servants today inspired in their exhortations, receiving guidance from beyond the veil in their preparation. As in times past, the Lord does not leave his servants alone as they instruct us; he is not absent from *his* conference. "The Lord has magnified each one who has spoken," President David O. McKay observed at the concluding session of a general conference, "to the end that his words have emanated from the presence of our Father" (*Improvement Era*, December 1965, p. 1161). Like King Benjamin of old, President

Joseph Fielding Smith instructed us on the significance of general conference as a time to be trained by the Lord, and invited all Saints everywhere to prepare their ears to hear, their minds to understand, and their hearts to hearken to the voice of the Lord.

> It is our prayer that all those who are present and all those who hear the broadcasts, and all those who read the conference messages will have their hearts open to the great truths which will be presented and the words of wise counsel which will fall from the lips of those who shall speak to us. . . .
>
> We are the servants of the Lord. We have received light and truth and revelation from him. He has commanded us to proclaim his truths and live his laws. And so now, in harmony with his mind and will, and as guided by his Holy Spirit, we give counsel and direction to the Saints, and to the world. . . .
>
> Now there is much more that the Lord would have us hear and know and do, and I shall rely upon [the First Presidency], upon the members of the Council of the Twelve and the other General Authorities to counsel further with you by the power of the Spirit about these things. (*Ensign,* July 1972, pp. 27–28.)

Purposes of General Conference

As the Church has expanded into an international entity and as its programs and members have diversified, the nature of conference (format, length, and so forth) has been altered. However, the fundamental purposes as stated in the revelations have remained constant. The scriptures and latter-day prophets have identified several important functions of general conference that serve to further the kingdom of God on earth and to strengthen individual members.

1. To Transact Church Business

As the first quoted scripture in this chapter indicates "conferences are to do whatever church business is necessary to be done at the time" (D&C 20:62). In the earliest days of the Church, when membership was small and concentrated, many of the matters that are handled today in wards and stakes were taken care of as part of the general conferences. Today the business that is transacted in general conference is composed of those matters that affect the entire membership of the Church. Such Church business includes canonization of new scriptures, reorganization of the presiding quorums or of auxiliaries, callings and releases of general officers of the Church, and announcement of changes in policies or programs. In the future the transaction of Church business may change somewhat to reflect the contemporary needs of the Church, but one of the fundamental functions of general conference will remain—"to do whatever church business is necessary to be done at the time."

2. To Receive Reports and Church Statistics and Commend True Merit

Closely related to the transaction of Church business is the presentation of reports. These reports come in a variety of ways—some formal and others less formal. The formal reports that are annually presented for the information of the Church (typically in the April conference) include the statistical report for the previous year and the auditors' financial report. The financial report assures the membership of the Church that sacred tithing funds and other donations are being expended according to the inspired policies and procedures of the Church, as administered under the direction of the First Presidency, the Twelve, and the Presiding Bishopric (see D&C 120). The audit of Church finances and the subsequent report to the general membership ensures institutional integrity and helps to establish financial stability in order "that the church may stand independent above all other creatures beneath the celestial world" (D&C 78:14). Other reports that are less formal and are given periodically would include stewardship reports from Church leaders and/or reports concerning special assignments or ministries that have impacted the Church in some manner. Sometimes the significant and exemplary service of prominent Church members is acknowledged and commended. President David O. McKay stated that such reports, as given in general conference, "inform the membership of general conditions— whether the Church is progressing or retrogressing, economically, ecclesiastically, or spiritually" (in Conference Report, October 1954, p. 7).

The statistical report is not delivered in general conference in order to boast or to impress the world with our growth as a church, but to report progress to the members. It also is a means of showing the fulfillment of Daniel's prophecy that the kingdom of God that started as a small stone is rolling forth and filling the earth. Seeing such rapid growth and recognizing in the modern church the fulfillment of ancient prophecies should instill in us a sense of gratitude for the blessings of the Lord, not a sense of pride in our own accomplishments. Reporting the growth of the Church and all the related statistical information also serves as a reminder to us that there is yet much work to be done and that, as President Spencer W. Kimball declared, "we have paused on some plateaus long enough" (in Conference Report, April 1979, p. 114). He further explained how an acknowledgment of the growth of the church should bring with it an increased sense of gratitude and obligation.

> I rejoice with you in the progress and expansion of the Lord's earthly kingdom in almost all parts of the free world. We are constantly opening up new areas, and we are continually establishing new missions and dividing others. . . .
>
> This growth is a cause for thanksgiving and praise to the Lord for divine direction of this program of saving souls and bringing them into the fold of Christ. While much has been done and accomplished, much more remains to be done. We must go forward in courage and great boldness to proclaim Jesus Christ as the resurrected Lord and the Redeemer of mankind. (In Conference Report, October 1978, p. 4.)

3. *To Approve or Disapprove of Names Proposed*

"And a commandment I give unto you," the Lord declared through the Prophet in Nauvoo, "that you should fill all these offices and approve of those names which I have mentioned, or else disapprove of them at my general conference" (D&C 124:144). From the time of the organization of the Church on April 6, 1830, sustaining those people who have been called of God to preside over and direct the affairs of the Church has always been one of the fundamental purposes of the conference. "All things shall be done by common consent in the church, by much prayer and faith" (D&C 26:2; see also D&C 20:65). As was discussed in chapter 5, the sustaining vote of common consent is in reality a personal covenant to sustain, strengthen, assist, be loyal to, pray for, and in all ways support those who are called to preside over and serve in the Church. For this reason we participate in a sustaining vote at each conference (ward, stake, and general), whether or not there have been changes in the officers since the previous conference. In this way each member of the Church is given the opportunity to renew that covenant. Just as the sacrament is administered in every sacrament meeting for the renewal of our baptismal covenants and is a central feature of our worship, so also the renewal of our covenant of common consent is critical to our gaining the spiritual insight and uplift that is central to general conference.

4. *To Receive Revelation, Inspired Instruction, and Counsel*

In the early days of the Church, leaders and missionaries, as well as the general membership, were often called to gather for a conference in which the Lord would give them instructions concerning the personal and collective challenges they were facing (see D&C 58:56, 61–62; 124:88). The commandment was issued to the Saints to gather from all directions to be taught from on high and to be strengthened in their callings and responsibilities. Accompanying the commandment to convene a conference were promised institutional instructions, as well as spiritual blessings for the Church.

> Behold, thus saith the Lord unto you my servants, it is expedient in me that the elders of my church should be called together, from the east and from the west, and from the north and from the south, by letter or some other way.
>
> And it shall come to pass, that inasmuch as they are faithful, and exercise faith in me, I will pour out my Spirit upon them in the day that they assemble themselves together.
>
> And it shall come to pass that they shall go forth into the regions round about, and preach repentance unto the people.
>
> And many shall be converted, insomuch that ye shall obtain power to organize yourselves according to the laws of man;
>
> That your enemies may not have power over you; that

you may be preserved in all things; that you may be enabled
to keep my laws; that every bond may be broken wherewith
the enemy seeketh to destroy my people. (D&C 44:1–5.)

General conference today fulfills this commandment. And
although it is somewhat different from that conference in 1831,
the purpose is the same—the spiritual outpouring still flows, inspired counsel is still delivered, and the magnification of individual leaders and members still results. Concerning this revealed
purpose and blessing of general conference Elder Marion G.
Romney stated: "We have come to this conference from many
nations of the world—not, however, as representatives of the
governments of these nations. We are here representing the
leadership of the kingdom of God. This Church is the literal
kingdom of God in the earth. We did not come to argue, to
jockey for position, to compromise differences and establish
policies. We came here to hear and learn the word of God as he
has and does now reveal it through his appointed servants, and
to take it back and teach it to our people." (In Conference Report, April 1961, p. 117.)

President Spencer W. Kimball also spoke of the manifold
long-term benefits that come from the veritable spiritual harvest
that attends the Lord's conference of his people.

My dear brothers and sisters, we came together to wait
upon the Lord, to be cleansed and edified by his Spirit, and
to know in our hearts the spirit of true worship.

We have not been disappointed. The Lord has been with
us by the power of his Spirit, and it has been good for us to
be here.

I hope we will go forth now, believing the doctrines that
have been preached, taking the counsels of the Brethren,
and basking in the same spirit that has uplifted and edified
us while here. . . .

Now this system of revealed religion which has come to
us by revelation is a very practical religion. It deals with
flocks and herds and properties; it teaches us how to get
along with each other here and now; it is a way of life that
turns a dreary and drab mortal existence into a glorious and
exhilarating experience. (*Ensign,* November 1978, p. 71.)

As circumstances in the world change, the challenges facing the Saints and the spiritual and temporal needs of the Church also change. For this reason, general conference has become a vital link between the eternal principles revealed in the past and the current application of those principles. Having made reference to the innumerable conferences and conventions held for various secular purposes, Elder Kimball observed: "All the conferences and conventions combined of all the years could not possibly be as important as [the] recent three-day conference of the Lord's Church. . . . Let no arrogant, self-assured, self-styled intellectual discard the truths there taught and the testimonies there borne, nor argue with the messages and instructions there given." ("In the World but Not of It," p. 2.)

Sometimes the counsel and instructions given are very direct and specific to contemporary challenges, societal trends, and personal problems. "We've never had a conference," President Harold B. Lee once said of general conference, "where there has been so much direct instruction, so much admonition, when the problems have been defined, and also the solution to the problem has been suggested. . . . I think you have never attended a conference where . . . you have heard more inspired declarations on almost every subject and problem about which you have been worrying." (In Conference Report, October 1973, p. 170.) President Spencer W. Kimball made a similar comment concerning a conference over which he presided. "The sermons from the Brethren have developed almost every theme and subject, and they have been rich and full of meat" (in Conference Report, October 1976, p. 163). Such observations perhaps could be made concerning every general conference. The Lord is eternally mindful of our need for unceasing guidance. "It is my humble opinion," President Joseph Fielding Smith testified, "that we are receiving counsel by inspiration, or revelation, at *every* general conference of the Church" (*Answers to Gospel Questions* 2:205).

Sometimes, however, the messages of general conference may be more general in nature, reemphasizing long-held beliefs and reminding the Saints of those things that they already know and have been taught to do. One must not minimize the significance of or ignore these inspired reminders and reiterations just because they do not appear to be new or unique. President Kimball taught:

Some may wonder why General Authorities speak of the same things from conference to conference. As I study the utterances of the prophets through the centuries, their pattern is very clear. We seek, in the words of Alma, to teach people "an everlasting hatred against sin and iniquity." We preach "repentance, and faith on the Lord Jesus Christ" (Alma 37:32–33). We praise humility. We seek to teach people "to withstand every temptation of the devil, with their faith on the Lord Jesus Christ" (Alma 37:33). We teach our people "to never be weary of good works" (Alma 37:34).

Prophets say the same things because we face basically the same problems. Brothers and sisters, the solutions to these problems have not changed. It would be a poor lighthouse that gave off a different signal to guide every ship entering a harbor. It would be a poor mountain guide who, knowing the safe route up a mountainside, took his trusting charges up unpredictable and perilous paths from which no traveler returns. (In Conference Report, April 1976, p. 7.)

Earlier in this dispensation the Lord promised that at general conference "it shall be made known unto you what you shall do" (D&C 73:2). As stated, this promise is fulfilled with each and every conference. Although the issues and problems may change and temptations may take on a new face, the living prophets provide the guidance on both temporal and spiritual matters that will enable us to stand "steadfast and immovable" amidst the storms of the day. "We meet together often in the Church in conferences," President Spencer W. Kimball testified, "to worship the Lord, to feast upon the word of Christ, and to be built up in faith and testimony. . . . The purpose of this conference is that we may refresh our faith, strengthen our testimonies, and learn the ways of the Lord from his duly appointed and authorized servants. May we take this opportunity, then, to remind each other of our covenants and promises and commitments." (*The Teachings of Spencer W. Kimball*, p. 521.)

5. *To Proclaim the Gospel to the World*

"The main purpose of general conferences," President N. Eldon Tanner stated, "the main purpose of *this* conference, is to sound the voice of warning. You who hear and are warned must warn your neighbors. If we fail to heed the warnings given, or fail to warn our neighbors, we all may be lost." (In Conference Report, October 1976, p. 124.) One of the primary missions of the Church—the earthly kingdom of God—is to proclaim the gospel and to take its message to every nation, kindred, tongue, and people. Likewise, it is the obligation of every member to "stand as witnesses of God at all times and in all things, and in all places" (Mosiah 18:9). General conference instructs and inspires us so that we can be spiritually enlarged and in turn teach and inspire others. "That ye may be prepared in all things," the Lord declared concerning the school of the prophets and elders held in the early days of the Church and which also applies to general conferences today, "to magnify [your] calling. . . . I sent you out to testify and warn the people." (D&C 88:80–81.)

Today general conference is able to fulfill an institutional charge by proclaiming the gospel through the use of current technologies such as radio, television, satellites, videos, and so forth. In the early days of the Church, general conference was used to teach and motivate members and missionaries to go forth and share the gospel with family, friends, and neighbors. That is likewise a desired outcome today, but with the advent of these modern inventions the Church is also able to proclaim the gospel directly to the world in general conference. It is not uncommon, therefore, to hear some of the Brethren address those who are not members of the Church. Perhaps in the future the missionary objective of conference will be expanded as technology increases the accessibility of the Church's general conferences throughout the world.

6. *To Bring About a Spiritual Revival and Personal Rededication*

The Lord promised the early Saints that "as they are faithful, and exercise faith in me, I will pour out my Spirit upon them in the day that they assemble themselves together" (D&C 44:2). The promise is the same for us today. When the much-awaited spiritual outpouring is realized in conjunction with general conference, hearts are changed, spirits are revived, souls are strengthened, and personal resolves of greater righteousness are renewed. Whether or not anything new is revealed or set forth in the conference, the fruits of the Spirit always include an individual rejuvenation and a rededication to those principles taught and testified of in general conference. Declared President Howard W. Hunter:

> Conference time is a season of spiritual revival when knowledge and testimony are increased and solidified that God lives and blesses those who are faithful. It is a time when an understanding that Jesus is the Christ, the Son of the living God, is burned into the hearts of those who have the determination to serve him and keep his commandments. Conference is the time when our leaders give us inspired direction in the conduct of our lives—a time when souls are stirred and resolutions are made to be better husbands and wives, fathers and mothers, more obedient sons and daughters, better friends and neighbors. (In Conference Report, October, 1981, p. 15.)

At the conclusion of one of the general conferences over which he presided, President Spencer W. Kimball spoke of the personal impact that conference had had on him and of his new resolve to apply its messages to his life. His humble and unassuming example taught the Saints that if the prophet of the Lord can find impetus for improvement in the inspired messages and personal, spiritual promptings that accompany each general conference, they, too, should find ample room for growth.

> Many suggestions have been given that will help you as leaders in the perfection of your work. Many helpful thoughts have been given for the perfection of our own lives, and that, of course, is the basic reason for our coming.
>
> While sitting here, I have made up my mind that when I go home from this conference this night there are many, many areas in my life that I can perfect. I have made a mental list of them, and I expect to go to work as soon as we get through with conference. (In Conference Report, October 1975, p. 164.)

Differing Responses to General Conference

Whether it be the transaction of Church business, the renewal of our covenant of common consent, the reception of inspired instruction, or the proclaiming of the gospel to the world, each of the purposes of general conference is spiritual in nature and intended to uplift and motivate each member of the Church. The success of any given general conference in fulfilling these purposes and achieving the Lord's overall objectives will be determined not only by quality or content of the talks given by the Brethren, but also, and chiefly, by our individual responses to the messages and the promptings of the Spirit which accompany them. Elder Marion G. Romney described the diversity of response to general conference that he had observed while visiting stake conferences. He then pointed out why such differences exist and, in so doing, affirmed to us what is required to enjoy the abundant outflow of the Spirit and to be strengthened and encouraged by general conference.

A number of the speakers had just attended for the first time a general conference. Their reports were soul stirring. One bishop wished that every member of his ward might attend just one conference in the tabernacle. Another, when he stood with the vast congregation for the first time, was so moved that tears ran down his cheeks, and his voice so choked that he could not join in the singing. A third was impressed with President Grant's closing remarks. He said as he finished his talk: "Three times the President said, 'I bless you, I bless you, I bless you.'"

In another outlying stake, an ex-bishop said to me that conference was nothing but a political convention. In another a man said that whether he would follow the counsel of the leaders depended upon what subject they discussed.

How are these different responses accounted for? I will tell you. The members of one group were observing and keeping the commandments of God, and the others were not; one group was walking in the light of truth, and the other was in the dark; one group enjoyed the Spirit of the Lord, and the others did not. (In Conference Report, April 1942, p. 19.)

How to Gain the Most from General Conference

Just as personal revelation is not received in a vacuum—that is, without individual effort and diligence—effectively recognizing and receiving the inspired messages of general conference also requires considerable effort on the part of each Church member. The extent to which general conference helps us acquire doctrinal knowledge and gospel insight, receive personal inspiration for meeting life's challenges, and achieve spiritual strength to resist temptations and more fully live the teachings of the Master will be commensurate with our own personal preparation for and study of general conference. These and many other "fruits" of general conference will be ours as we put forth our best efforts to obtain them *before, during,* and *after* each general conference.

1. *Make Personal Spiritual Preparation*

Our perception of the spiritual success of any conference depends not so much upon the preparation and skill of the speakers as on our own preparation for the conference (see Boyd K. Packer, "Follow the Brethren," Appendix E). It is not uncommon for a family or individual to exert considerable effort, time, and resources in preparing for a much-awaited vacation or personal project, yet we often approach general conference with little thought or effort. One of the ways in which we should prepare for general conference is to pray for the Brethren. "When the Brethren arise to speak," President Lorenzo Snow counseled, "you should ask the Lord to let them say something that you want to know, that they may suggest something to you that will be of some advantage. If you have any desire to know certain matters that you do not understand, pray that these brethren in their talks may say something that shall enlighten your mind in reference to that which troubles you, and we will have a grand and glorious conference, a better one than we have ever had before." (*The Teachings of Lorenzo Snow,* p. 89.)

It is true that we should and often do pray, both personally and with our families, for the Brethren as *they* prepare for conference. Yet we sometimes fail to seek the Lord's influence as *we* prepare ourselves. Just as the quality of the produce from a farm or backyard garden is largely dependent upon the preparation of the soil, so too must our hearts and minds be prepared to become fertile receptors for the seeds of the gospel which are sown during general conference.

One significant thing we could do to enable us to gain the most from general conference is to prepare our hearts and minds in the weeks and days prior to conference through prayer and, in some cases, fasting. This will not only help us to focus on the true intent of general conference but it will also create an attitude of spiritual anticipation in that we will look forward to the conference "hungering and thirsting after righteousness." Rather than passively viewing it as a televised substitute for Sabbath meetings wherein our obligation to worship is fulfilled simply by watching or attending the Sunday morning session, we will be filled with spiritual cravings to hear and live by "every word that proceedeth out of the mouth of God" (Matthew 4:4).

All spiritual experiences in life are enhanced through proper personal preparation, and general conference should receive the same type of consideration. We usually prepare for patriarchal blessings through fasting and prayer so that the experience will have greater significance in our lives. Missionaries enhance their effectiveness dramatically when they diligently prepare to teach the gospel through conscientious scripture study and personal prayer. Temple ordinances become more instructional and covenants and promises become more meaningful as daily guides in life when a person has prepared himself to be "taught from on high" (see D&C 43:16). Preparation precedes power. With general conference, it is no different.

The success of any general conference for us as individuals begins well before the first weekends in April and October. "In a few days there opens another general conference of the Church," said Elder Boyd K. Packer at a BYU Devotional just days before the commencement of general conference. "The servants of the Lord will counsel us. . . . What you shall gain will depend not so much upon their preparation *of* the messages as upon your preparation *for* them." (*That All May Be Edified,* p. 244.) If, like the sons of Mosiah, we give ourselves to "much prayer and fasting" in preparation for general conference, we too can be filled with "the spirit of prophecy, and the spirit of revelation" (see Alma 17:3) and be magnified in our callings and spiritually strengthened individually.

2. *Listen Carefully to the Speakers and the Spirit*

Attendance at general conference—whether it be in the Tabernacle in Salt Lake City or watching the telecast via satellite in stake centers or on the television in our homes—provides the capstone to one's personal preparation. As we attend conference, in whatever manner or capacity, we receive both instruction by the speakers and inspiration by the promptings of the Spirit. "You have heard many sermons in [general conference], many sermons that could be of great value to you," President Spencer W. Kimball taught. "But it isn't so much what has been said that is important as it is what you have heard." (*The Teachings of Spencer W. Kimball,* p. 522.) It becomes imperative, therefore, that we pay close attention not only to what we hear but also to what we feel.

One of the ways in which we learn and retain something is to take notes on what we hear and are taught. This practice is a valuable instructional tool and a significant spiritual exercise in listening to and learning from general conference. It may not be necessary to write down extensive notes on every presentation, inasmuch as the talks are soon published in their entirety. What notes should we take, then, as we attentively listen to conference? President Kimball encouraged the Saints to make "copious notes of the thoughts that have come to your mind as the Brethren have addressed you" (in *Ensign,* November 1975, p. 111). The actual words of the talks are the same for everyone, but the spiritual insights and the promptings and proddings of the Spirit will not be the same for all. Therefore the most important notes to record in our journals would be those personal "flashes" of insight and inspiration—when we learn something new, when something that has personal relevance and application is spoken to the mind and heart, or when the Spirit prompts us to make changes in our life. As we listen to the speakers we can, as Nephi said of the scriptures, liken their words to ourselves, our unique circumstances, the needs and desires of our hearts. In this manner general conference is transformed from institutional instruction to inspiration of individuals.

3. *Diligently Study the Conference Issue of the* Ensign

King Benjamin had his great discourse written and distributed among the people so that those who could not hear would have access to his important counsel and teachings. Besides making them accessible to those who didn't or couldn't attend or hear conference, there is an additional value to having the conference discourses published and available to all the Saints. Thereby we may refresh in our memories the words we heard, the feelings we felt. We also gain new insights and "hear" and feel new promptings as we study the printed talks again and again. In this way we continue to be blessed and taught by general conference long after the last sermon and the closing prayer.

Through the years several of the Lord's prophets have urged the Latter-day Saints to make general conference a continual blessing by re-reading the messages and studying the conference reports just as we would study the standard works. "If you want to know what the Lord would have the Saints know and to have his guidance and direction for the next six months," declared President Harold B. Lee, "get a copy of the proceedings of this conference, and you will have the latest word of the Lord as far as the Saints are concerned" (in Conference Report, October 1973, p. 168). President Spencer W. Kimball counseled us on several occasions to carefully study the talks that were given in general conference. To students at BYU he said: "I hope you young people all heard the messages of the ages delivered [in the previous general conference]. There will be other conferences every six months. I hope that you will get your copy of [the *Ensign* containing the conference talks] and underline the pertinent thoughts and keep it with you for continual reference. No text or volume outside the standard works of the Church should have such prominent place on your personal library shelves." ("In the World but Not of It," p. 3.)

While serving as President of the Church, he likewise often closed general conference with counsel to the Saints to continue to study, ponder, and live the principles that were set forth in the conference. "I urge you to take much thought in your return home from this conference and think again of the things that have been brought to your attention," he declared on one occasion (in Conference Report, October 1977, p. 113). At another conference he said, "May I stress again the value of reading the addresses given at our general conferences in the *Ensign* magazine" (in *Ensign*, May 1978, p. 77).

At the conclusion of the April 1988 general conference, President Ezra Taft Benson stated: "I commend my Brethren of the General Authorities for the excellent addresses they have given. My humble prayer is that all of us will follow the counsel and instruction we have received. As we have felt the Spirit and made new and sacred resolves, may we now have the courage and fortitude to carry out those resolves. For the next six months your conference edition of the *Ensign* should stand next to your standard works and be referred to frequently." (In Conference Report, April 1988, p. 84.)

As with the study of the scriptures, our reading and marking of the conference addresses can continue to bless our lives and those of our families and friends when we use those messages in talks and lessons and in counseling and conversation in the Church and at home. President Kimball encouraged us, "Let the messages and spirit of this conference radiate and find expression in all that you do henceforth—in your homes, in your work, in your meetings, and in all your comings and goings" (*Ensign,* November 1978, p. 73).

4. *Hearken to the Words of the Prophets*

Preparation, attention, and note-taking are of limited consequence if what is said and done in general conference does not translate into increased obedience and personal righteousness. *Hearing* conference is of little value if we do not also *hearken to* the words of the prophets and the promptings of the Spirit.

Throughout the scriptures, the term *hearken* is inextricably linked to obedience. Different terms were used in the Hebrew text whenever reference was made to hearing *without* implied obedience (see Russell M. Nelson, "Listen to Learn," *Ensign,* May 1991, pp. 22–25). General conference "will have been lost motion," President Spencer W. Kimball boldly declared, "a waste of time, energy, and money if its messages are not heeded" ("In the World but Not of It," p. 2). James the Apostle commanded the early Saints, "But be ye doers of the word, and not hearers only." His charge is relevant to the Saints today. "For if any be a hearer of the word, and not a doer, he is like unto a man beholding his natural face in a glass: for he beholdeth himself, and goeth his way, and straightway forgetteth what manner of man he was." (James 1:22–24.) Let us not go our way after general conference and forget to implement the lessons we learned from the speakers as well as from the Spirit. Our most important, even imperative, duty with regard to general conference is not merely to hear and know but also to do.

Of the importance of general conference and the eternal significance of our response to it, Elder Mark E. Petersen testified:

A general conference of The Church of Jesus Christ of Latter-day Saints is far more significant than most people realize. . . .

The spirituality which characterizes these conference sessions leaves its stamp indelibly upon many who see and hear. It is different from the religious worship to which most people are accustomed, and is impressive to say the least.

And so it should be, for it is one of the most important events of the present day. Many do not so regard it, even among the Latter-day Saints. But for those who appreciate its true significance, it is of transcending importance, for in it *prophets of God speak,* living prophets.

When God gives a message to mankind, it is not something to be lightly cast aside. Whether He speaks personally or through His prophets. He Himself said, it is the same.

And in this conference *His prophets speak!* . . .

Shall we not take our modern prophets seriously and accept them as the servants of God? Will we choose to follow the wisdom of the world or the wisdom of these inspired men? Will we consider worldly deductions of greater value than the advice of our spiritual leaders?

We of today do not kill our prophets, nor do we put them into prison as was the case with Jeremiah and his contemporaries. But do we believe them? Or do we nullify what they say by our indifference? . . .

When the prophets of God speak today it is as significant as when Moses or Jeremiah spoke. Their words are as valid and as binding as were the teachings of the prophets anciently. . . .

In general conference the modern prophets speak to a modern world, by modern facilities, with a modern message. And that message is the Gospel of Christ, brought to earth once again in its purity. It alone can save. (*Why the Religious Life,* pp. 203–6.)

We should learn to accept counsel. All of us need counsel. . . . If you can receive counsel, and will seek it, you will prosper in the work; if you cannot, you will not be magnified. . . . I have come to see that receiving counsel is a test of obedience by which the Lord magnifies His servants.

—Ezra Taft Benson
The Teachings of Ezra Taft Benson, pp. 332–33

CHAPTER 8

Counsel:
Responses and Their Consequences

The Lord has always counseled his people through his living servants. The importance of such admonitions cannot be overemphasized. In many cases, both ancient and modern, the very lives and well-being of the Saints were dependent upon their hearkening to prophetic counsel. "Hearken unto me," declared the Lord to a group of priesthood holders in the early days of the Restoration. Speaking of the Prophet, the Lord further admonished, "and listen to the counsel of him who has ordained you from on high, who shall speak in your ears the words of wisdom, that salvation may be unto you in that thing which you have presented before me, saith the Lord God." (D&C 78:1–2.)

Salvation, sometimes temporal as well as spiritual salvation, is dependent upon receiving and obeying counsel from the Lord's anointed. "You cannot say that you submit to the law of God," President John Taylor declared, "while you reject the word and counsel of his servants" (in *Journal of Discourses* 7:325). Such is the eternal pattern that repeatedly has been reiterated and demonstrated throughout all dispensations. From the earliest of times, failure to hearken to—by hearing and obeying—the counsel of prophets has resulted in tragic consequences. "Where no counsel is, the people fall," observed wise King Solomon, "but in the multitude of counsellors there is safety" (Proverbs 11:14). The cycles of righteousness and prosperity followed by pride, apostasy, and destruction recorded in both the Bible and the Book of Mormon bear witness of the blessings for obedience to and the judgments for rejection of the counsels of prophets and Apostles.

In our day some pick and choose which words of the prophets they will accept and abide by. The Lord decries this type of selective obedience. One who is so personally "picky" about prophetic teachings reflects "littleness of soul" (D&C 117:11). "Our relationship to living prophets," wrote Elder Neal A. Maxwell, "is *not* one in which their sayings are a smorgasbord from which we may take only that which pleases us. We are to partake of all that is placed before us, including the spinach, and to leave a clean plate." (*Things As They Really Are*, p. 74.) Some seek to dismiss or minimize the counsel of living prophets by asserting that they are obligated to obey only *commandment*, but not *counsel*. Such a view reflects an ignorance of the role of prophets and the workings of the Lord; nowhere in the standard works or in the inspired utterances of modern prophets is such an idea implied or endorsed. To the contrary, numerous scriptural passages and examples testify of the fundamental need for us to listen to all counsel of the prophet, and to "give heed unto all his words and commandments which he shall give unto you" (D&C 21:4). President Wilford Woodruff taught:

> We have been governed by counsel instead of command-ment in many things, which has been a blessing to the Saints, for "he that is commanded in all things" and obeyeth it with slothfulness and not a willing mind, is not qualified before the Lord as that man is who, having the power within him, bringeth to pass much righteousness without being commanded in all that he does (in *Journal of Discourses* 14:36).

> We, as a people, should not treat lightly . . . counsel, for I will tell you in the name of the Lord—and I have watched it from the time I became a member of this Church—there is no man who undertakes to run counter to the counsel of the

legally authorized leader of this people that ever prospers, and no such man will ever prosper. . . . When counsel comes we should not treat it lightly, no matter to what subject it pertains, for if we do it will work evil unto us. (In *Journal of Discourses* 14:33.)

Just as the Old Testament and the Book of Mormon chronicle the blessings for obedience and the tragic consequences of rejection of the prophets, so the history of the restored Church presents many examples that serve to remind us of the reality of the Lord's declaration: "And the arm of the Lord shall be revealed; and the day cometh that they who will not hear the voice of the Lord, neither the voice of his servants, neither give heed to the words of the prophets and apostles, shall be cut off from among the people" (D&C 1:14).

One of the most tragic of such events in early Church history occurred during the difficulties in Missouri when the ignoble Extermination Order of Governor Boggs precipitated the infamous massacre of Saints at Haun's Mill. The Prophet Joseph used this terrible event as an example of suffering and destruction that could have been averted had counsel been strictly obeyed. At a special conference of the Saints in Nauvoo in August 1842, the Prophet taught that despite the persecutions "there would be no lives lost, if they would hearken to my counsel. Up to this day God had given me wisdom to save the people who took counsel. None had ever been killed who abode by my counsel. At Haun's Mill the brethren went contrary to my counsel; if they had not, their lives would have been spared." (*HC* 5:137.) What Joseph meant by this statement can be seen in a revealing conversation between Jacob Haun and the Prophet in October 1838.

It will be recalled that prior to the Battle of Crooked River, Joseph Smith had advised all of the Saints in smaller communities to gather to the larger population centers. Apparently Jacob Haun was unwilling to abandon his property as advised, particularly in view of what had happened in Daviess County a few weeks before. Haun went to Far West to consult with the Mormon Prophet about the matter. The following is an account of their meeting:

The morning after the Battle of Crooked River, Haughn [sic] came to Far West to consult with the Prophet concerning the policy of the removal of the settlers on Log Creek to the fortified camps. Col. White [i.e., Wight] and myself [John D. Lee] were standing by when the Prophet said to him: "Move in, by all means, if you wish to save your lives." Haughn [sic] replied that if the settlers left their homes, all of their property would be lost and the Gentiles would burn their houses and other buildings. The Prophet said: "You had better lose your property than your lives; one can be replaced, the other cannot be restored; but there is no need of losing either if you will only do as you are commanded." Haughn [sic] said that he considered the best plan was for all the settlers to move into and around the mill, and use the blacksmith's shop and other buildings as a fort in case of attack; in this way he thought they would be perfectly safe. "You are at liberty to do so if you think best," said the Prophet. Haughn [sic] then departed, well satisfied that he had carried his point.

The Prophet turned to Col. White [sic] and said: "That man did not come for counsel, but to induce me to tell him to do as he pleased; which I did. Had I commanded them to move in here and leave their property, they would have called me a tyrant. I wish they were here for their own safety. I am confident that we will soon learn that they have been butchered in a fearful manner." (In Leland H. Gentry, "A History of the Latter-day Saints in Northern Missouri from 1836 to 1839," 1965, pp. 432–33.)

The Prophet's feelings of impending doom were soon realized. Many of the survivors of the massacre later felt betrayed by Jacob Haun, whose unwillingness to follow the Prophet's original urging cost them dearly.

Incredibly, the same tragedy befell another party of Saints in relation to this same episode, demonstrating again the regrettable results of failing to take prophetic counsel seriously. The last group of Saints to leave Kirtland for Missouri was known as Kirtland Camp. They had been counseled by the Prophet to stay together and travel straight through to Far West. An entry from the journal of Charles Pulsipher chronicles a fateful decision by some to disregard this directive.

We moved quietly and peacefully until we came to the border of the Missouri, hearing many reports from our enemies telling us we had better not go any farther. We Mormons were all being driven out and if we went on we would share the same fate. Some of our brethren became faint hearted and wished to turn by the wayside and stop. A council was called that night, in which the majority were in favor of going on together, but when a portion still wanted to stop, the council bore a powerful testimony urging them all to hang together, and fulfill the covenants that had been made in the temple. He said, "I can promise you, in the name of the Lord, if you will hang together, and fulfill the covenants, you shall go through and not one hair of your head shall be harmed, but if you fall by the wayside there is no such promise given unto me to make to you." When we rolled out next morning there were a little over twenty wagons pulled off with their families and went to Haun's Mill. Most of the men were massacred. (In Gordon Orvill Hill, "A History of Kirtland Camp; Its Initial Purpose and Notable Accomplishments," 1975, p. 113.)

Heeding the counsel of the prophets of God was often a theme of the Prophet Joseph Smith's. Undoubtedly, he taught the Saints what he had been taught by the Lord. Indeed, the importance of following counsel is found throughout the revelations contained in the Doctrine and Covenants.

For although a man may have many revelations, and have power to do many mighty works, yet if he boasts in his own strength, and sets at naught the counsels of God, and follows after the dictates of his own will and carnal desires, he must fall and incur the vengeance of a just God upon him (D&C 3:4).

Behold, thus saith the Lord unto my people—you have many things to do and to repent of; for behold, your sins have come up unto me, and are not pardoned, because you seek to counsel in your own ways (D&C 56:14).

And behold, verily I say unto you, blessed are you who are now hearing these words of mine from the mouth of my servant, for your sins are forgiven you (D&C 50:36).

They were slow to hearken unto the voice of the Lord their God; therefore, the Lord their God is slow to hearken unto their prayers, to answer them in the day of their trouble. In the day of their peace they esteemed lightly my counsel; but in the day of their trouble, of necessity they feel after me. (D&C 101:7–8.)

And inasmuch as they follow the counsel which they receive, they shall have power after many days to accomplish all things pertaining to Zion (D&C 105:37).

Verily thus saith the Lord unto you, my servant Lyman: Your sins are forgiven you, because you have obeyed my voice in coming up hither this morning to receive counsel of him whom I have appointed (D&C 108:1).

While the pure in heart, and the wise, and the noble, and the virtuous, shall seek counsel, and authority, and blessings constantly from under thy hand (D&C 122:2).

His reward shall not fail if he receive counsel (D&C 124:16).

And with my servant Almon Babbit, there are many things with which I am not pleased; behold he aspireth to establish his counsel instead of the counsel which I have ordained, even that of the Presidency of my Church; and he setteth up a golden calf for the worship of my people (D&C 124:84).

Teaching the Saints that which had been powerfully impressed upon him by the Lord, Joseph repeatedly warned that failure to abide prophetic counsel would result in the loss of the Spirit and other negative consequences. On one occasion, speaking to convert Saints who had just arrived in Nauvoo, the Prophet cautioned "that it was generally in consequence of the brethren disregarding or disobeying counsel that [some] became dissatisfied and murmured" (*The Words of Joseph Smith,* p. 132).

All of the Presidents of the Church, from Joseph Smith to the present day, have maintained the importance of following counsel. In each era there have been instances, involving both the Church and individuals, that testify of the blessings that flow from obedience and of the problems and pain that naturally result from disobedience. As an example, during the lifetime of Brigham Young many of the Saints who were called to colonize parts of the Great Basin encountered difficulties with the Indians. These hostilities resulted in bloodshed and destruction. President George A. Smith, who served as a Counselor to Brigham Young in the First Presidency, explained the cause of these problems:

> For when God has a Prophet on the earth, and that Prophet tells the people what to do, and they neglect to do it, they must suffer for it. I bear witness before you this day, in the name of the Lord God of Israel, that no people can treat lightly the sayings of a Prophet of God, whom He places on the earth to direct His people, and prosper. I know it is impossible. . . .
>
> Had the people listened to the counsel of President Young, in the first place, and put their property in a proper place, it would have been protected. . . .
>
> And I do further know, to my satisfaction, that if the counsel of President Young had been observed, not one of the Saints would have lost his life by an Indian. I am certain of these facts; and yet occasionally some man falls a prey to some cruel savage, and whole villages have to be removed, and farms vacated, and tens of thousands of dollars' worth of damage is done all the time, because men will not live according to the instructions given to them by the Prophet of God. . . .
>
> The Indian War is the result of our thinking we know better than our President, the result of following our own counsel instead of the counsel of Brigham Young. (In *Journal of Discourses* 1:193–95.)

President Brigham Young told the early Saints that many of the difficulties encountered in crossing the plains and the economic problems faced after arriving in the Salt Lake Valley were caused by their own shortsightedness and selfishness as reflected in their unwillingness to follow his inspired instructions.

During the migration West, Brigham Young spoke of the anxiety he was experiencing and the problems he was encountering because the Saints had not hearkened to counsel:

> When the removal westward was in contemplation at Nauvoo, had the brethren submitted to our counsel and brought their teams and means to me and authorized me to do as the Spirit and wisdom of the Lord directed with them, then we could have outfitted a company of men that were not encumbered with large families and sent them over the mountains to put in crops and build houses, and the residue could have been gathered. . . . None would be found crying for bread, or none destitute for clothing, but all would be provided for as designed by the Almighty. But instead of taking this course, the Saints have crowded on us all the while and have completely tied our hands by importuning, saying do not leave us behind. . . . They are afraid to let us go on and leave them behind; forgetting that they have covenanted to help the poor away at the sacrifice of all their property. . . .
>
> I know that the same cause caused Joseph to lose his life, and unless this people are more united in spirit and cease to pray against counsel, it will bring me down to my grave. (In Manuscript History, 3 May 1846.)

President Brigham Young continued to teach the Saints, long after their establishment in Salt Lake, of the importance of obedience to the counsel, instructions, and directions given to them by the living prophets. He enumerated the blessings that could result from obedience and testified of the consequence that would befall those who ignored such:

> If the Spirit of God whispers this to His people through their leader, and they will not listen nor obey, what will be the consequence of their disobedience? Darkness and blindness of mind with regard to the things of God will be their lot; they will cease to have the spirit of prayer, and the spirit of the world will increase in them in proportion to their disobedience until they apostatize entirely from God and His ways. . . .

The history of the people of God in all ages testifies that whenever they have listened to the counsel of heaven they have always been blessed. All this people are satisfied that they will be more blessed to hearken to good counsel than not to do so. (In *Journal of Discourses* 12:117, 122.)

I believe the Latter-day Saints are the best people on the earth of whom we have any knowledge. Still, I believe that we are, in many things, very negligent, slothful and slow to obey the words of the Lord. Many seem to act upon the faith that God will sustain us instead of our trying to sustain ourselves. . . . I have paid attention to the counsel that has been given me. For years past it has been sounded in my ears, year after year, to lay up grain, so that we might have an abundance in the day of want. Perhaps the Lord would bring a partial famine on us; perhaps a famine would come upon our neighbors. I have been told that He might bring just such a time as we are now having. But suppose I had taken no heed to this counsel, and had not regarded the coming time, what would have been my condition today.

View the actions of the Latter-day Saints on this matter, and their neglect of the counsel given. . . . Now the people are running distracted here and there. . . . They are in want and in trouble, and they are perplexed. They do not know what to do. They have been told what to do, but they did not hearken to this counsel. . . .

We must learn to listen to the whispering of the Holy Spirit, and the counsels of the servants of God, until we come to the unity of the faith. If we had obeyed counsel we would have had granaries today, and they would have been full of grain; and we would have had wheat and oats and barley for ourselves and for our animals, to last us for years. (In *Journal of Discourses* 12:240–41.)

Today the issues may be different, but the need to follow the counsel of living prophets remains the same. Our temporal well-being and our spiritual strength and salvation are just as dependent upon such counsel as they were for the early Saints. The current counsel of the prophets is as vital to us today as was

Joseph Smith's counsel to the people at Haun's Mill to gather for safety at Far West. Contemporary counsel may not seem as dramatic or urgent to us as these historical examples, yet to those people such counsel also did not seem urgent in their time. Sometimes the Saints seem to desire the sensational and dramatic, as if they would be more responsive to counsel that appears more pressing or extreme. Most of the time, however, the prophets teach with what President Kimball called "gentle counsel" rather than pulpit-pounding demands (see Conference Report, April 1981, p. 108). We need to be responsive to those "gentle counsels" and recognize urgency even when counsel seems basic and ordinary. Just as the Spirit of the Lord speaks to us in a still, small voice, so will some of the most vital instruction from the Lord's anointed come to us in a simple and unspectacular manner. Although prophetic counsel may not be dramatic, receive network news coverage, or be heralded by the world, those admonitions, as simple and gentle as they may appear have the power, as President Kimball testified, to "save the whole world from all its ills—and I mean from *all* its ills" ("In the World, but Not of It," p. 2).

Perhaps many of the social ills we face in these tempestuous times can be traced to a rejection of prophetic counsel by both member and nonmember alike. Maybe the onslaught of drug abuse and the terrible toll of addiction and alcoholism can, in part, be traced back to the ignoring of President Heber J. Grant's counsel concerning the Word of Wisdom and his opposition to the repealing of the Eighteenth Amendment. The state of Utah, with its predominantly LDS population, became the decisive vote on the matter. "One of the saddest days in all of Utah's history," observed President Spencer W. Kimball, "was when the people, including the Latter-day Saints (for it could not have been done without them), rejected the counsel and urging of the Lord's prophet, Heber J. Grant, and repealed Prohibition long years ago—yet many of those voters had sung numerous times, 'We Thank Thee, O God, for a Prophet.'" (*The Teachings of Spencer W. Kimball*, p. 412.) Many Church members viewed President Grant's counsel as nothing more than his political opinion. They failed to recognize that through their disobedience they were sowing seeds of subsequent sorrow and heartache. Of this result, President George Albert Smith said:

We are fortunate today to have the servant of the Lord who presides over the Church, the mouthpiece of the Lord to us, sitting in our midst. There are thousands of people who would walk any distance they were able, in order that they might see the face and touch the hand of the Prophet of the Lord, and yet there are many of our own people who disregard his guidance and his counsel. From this very stand he pleaded with us not to repeal the Eighteenth Amendment to the Constitution of the United States. He didn't speak as Heber J. Grant, the man. He spoke as the President of the Church and the representative of our Heavenly Father. And yet in a state where we could have retained what we had, there were enough Latter-day Saints, so called (some of them hold positions in the Church, or did at that time), who paid no attention to what the Lord wanted, ignored what he had said through his prophet, and what is the result? Such delinquency as we have never known is in our own community today, and the sons and daughters and grandchildren, and in many cases the fathers and mothers, who defied the advice of our Heavenly Father and said, "We will do as we please," are paying the penalty and will continue to do so until they turn away from their foolishness and desire with all their hearts to do what our Heavenly Father desires us to do. (In Conference Report, October 1943, p. 47.)

In similar manner and closer to our day, could the many broken families and the high scale of divorce in the modern Church be resulting in part from failure to follow the counsel of prophets concerning families and marriages (e.g., family home evening, family prayer, scripture study, unselfishness, priorities)? Are the growing problems of child abuse and neglect, increased delinquency, and disregard for others stemming somewhat from a failure to heed the words of prophets about the divinely assigned roles of mother and father? Could some of the economic problems we face as families or as individuals be the by-products of our indifference to prophetic admonitions concerning thrift and industry, faithful payment of tithes and offerings, choices in entertainment, and cautions against materialism and excessive debt? Could droughts, famines, or floods be sent from the Lord because many of his people have ignored the counsel of his servants concerning the sanctity of the Sabbath day? "The Lord uses the weather sometimes," President Kimball taught, "to discipline his people for the violation of his laws" (in *Ensign,* May 1977, p. 4). Prophets give us guidance in regard to virtually every potential problem or societal challenge that we may face either institutionally or individually. As in days of old, there is security and serenity in obeying and peril and pain in rejecting such advice. "The great test that confronts us, as in every age when the Lord has a people on earth," observed Elder Bruce R. McConkie, "is whether we will give heed to the words of his living oracles and follow the counsel and direction they give for our day and time" (*Ensign,* May 1974, pp. 71–72). President Spencer W. Kimball on several occasions pleaded with Saints to follow the words of the prophets in order that they might receive the blessings and protection of the Lord.

> Beloved brothers and sisters, you are facing the trial of your faith. Will you listen to your leaders? . . . Will you listen? Will you follow the advice and counsel of your leaders, local and general? Or will you choose your own paths though they lead you into the dark wilderness? . . . Listen to the words of heaven. (In Conference Report, October 1974, pp. 9–10.)

> May I remind all of us that if we will live the gospel and follow the counsel of the leaders of the Church, we will be blessed to avoid many of the problems that plague the world. The Lord knows the challenges we face. If we keep his commandments, we will be entitled to the wisdom and blessings of heaven in solving them. (In Conference Report, April 1980, p. 128.)

Following counsel not only helps us "to avoid many of the problems that plague the world," but also is in itself a test of our discipleship. "One who rationalizes that he or she has a testimony of Jesus Christ," President Ezra Taft Benson stated, "but cannot accept direction and counsel from the leadership of His Church is in a fundamentally unsound position and is in jeopardy of losing exaltation" (in Conference Report, April 1982, p. 90). Obtaining a crown of eternal life requires strict, not selective, obedience. "For he that receiveth my servants receiveth me," declared the Lord in the oath and covenant of the Priesthood. "And he that receiveth me receiveth my Father; and he that receiveth my Father receiveth my Father's kingdom; therefore all that my Father hath shall be given unto him." (D&C 84:36–38.)

At the conclusion of a general conference, President Kimball testified of the relationship between heeding the prophets and our personal salvation and exaltation. "Now as we conclude this general conference, let us all give heed to what was said to us. Let us assume the counsel given applies to *us*, to me. Let us hearken to those we sustain as prophets and seers, as well as the other brethren, as if our eternal life depended upon it, because it does!" (In Conference Report, April 1978, p. 117.)

While many examples of the negative consequences of rejecting counsel have been cited in this chapter, it is even more important that we also recognize the positive promises and blessings that are reserved for those who hearken to the words of the prophets. As we strive to meet the challenges of life faithfully, resist the temptations of the devil, and serve the Lord and our fellowman, we need a special endowment of power and an outpouring of the Spirit. On April 6, 1830, at the organization of the restored Church, the Lord not only commanded his people to follow the Prophet, but also promised a most significant blessing.

> Wherefore, meaning the church, thou shalt give heed unto all his words and commandments which he shall give unto you as he receiveth them, walking in all holiness before me;
>
> For his word ye shall receive, as if from mine own mouth, in all patience and faith.
>
> For by doing these things the gates of hell shall not prevail against you; yea, and the Lord God will disperse the powers of darkness from before you, and cause the heavens to shake for your good, and his name's glory. . . .
>
> For behold, I will bless all those who labor in my vineyard with a mighty blessing. (D&C 21:4–6, 9.)

The gates of hell are closed, the powers of darkness are dispersed, and the heavens shake for our good only as we are

illuminated and led by the power of the Spirit. The guidance of
the Holy Spirit is conditioned upon our adherence to the teachings of the Lord's servants. Elder Neal A. Maxwell wrote: "A
lack of obedience to the leaders will, therefore, mean that we
will not have the precious promptings of the Spirit, which we
need personally—so much and so often. This potential loss
would be reason enough for us to be obedient to the prophets,
for apparently we cannot have one without the other. Vital as
the words of the prophets are, these come to us only periodically. We need the directions of the Spirit daily, even hourly."
(*All These Things Shall Give Thee Experience*, p. 104.)

A poignant example from Church history portrays the spiritual power that attends one who follows the counsel of
prophets. Ephraim Hanks had known Brigham Young since the
Nauvoo days. Eph's loyalty to the Brethren and his willingness
to obey strictly the counsel of the prophet on any matter caused
him to be much beloved and trusted by President Young, by
whom Eph had been tested on more than one occasion.

On a fall morning in 1848, President Young drove to
where Eph was building an adobe house inside the Old
Fort. Looking over the completed foundation, he inquired
as to the thickness of the rock wall. "Eight inches," replied
Eph. "Tear it down and build it twice that thick," suggested
Brigham, who then promptly drove away before Eph could
answer. To rebuild meant hauling more rock and doing twice
the work they thought was necessary. . . . Nevertheless, they
widened the foundation to sixteen inches according to the
leader's instruction. Eph was fitting the rafters on the house
a month later when a heavy rain began falling, ultimately
causing widespread flooding and considerable damage in
parts of the valley. Eph's reinforced walls stood firm against
the resulting deluge, however, thus preventing a possible
collapse of the entire structure. Others were not so fortunate. From then on when Brigham talked, Eph listened.

Not long following this incident with Brigham Young,
Eph met the Mormon leader at a dance in Salt Lake City.
Again he counseled Eph. This time Eph was to go home and
shave his face. Like many men of his day, Eph wore a beard
almost to his waist. Somewhat puzzled, he left the social and

rode home, pondering the unusual request. In an hour, however, he returned to the dance without a beard, but still wearing a mustache which he hadn't shaved. Still not satisfied with his appearance, Brigham Young indicated with a sweep of the hand across Eph's face that he wanted a clean shave. Excusing himself a second time, Eph complied by shaving his entire face. It was perhaps this type of obedience to counsel that prompted the Mormon Church President to later say of Eph that "Here was a man always ready to lay down his life for the authorities of the Church as well as for the cause of Zion and her people." (Richard K. Hanks, "Eph Hanks, Pioneer Scout," unpublished master's thesis, BYU, 1973, pp. 26–27.)

Because of his obedience to counsel and his loyalty to the Brethren, Eph Hanks became a spiritual giant in his own right and was able to render significant service to the Church and to his fellowmen. One experience in his life seems to epitomize the blessing of spiritual guidance with which those who hearken to prophetic counsel are endowed. Because of this gift, Eph Hanks was able not only to serve but also to actually save lives that would have been lost had he not been able to discern the workings of the Spirit. In his own words he tells the story:

In the fall of 1856, I spent considerable of my time fishing in Utah Lake; and in traveling backward and forward between that lake and Salt Lake City, I had occasion to stop once overnight with Gurney Brown, in Draper, about nineteen miles south of Salt Lake City. Being somewhat fatigued after the day's journey, I retired to rest quite early, and while I still lay wide awake in my bed I heard a voice calling me by name, and then saying: "The hand-cart people are in trouble and you are wanted; will you go and help them?" I turned instinctively in the direction from whence the voice came and beheld an ordinary-sized man in the room. Without any hesitation I answered, "Yes, I will go if I am called." I then turned around to go to sleep, but had laid only a few minutes when the voice called a second time, repeating almost the same words as on the first occasion. My answer was the same as before. This was repeated a third time.

When I got up the next morning I said to Brother Brown, "The hand-cart people are in trouble and I have promised to go out and help them;" but I did not tell him of my experience during the night.

I now hastened to Salt Lake City, and arrived there on the Saturday, preceding the Sunday on which the call was made for volunteers to go out and help the last hand-cart companies in. When some of the brethren responded by explaining that they could get ready to start in a few days, I spoke at once saying, "I am ready now!" The next day I was wending my way eastward over the mountains with a light wagon all alone.

The terrific storm which caused the immigrants so much suffering and loss overtook me near the South Pass, where I stopped about three days with Reddick N. Allred, who had come out with provisions for the immigrants. The storm during these three days was simply awful. In all my travels in the Rocky Mountains both before and afterwards, I have seen no worse. When the snow at length ceased falling, it lay on the ground so deep that for many days it was impossible to move wagons through it.

Being deeply concerned about the possible fate of the immigrants, and feeling anxious to learn of their condition, I determined to start out on horseback to meet them; and for this purpose I secured a pack-saddle and two animals (one to ride and one to pack), from Brother Allred, and began to make my way slowly through the snow, alone. After traveling for some time I met Joseph A. Young and one of the Garr boys, two of the relief company which had been sent out from Salt Lake City to help the companies. They had met the immigrants and were now returning with important dispatches from the camps to the headquarters of the Church, reporting the awful condition of the companies.

In the meantime I continued my lonely journey, and the night after meeting Elders Young and Garr, I camped in the snow in the mountains. As I was preparing to make a bed in the snow with the few articles that my pack animal carried for me, I thought how comfortable a buffalo robe would be on such an occasion, and also how I could relish a little buffalo meat for supper, and before lying down for the night I was instinctively led to ask the Lord to send me a buffalo. Now, I am a firm believer in the efficacy of prayer, for I have on many different occasions asked the Lord for blessings, which He in His mercy has bestowed upon me. But when I, after praying as I did on that lonely night in the South Pass, looked around me and spied a buffalo bull within fifty yards of my camp, my surprise was complete; I had certainly not expected so immediate an answer to my prayer. However, I soon collected myself and was not at a loss to know what to do. Taking deliberate aim at the animal, my first shot brought him down. . . . I was soon busily engaged skinning my game, finishing which, I spread the hide on the snow and placed my bed upon it. I next prepared supper, eating . . . to my heart's content. After this I enjoyed a refreshing night's sleep, while my horses were browsing on the sage brush.

Early the next morning I was on my way again, and soon reached what is known as the Ice Springs Bench. There I happened upon a herd of buffalo and killed a nice cow. I was impressed to do this, although I did not know why until a few hours later, but the thought occurred to my mind that the hand of the Lord was in it, as it was a rare thing to find bufallo herds around that place at this late part of the season. I skinned and dressed the cow; then cut up part of its meat in long strips and loaded both my horses with it. Thereupon I resumed my journey, and traveled on till towards evening. I think the sun was about an hour high in the west when I spied something in the distance that looked like a black streak in the snow. As I got near to it, I perceived it moved; then I was satisfied that this was the long looked for hand-cart company, led by Captain Edward Martin. I reached the ill-fated train just as the immigrants were camping for the night. The sight that met my gaze as I entered their camp can never be erased from my memory. The starved forms and haggard countenances of the poor sufferers, as they moved about slowly, shivering with cold, to prepare their scanty evening meal was enough to touch the stoutest heart. When they saw me coming, they hailed me with joy inexpressible, and when they further beheld the supply of fresh meat I brought into camp, their gratitude knew no bounds. Flocking around me, one would say, "Oh please, give me a small piece of meat;" another would exclaim, "My poor children are starving, do give me a little;" and children with tears in their eyes would call out, "Give me some, give me some." At first I tried to wait on them and handed out the meat as they called for it; but finally I told them to help themselves. Five minutes later both my horses had been released of their extra burden—the meat was all gone, and the next few hours found the people in camp busily engaged cooking and eating it, with thankful hearts.

A prophecy had been made by one of the brethren that the company should feast on buffalo meat, when their provisions might run short; my arrival in their camp, loaded with meat, was the beginning of the fulfillment of that prediction; but only the beginning, as I afterwards shot and killed a number of buffalo for them as we journeyed along. . . .

Soon more relief companies were met and as fast as the baggage was transferred into the wagons, the hand carts were abandoned one after another, until none were left.

I remained with the immigrants until the last of Captain Martin's company arrived in Salt Lake City on thirtieth of November, 1856. (Andrew Jenson, "Church Emigration: Ephraim K. Hank's Narrative," *Contributor,* XIV (1893): 202–5; cited in Richard K. Hanks, "Eph Hanks, Pioneer Scout," pp. 77–79.)

As we follow the counsel of the living prophets, whether gentle or direct, we will be filled with the Spirit and be magnified, as Eph Hanks was, in our ministry in the Lord's kingdom and our service to others (see *The Teachings of Ezra Taft Benson,* p. 332). Untold blessings, both here and hereafter, await those who seek counsel from the Lord's servants and faithfully follow it. President Lorenzo Snow gave this glorious promise:

No man can be more happy than by obeying the living prophet's counsel. You may go from east to west, from north to south, and tread this footstool of the Lord all over, and you cannot find a man that can make himself happy in this Church, only by applying the counsel of the living prophet in this life; it is a matter of impossibility for a man to receive a fulness who is not susceptible of receiving and carrying out the living prophet's counsel. An individual that applies the counsel of this Church is bound to increase in all that is good, for there is a fountain of counsel which the Lord has established. He has made it, has deposited that counsel, that wisdom and those riches, and it will circumscribe all that pertains unto good, unto salvation; all that pertains unto peace and unto happiness; all things that pertain to glory and to the exaltation of the Saints in this world and in the world to come. (*The Teachings of Lorenzo Snow*, pp. 86–87.)

It is an eternal principle: That man who rises up to condemn others, finding fault with the Church . . . is on the high road to apostasy; and if he does not repent, will apostatize, as God lives.

—Joseph Smith, *Teachings*, pp. 156–57

CHAPTER 9

Patterns of Apostasy: Murmuring, Criticism, and Rebellion

A major theme of the scriptures, as demonstrated by both doctrinal teaching and historical example, is the spiritual danger of speaking evil of the Lord's anointed. Numerous passages reflect the Lord's expectation that his people will not only hearken to the prophets but also respect and esteem them, avoiding all forms of murmuring and criticism. In Old Testament times, Moses taught the ancient Israelites that such evil speaking against the Lord's prophets and other leaders of his earthly kingdom is really aimed at the Lord, not his appointed spokesmen. The Lord "heareth your murmurings which ye murmur against him," Moses declared. "And what are we? your murmurings are not against us, but against the Lord." (Exodus 16:7–8.) Peter, Paul, James, and Jude all admonished the Saints of New Testament times not to "speak evil of dignities" (Jude 1:8; see also 2 Peter 2:10; James 4:10–11; 1 Corinthians 15:33; Ephesians 4:31; Titus 3:2). The ancient peoples of the Book of Mormon also knew that it was spiritually perilous to murmur and contend against the prophets of God but some of them still did it, even to the point of murder (see 1 Nephi 2:11; 3:6; 2 Nephi 26:5; Alma 22:24; Alma 37:30; Helaman 13:24; Ether 7:24).

Such scriptural examples and teachings embody the Lord's merciful warnings to us concerning the dangers of the rocky road to apostasy. "The journey of a thousand miles," states an ancient Chinese proverb, "begins with the first step." It is unlikely that anyone would spontaneously and immediately apostatize and fight against Zion. That ultimate destination is reached step by step, starting with one small unchecked act or attitude that in time exponentially escalates to the point of open rebellion against the servants of the Lord. It might begin with a seemingly innocuous doubting or "second guessing" of the prophets. These seeds of doubt may then sprout into tiny seedlings of murmuring and grumbling within one's own heart. If these weeds are not uprooted they can then rapidly grow and take firm root, blossoming into open criticism and mocking of the Lord's anointed. From criticism and faultfinding are eventually born the evil "fruits" of rebellion, apostasy, and an ultimate spiritual death. Elder Spencer W. Kimball gave an example of this tragic cycle and the potential pitfalls of even "mild criticism".

There is the man who, to satisfy his own egotism, took a stand against the Authorities of the Church. He followed the usual pattern, not apostasy at first, only superiority of knowledge and mild criticism. He loved the Brethren, he said, but they failed to see and interpret as he would like. He would still love the Church, he maintained, but his criticism grew and developed into everwidening circles. He was right, he assured himself; he could not yield in good conscience; he had his pride. His children did not accept his philosophy wholly, but their confidence was shaken. In their frustration, they married out of the Church, and he lost them. He later realized his folly and returned to humbleness, but so very late. He had lost his children. "It is hard for thee to kick against the pricks." (In Conference Report, April 1955, pp. 94–95.)

When we recognize that murmuring, criticizing, or any manner of evil speaking of the Lord's chosen servants is in reality a form of rebellion against God, we begin to understand why the scriptures contain so many examples of tragic consequences that befell both individuals and entire nations who derided and demeaned the Lord's servants. Although the consequences surrounding these ancient incidents may differ drastically from what we might experience today, the principles are the same. We can perceive the modern relevance of these ancient warnings by "likening the scriptures" to ourselves and applying these eternal principles to our generation and to our personal circumstances.

Murmuring and Criticism

One of the most graphic examples of the consequences of murmuring and criticism in relation to the prophets is found in the Old Testament. Miriam and Aaron called into question Moses' marriage to an Ethiopian woman and, apparently, his right to be the sole revelator (see Numbers 12:1–2; also Josephus, *Antiquities of the Jews,* 2.10.2). Moses was their younger brother, and they apparently felt they could criticize and correct him. Jehovah taught them that though he was their brother, Moses was His chosen mouthpiece, and they had no right to criticize and find fault with him in any matter. To emphasize this point to them, the Lord caused a unique consequence to befall them.

> And the Lord came down in the pillar of the cloud, and stood in the door of the tabernacle, and called Aaron and Miriam: and they both came forth.
>
> And he said, Hear now my words: If there be a prophet among you, I the Lord will make myself known unto him in a vision, and will speak unto him in a dream.
>
> My servant Moses is not so, who is faithful in all mine house.
>
> With him will I speak mouth to mouth, even apparently, and not in dark speeches; and the similitude of the Lord shall he behold: wherefore then were ye not afraid to speak against my servant Moses?
>
> And the anger of the Lord was kindled against them; and he departed.
>
> And the cloud departed from off the tabernacle; and, behold, Miriam became leprous, white as snow: and Aaron looked upon Miriam, and, behold, she was leprous.

And Aaron said unto Moses, Alas, my lord, I beseech thee, lay not the sin upon us, wherein we have done foolishly, and wherein we have sinned. (Numbers 12:5–10.)

It may seem to some that Jehovah treated Miriam and Aaron harshly by using a temporary case of leprosy in making his point. They were not blatantly wicked or rebellious. They felt justified in their criticism and attempted correction of the prophet. From this episode we see that criticizing the prophets of God, whatever the issue, is no light matter to the Lord—even if one feels right or justified in the criticism. Today some murmur against, criticize, and/or reject living prophets by virtue of some similarly misconceived justification—the obscurity of the prophets' background, their lack of academic credentials or professional training, a familiarity with their failings, or any other supposed deficiency. President Spencer W. Kimball taught:

> Various excuses have been used over the centuries to dismiss these divine messengers. There has been denial because the prophet came from an obscure place. "Can any good thing come out of Nazareth?" (John 1:46.) Jesus was also met with the question, "Is not this the carpenter's son?" (Matthew 13:55.) By one means or another, the swiftest method of rejection of the holy prophets has been to find a pretext, however false or absurd, to dismiss the man so that his message could also be dismissed. Prophets who were not glib, but slow of speech, were esteemed as naught. . . .
>
> But while there are various excuses for rejection, there's a certain cause for this sad record. It must not be passed over. The cares of the world, the honors of the world, and looking beyond the mark are all determined by a persuasive few who presume to speak for all. . . .
>
> These excuses for rejection of the prophets are poor excuses. The trouble with using obscurity as a test of validity is that God has so often chosen to bring forth his work out of obscurity. He has even said it would be so. (See D&C 1:30). . . .
>
> The trouble with rejection because of personal familiarity with the prophets is that the prophets are always somebody's son or somebody's neighbor. They are chosen from

among the people, not transported here from another planet, dramatic as that would be! . . .

The trouble with rejecting the prophets because they lack prestige is that Paul, who knew something of rejection, forewarned us when he said, speaking of the work of God, "For ye see your calling, brethren, how that not many wise men after the flesh, not many mighty, not many noble are called" (1 Corinthians 1:26).

In multiple scriptures the Lord has indicated that he will perform his work through those whom the world regards as weak and despised. (In Conference Report, April 1978, pp. 115–17.)

The lesson to be learned from the example of Miriam and Aaron is that it is the Lord who calls his servants and it is he who will correct them. No matter what some feel the prophets' shortcomings and deficiencies may be, he upholds them; and those who "speak evil dignities" will ultimately be brought to account for it. Those who in our day criticize the Brethren and call in question their decisions and counsel may not show outward symptoms like those of leprosy; but they will be afflicted with an inward, more serious spiritual sickness that, if left untreated by repentance, can cause the person's spiritual demise. President Harold B. Lee testified:

Mark well those who speak evil of the Lord's anointed, for they speak from impure hearts. Only the "pure in heart" see the "God" or the divine in man and accept our leaders and accept them as prophets of the Living God. . . .

I want to bear you my testimony that the experience I have had has taught me that those who criticize the leaders of this Church are showing signs of a spiritual sickness which, unless curbed, will bring about eventually spiritual death. I want to bear my testimony as well that those who in public seek by their criticism to belittle our leaders or bring them into disrepute, will bring upon themselves more hurt than upon those whom they seek thus to malign. I have watched over the years, and I have read of the history of many of those who fell away from this Church, and I want to bear testimony that no apostate who ever left this Church

ever prospered as an influence in his community thereafter.
(In Conference Report, October 1947, p. 67.)

Surely members of the Church who undertake to criticize
living prophets have no overt desire to destroy the Church or
undermine the Brethren. They think they are being true and
faithful to their principles and that their well-intentioned criticism will help the Church in some way. Such a stance is "wholly
inconsistent" with the principles of the restored gospel. Thinking that one can be faithful in the kingdom which taking it upon
oneself to murmur, criticize, or attempt to correct the Lord's
anointed is, as Elder Marion G. Romney explained, "assuming
an indefensible position."

> I desire to call your attention to the principle of loyalty,
> loyalty to the truth and loyalty to the men whom God has
> chosen to lead the cause of truth. I speak of "the truth" and
> these "men" jointly, because it is impossible fully to accept
> the one and partly reject the other.
> I raise my voice on this matter to warn and counsel you
> to be on your guard against criticism. . . . It comes, in part,
> from those who hold, or have held, prominent positions. Os-
> tensibly, they are in good standing in the Church. In ex-
> pressing their feelings, they frequently say, "We are mem-
> bers of the Church, too, you know, and our feelings should
> be considered."
> They assume that one can be in full harmony with the
> spirit of the gospel, enjoy full fellowship in the Church, and
> at the same time be out of harmony with the leaders of the
> Church and the counsel and directions they give. Such a po-
> sition is wholly inconsistent, because the guidance of this
> Church comes, not alone from the written word, but also
> from continuous revelation, and the Lord gives that revela-
> tion to the Church through His chosen leaders and none
> else. It follows, therefore, that those who profess to accept
> the gospel and who at the same time criticize and refuse to
> follow the counsel of the leaders, are assuming an indefensi-
> ble position. (In Conference Report, April 1942, pp. 17–18.)

Why does the Lord command us not to criticize his servants,
recognizing that even they are human and make mistakes? Why

does he condemn "evil speaking" and "corrupt communication" in such harsh terms? Why are the consequences of such behavior frequently so severe? Perhaps the answers to each of these questions can be found in the following experience of President Brigham Young.

> I can tell the people that once in my life I felt a want of confidence in brother Joseph Smith, soon after I became acquainted with him. It was not concerning religious matters—it was not about his revelations—but it was in relation to his financiering—to his managing the temporal affairs which he undertook. A feeling came over me that Joseph was not right in his financial management, though I presume the feeling did not last sixty seconds, and perhaps not thirty. But that feeling came on me once and once only, from the time I first knew him to the day of his death. It gave me sorrow of heart, and I clearly saw and understood, by the spirit of revelation manifested to me, that if I was to harbor a thought in my heart that Joseph could be wrong in anything, I would begin to lose confidence in him, and that feeling would grow from step to step, and from one degree to another, until at last I would have the same lack of confidence in his being the mouthpiece for the Almighty. . . . Though I admitted in my feelings and knew all the time that Joseph was a human being and subject to err, still it was none of my business to look after his faults.
>
> I repented of my unbelief, and that too, very suddenly; I repented about as quickly as I committed the error. It was not for me to question whether Joseph was dictated by the Lord at all times and under all circumstances or not. I never had the feeling for one moment, to believe that any man or set of men or beings upon the face of the whole earth had anything to do with him, for he was superior to them all, and held the keys of salvation over them. Had I not thoroughly understood this and believed it, I much doubt whether I should ever have embraced what is called "Mormonism." He was called of God; God dictated him, and if He had a mind to leave him to himself and let him commit an error, that was no business of mine. And it was not for me to question it, if the Lord was disposed to let Joseph lead the people astray, for He had called him and instructed

him to gather Israel and restore the Priesthood and king-dom to them.

It was not my prerogative to call him in question with re-gard to any act of his life. He was God's servant, and not mine. He did not belong to the people but to the Lord, and was doing the work of the Lord, and if He should suffer him to lead the people astray, it would be because they ought to be led astray. If he should suffer them to be chastised, and some of them destroyed, it would be because they deserved it, or to accomplish some righteous purpose. That was my faith, and it is my faith still. (In *Journal of Discourses* 4:297–98.)

Thus the Lord's commandment to avoid murmuring and contending against the living prophets and their counsel is not designed to insulate or protect them from criticism; rather, it is to protect us from the deadly spiritual toxins that poison our own souls. In his love and mercy, the Lord seeks to insulate us from the soul-damaging consequences that always result from murmuring and criticism. Elder Dallin H. Oaks explained:

Criticism is particularly objectionable when it is directed toward Church authorities, general or local. Jude condemns those who "speak evil of dignities." (Jude 1:8.) Evil speaking of the Lord's anointed is in a class by itself. It is one thing to depreciate a person who exercises corporate power or even government power. It is quite another thing to criticize or depreciate a person for the performance of an office to which he or she has been called of God. It does not matter that the criticism is true. As Elder George F. Richards, Pres-ident of the Council of the Twelve, said in a conference ad-dress in April 1947, "When we say anything bad about the leaders of the Church, whether true or false, we tend to im-pair their influence and their usefulness and are thus work-ing against the Lord and his cause." (In Conference Report, April 1947, p. 24.) . . .

The counsel against speaking evil of Church leaders is not so much for the benefit of the leaders as it is for the spir-itual well-being of members who are prone to murmur and find fault. The Church leaders I know are durable people. They made their way successfully in a world of unrestrained criticism before they received their current callings. They have no personal need for protection; they seek no personal immunities from criticism—constructive or destructive. They only seek to declare what they understand to be the word of the Lord to his people. (*Ensign*, February 1987, p. 70.)

Murmuring and criticism in any matter sow the seeds of *doubt*, which may spring forth into *disbelief*. This in turn causes us to *disregard* the prophets' teachings, which nearly always leads to spiritual *defiance* and eventual *destruction*. While many may feel that today they can criticize and make fun of the leaders of the kingdom of God without fear of being cursed with leprosy or an attack of she-bears (see 2 Kings 2:23–24), it would be wise to remember the warnings in modern revelation. God will not allow anyone to criticize, contend against, or demean his servants with impunity. The judgments reserved for those who do these things make leprosy and she-bears pale in comparison. They may not seem as sensational nor as visible as some of the Old Testament penalties, but they are real nonetheless. Concerning those who criticized and persecuted the Prophet Joseph and claimed that he was a "fallen prophet," the Lord declared:

> And they who do charge thee with transgression, their hope shall be blasted, and their prospects shall melt away as the hoar frost melteth before the burning rays of the rising sun;
>
> And also that God hath set his hand and seal to change the times and seasons, and to blind their minds, that they may not understand his marvelous workings; that he may prove them also and take them in their own craftiness;
>
> Also because their hearts are corrupted, and the things which they are willing to bring upon others, and love to have others suffer, may come upon themselves to the very uttermost;
>
> That they may be disappointed also, and their hopes may be cut off;
>
> And not many years hence, that they and their posterity shall be swept from under heaven, saith God, that not one of them is left to stand by the wall (D&C 121:11–15).

In that same revelation, given to Joseph Smith while he was incarcerated in Liberty Jail, the Lord spoke further in terms that have general relevance and application to all who speak evil of the living prophets.

> Cursed are all those that shall lift up the heel against mine anointed, saith the Lord, and cry they have sinned when they have not sinned before me, saith the Lord, but have done that which was meet in mine eyes, and which I commanded them.
>
> But those who cry transgression do it because they are the servants of sin, and are the children of disobedience themselves.
>
> And those who swear falsely against my servants, that they may bring them into bondage and death—
>
> Wo unto them; because they have offended my little ones they shall be severed from the ordinances of mine house.
>
> Their basket shall not be full, their houses and their barns shall perish, and they themselves shall be despised by those that flattered them.
>
> They shall not have right to the priesthood, nor their posterity after them from generation to generation. (D&C 121:16–21.)

Being cut off from the blessings of the temple and the priesthood, losing the comfort and guidance of the Holy Spirit, suffering feelings of insecurity and disappointment, and forfeiting the prosperity of the Lord are among those curses that can follow murmuring and criticism of the living prophets. Who among us would not choose to have the physical malady of leprosy or the wounds inflicted by wild animals that heal in time, rather than experience those irreversible, eternal spiritual consequences? It is against these latter judgments that the Lord lovingly seeks to shield us. President George Q. Cannon taught:

> If any of you have indulged in the spirit of murmuring and fault-finding and have allowed your tongues to give utterance to thoughts and words that were wrong and not in accordance with the spirit of the Gospel, . . . you ought to re-

pent of it with all your hearts and get down into the depths of humility and implore Him for the forgiveness of that sin—for it is a most deadly sin.

The men who hold the Priesthood are but mortal men; they are fallible men. . . . No human being that ever trod this earth was free from sin, excepting the Son of God. . . .

Nevertheless, God has chosen these men. He has singled them out. . . . He has selected them, and He has placed upon them the authority of the Holy Priesthood, and they have become His representatives in the earth. He places them as shepherds over the flock of Christ, and as watchmen upon the walls of Zion. And He holds them to a strict accountability . . . for the authority which He has given to them, and in the day of the Lord Jesus they will have to stand and be judged for . . . the manner in which they have exercised this authority. If they have exercised it wrongfully and against the interests of His work and the salvation of His people, woe unto them in the day of the Lord Jesus! He will judge them. (*Gospel Truth*, p. 215.)

God has chosen his servants. He claims it as His prerogative to condemn them, if they need condemnation. He has not given it to us individually to censure and condemn them. No man, however strong he may be in the faith, however high in the Priesthood, can speak evil of the Lord's anointed and find fault with God's authority on the earth without incurring His displeasure. The Holy Spirit will withdraw itself from such a man, and he will go into darkness. This being the case, do you not see how important it is that we should be careful? However difficult it may be for us to understand the reason for any action of the authorities of the Church, we should not too hastily call their acts in question and pronounce them wrong. (*Gospel Truth*, p. 217.)

Men do not obtain place in this Church because they seek for it. If it were known that a man was ambitious to hold a certain office in the Church, that fact itself would lead to his defeat because his desire would not be granted unto him. This is the case with the officers of this Church. . . . [They] are responsible to God. God chose and nominated

[them], and it is for him to straighten [them] out if [they] do wrong. (In *Deseret Weekly*, 21 May 1898, p. 708; also quoted by President Spencer W. Kimball in *Ensign,* January 1973, p. 35.)

All of us should seek to clothe ourselves in the armor of God that protects us from the "fiery darts" of the adversary. Putting on this spiritually protective clothing includes developing a loyalty to the living prophets and an aversion to murmuring against and criticizing them. "What can we do to combat this canker of contention?" asked Elder Russell M. Nelson in the April 1989 general conference. "Control the tongue, the pen, and the word processor," he answered. It would be wise for each of us, when tempted to murmur against or second-guess the prophets and/or their counsel and teachings, to remember the inspired proverb, "A man of understanding holdeth his peace" (Proverbs 11:12). We may not always understand or agree with the Brethren, but we can choose to eliminate from our lives any forms of "evil speaking."

Avoiding criticism does not mean that we have to ignore any concerns we may have or be in total, unthinking agreement with the leaders on every issue. President George Q. Cannon explained:

> A friend . . . wished to know whether we . . . considered an honest difference of opinion between a member of the Church and the Authorities of the Church was apostasy. . . . We replied that we had not stated that an honest difference of opinion between a member of the Church and the Authorities constituted apostasy, for we could conceive of a man honestly differing in opinion from the Authorities of the Church and yet not be an apostate; but we could not conceive of a man publishing these differences of opinion, and seeking by arguments, sophistry and special pleading to enforce them upon the people to produce division and strife and to place the acts and counsels of the Authorities of the Church, if possible, in a wrong light, and not be an apostate, for such conduct was apostasy as we understood the term.
>
> We further said that while a man might honestly differ in opinion from the Authorities through a want of understand-

ing, he had to be exceedingly careful how he acted in relation to such differences, or the adversary would take advantage of him, and he would soon become imbued with the spirit of apostasy and be found fighting against God and the authority which He had placed here to govern His Church. (*Gospel Truth*, p. 493.)

Even if we feel that the Lord's anointed has done wrong or that he is in error in some manner we must recognize that there are proper means whereby our concerns can be heard (see Dallin H. Oaks, *Ensign*, February 1987, pp. 68–73). Because of the spiritual side effects of "evil speaking of the Lord's anointed," we must never resort to undermining the Brethren with our criticism. We must remember that they are the Lord's chosen servants—accountable to him and not to us.

David demonstrated this kind of noble loyalty in an encounter he had with King Saul. Saul had done things that were not right in the sight of the Lord, and at this time he was in fact seeking David's life; yet when David had the chance to kill the king, who had fallen into his hands, he would not. When David's companion was about to raise his spear to slay Saul, David stopped him and declared, "Who can stretch forth his hand against the Lord's anointed, and be guiltless?" (1 Samuel 26:9.) Thus it is an eternal principle that such "evil speaking" will not only stunt our spiritual growth but also, if continued, will eventually lead to other forms of rebellion and apostasy.

The Prophet Joseph Smith declared: "I will give you one of the Keys of the mysteries of the Kingdom. It is an eternal principle, that has existed with God from all eternity: That man who rises up to condemn others, finding fault with the Church, saying that they are out of the way, while he himself is righteous, then know assuredly, that that man is in the high road to apostasy; and if he does not repent, will apostatize, as God lives." (*Teachings*, pp. 156–57.)

Rebellion and Apostasy

As Moses led the children of Israel in the wilderness, it was not uncommon for some to grumble and murmur about various

conditions and wonder both privately and aloud whether Moses
had lost his way. For some, the seeds of doubt sown by murmuring against the Lord's anointed grew into dissension and ultimate rebellion. A group of murmurers—led by Korah, Dathan,
Abiram and two hundred and fifty of the leaders of the camp—
rebelled against the authority of Moses and Aaron. They
claimed that they, and for that matter all the congregation, were
every bit as holy as Moses and Aaron and therefore were entitled to lead in priesthood functions that the two brothers had
reserved for themselves, in which, the rebels said, you "lift up
yourselves above the congregation of the Lord." This challenge
to their priesthood leaders' authority no doubt had started as secret doubts about the inspiration and authority of Moses and
had developed to open defiance and to seeking to assert their
will instead of the Lord's. Their criticism and contempt no
longer was internal and personal. They had expanded it like
leaven among the people in an effort that, if successful, would
have resulted in their usurping the authority to lead the camp of
Israel.

The rebellion was put down in a most dramatic and terrible
way when "Korah gathered all the congregation" for the show-
down "and the glory of the Lord appeared unto all the congregation."

> And the Lord spake unto Moses and unto Aaron, saying,
> Separate yourselves from among this congregation, that
> I may consume them in a moment.
> And they fell upon their faces, and said, O God, the
> God of the spirits of all flesh, shall one man sin, and wilt
> thou be wroth with all the congregation?
> And the Lord spake unto Moses, saying,
> Speak unto the congregation, saying, Get you up from
> about the tabernacle of Korah, Dathan, and Abiram.
> And Moses rose up and went unto Dathan and Abiram;
> and the elders of Israel followed him.
> And he spake unto the congregation, saying, Depart, I
> pray you, from the tents of these wicked men, and touch
> nothing of theirs, lest ye be consumed in all their sins.
> So they gat up from the tabernacle of Korah, Dathan,
> and Abiram, on every side: and Dathan and Abiram came

out and stood in the door of their tents, and their wives, and their sons, and their little children.

And Moses said, Hereby ye shall know that the Lord hath sent me to do all these works; for I have not done them of mine own mind.

If these men die the common death of all men, or if they be visited after the visitation of all men; then the Lord hath not sent me.

But if the Lord make a new thing, and the earth open her mouth, and swallow them up, with all that appertain unto them, and they go down quick into the pit; then ye shall understand that these men have provoked the Lord.

And it came to pass, as he had made an end of speaking all these words, that the ground clave asunder that was under them:

And the earth opened her mouth, and swallowed them up, and their houses, and all the men that appertained unto Korah, and all their goods.

They, and all that appertained to them, went down alive into the pit, and the earth closed upon them: and they perished from among the congregation.

And all Israel that were round about them fled at the cry of them: for they said, Lest the earth swallow us up also.

And there came out a fire from the Lord, and consumed the two hundred and fifty men that offered incense. (Numbers 16:20–35.)

Could any object lesson more dramatically impress upon the minds of the children of Israel the gravity of rebelling against the servants of the great Jehovah? Although they had witnessed numerous demonstrations of Moses' power and authority from God, the rebels chose instead to rely on the arm of flesh, thinking they knew better than the prophet. And, though this remarkable event further confirmed Moses' standing before the Lord, the scriptures record that "on the morrow all the congregation of Israel murmured against Moses and against Aaron" (Numbers 16:41). Incredibly, they still had not learned. The Lord's anger was kindled against them and a plague took the lives of 14,700 of the camp of Israel.

Today those who rebel against the prophets—disobeying

and openly defying their counsel and teachings—are not swallowed up in giant sinkholes or consumed by fire from heaven. Rather, they expose themselves to plagues and problems which, though not as visible, are more spiritually frightening and eternally deadly. "If they will not hearken to my voice, nor unto the voice of these men whom I have appointed, they shall not be blest," declared the Lord in this dispensation. "Instead of blessings, ye, by your own works, bring cursings, wrath, indignation, and judgments upon your own heads, by your follies." (D&C 124:46, 48.)

Steadying the Ark: Subtle Rebellion

Today few members apostatize or contend against the Church and its ordained leaders in open rebellion as did Korah and his followers. Usually the rebellion comes in a more subtle guise. Perhaps another Old Testament example can illustrate this principle.

As King David was transporting the ark of the covenant to the city of David, the oxcart in which the ark was being carried shook, tipping the sacred relic. In an attempt to steady the ark, a man named Uzzah, who was helping with this important task, touched the ark (which was strictly forbidden), and as a result was stricken and died on the spot. (See 2 Samuel 6:1–7.) The penalty may appear to us severe, but we must remember that the people had been repeatedly told that only certain authorized persons could touch the ark under any circumstances, and they had likewise been warned of the consequences of disobedience to this edict.

Today some well-intentioned people, not willing to fully entrust the administration of the Lord's earthly kingdom to his chosen servants (and by corollary to him), seek to "steady the ark." They feel some need to counsel the prophets and seek to shape the Church and its practices (and even doctrines) after their own pattern. They call in question the actions of the Lord's anointed and offer unsolicited and uninspired suggestions. Often their murmuring is really an attempt to introduce government by popular demand—changing the Church from a theocracy to a democracy. "Perhaps when we murmur we are unconsciously complaining over not being able to cut a special deal with the Lord," observed Elder Neal A. Maxwell. "We want full blessings but without full obedience to the laws upon which those blessings are predicated. For instance, some murmurers seem to hope to reshape the Church to their liking by virtue of their murmuring. But why would one want to belong to a church that he could remake in his own image, when it is the Lord's image that we should come to have in our countenances? (See Alma 5:19.) The doctrines are His, brothers and sisters, not ours. The power is His to delegate, not ours to manipulate!" (In *Ensign*, November 1989, p. 83.)

President Brigham Young taught that the Lord will "steady the ark" if necessary. He can better direct the work of the Church in his appointed ways than can mere mortals who lack the eternal revelatory perspective.

> Let the kingdom alone, the Lord steadies the ark; and if it does jostle, and appear to need steadying, if the way is a little sideling sometimes, and to all appearance threatens its overthrow, be careful how you stretch forth your hands to steady it; let us not be too officious in meddling with that which does not concern us; let it alone, it is the Lord's work. I know enough to let the kingdom alone, and do my duty. It carries me, I do not carry the kingdom. I sail in the old ship Zion, and it bears me safely above the raging elements. I have my sphere of action and duties to perform on board that ship; to faithfully perform them should be my constant and unceasing endeavor. If every bishop, every president, every person holding any portion of the holy priesthood, every person who holds a membership in this church and kingdom would take this course the kingdom would roll without our help. (In *Journal of Discourses* 11:252.)

The Lord directs the affairs of his church through proper channels of authority by the keys of the kingdom. The inspiration given to administer the Church also stays within those parameters. When we doubt that inspiration, questioning and seeking to undermine the authorized administration, we presume to steady the ark—a right that is not ours to take. When those inspired leaders pay little attention to our suggestions and do not make the changes that we may desire, we may become more vocal and critical of them. This pattern of apostasy leads from well-intentioned criticism to ever-increasing dissension and disaffection. There are many modern methods of steadying the ark by seeking to "straighten out" the Lord's appointed leaders. Elder Spencer W. Kimball declared that apostasy often begins with criticism of current leaders. He spoke of various forms of rebellion that contribute to the "devolutionary process" of apostasy.

> Apostasy usually begins with question and doubt and criticism. It is a retrograding and devolutionary process. The seeds of doubt are planted by unscrupulous or misguided people, and seldom directed against the doctrine at first, but more often against the leaders.
>
> They who garnish the sepulchres of the dead prophets begin now by stoning the living ones. They return to the pronouncements of the dead leaders and interpret them to be incompatible with present programs. They convince themselves that there are discrepancies between the practices of the deceased and the leaders of the present. . . . They allege love for the gospel and the Church but charge that leaders are a little "off the beam"! Soon they claim that the leaders are making changes and not following the original programs. Next they say that while the gospel and the Church are divine, the leaders are fallen. Up to this time it may be a passive thing, but now it becomes an active resistance, and frequently the blooming apostate begins to air his views and to crusade. He is likely now to join groups who are slipping away. He may become a student of the *Journal of Discourses* and is flattered by the evil one that he knows more about the scriptures and doctrines than the Church leaders who, he says, are now persecuting him. He generally wants all the blessings of the Church: membership, its priesthood, its temple privileges, and expects them from the leaders of the Church, though at the same time claiming that those same leaders have departed from the path. He now begins to expect persecution and adopts a martyr complex, and when finally excommunication comes he associates himself with other apostates to develop and strengthen cults. At this

stage he is likely to claim revelation for himself, revelations from the Lord directing him in his interpretations and his actions. These manifestations are superior to anything from living leaders, he claims. He is now becoming quite independent. (*The Teachings of Spencer W. Kimball,* p. 462.)

Manipulating the Words of the Prophets

Another insidious form of rebellion that leads to apostasy manifests itself when members refuse to hearken to the words of the prophets as they were spoken, but instead seek to manipulate those words to justify their own actions and perceptions. This may occur by taking the words of the prophets out of their proper context, by misinterpreting the original meaning or motive behind the words, or by purposely excluding other teachings that clarify the matter. This is a futile attempt to justify disobedience. A manipulator of prophetic words is not willing to follow submissively and seek faithfully to do the Lord's will; rather, he selectively uses the prophets to validate his own self-interests. Such actions may disguise true motives and actions to others, but he who knows the hearts of all men is not fooled. Elder Dallin H. Oaks explained:

A desire to follow a prophet is surely a great and appropriate strength, but even this has its potentially dangerous manifestations. I have heard of more than one group who are so intent on following the words of a dead prophet that they have rejected the teachings and counsel of the living ones. Satan has used that corruption from the beginning of the Restoration. You will recall Joseph Smith's direction for the Saints to gather in Kirtland, Ohio, then in Missouri, and then in Illinois. At each place along the way, a certain number of Saints fell away, crying "fallen prophet" as their excuse for adhering to the earlier words and rejecting the current direction. The same thing happened after the death of the Prophet Joseph Smith, when some Saints seized upon one statement or another by the deceased prophet as a basis for sponsoring or joining a new group that rejected the counsel of the living ones.

Following the prophet is a great strength, but it needs to be consistent and current lest it lead to the spiritual downfall that comes from rejecting continuous revelation. Under that principle, the most important difference between dead prophets and living ones is that those who are dead are not here to receive and declare the Lord's latest words to his people. If they were, there would be no differences among the messages of the prophets.

A related distortion is seen in the practice of those who select a few sentences from the teachings of a prophet and use these to support their political agenda or other personal purposes. In doing so, they typically ignore the contrary implications of other prophetic words, or even the clear example of the prophet's own actions. . . . The servants of God are under the Master's commands to follow him and to be examples to the flock (1 Timothy 4:12; 1 Peter 5:3). We should interpret their words in the light of their walk. To wrest the words of a prophet to support a private agenda, political or financial or otherwise, is to try to *manipulate* the prophet, not to *follow* him. ("Our Strengths Can Become Our Downfall," pp. 8–9.)

Picking and choosing which prophetic declarations we will accept and which we will ignore is also a form of manipulation. With this activity, we are in subtle rebellion against the Lord's anointed by seeking to set ourselves up as our own prophet. President N. Eldon Tanner illustrated how some become false prophets to themselves.

The Prophet spoke out clearly on Friday morning, telling us what our responsibilities are. He mentioned and spoke emphatically of liquor by the drink. A man said to me after that, "You know, there are people in our state who believe in following the Prophet in everything they think is right, but when it is something they think isn't right, and it doesn't appeal to them, then that's different." He said, "Then they become their own prophet. They decide what the Lord wants and what the Lord doesn't want."

I thought how true, and how serious when we begin to choose which of the covenants, which of the commandments we will keep and follow. When we decide that there are some of them that we will not keep or follow, we are taking the law of the Lord into our own hands and become our own prophets, and believe me, we will be led astray, because we are false prophets to ourselves when we do not follow the Prophet of God. No, we should never discriminate between these commandments, as to those we should and should not keep. (In Conference Report, October 1966, p. 98.)

Inappropriate Intellectualism

"To be learned is good," declared Jacob, "if they hearken unto the counsels of God" (2 Nephi 9:29). When one ignores the inspired teachings of the prophets simply because those prophets lack academic credentials or because their words fly in the face of the accepted theories and views of the world, that person is, in a way, rebelling against the "wisdom of God" and relying on the "arm of flesh." President Joseph F. Smith nearly a century ago warned that false educational ideas would be one of the major threats within the Church in the last days (see *Gospel Doctrine*, pp. 312–13). Judging prophetic teachings by the measure of mortal intellect alone instead of viewing them through the lenses of the restored gospel and the infinite perspective of God inevitably leads man astray. Jacob testified: "O that cunning plan of the evil one! O the vainness, and the frailties, and the foolishness of men! When they are learned they think they are wise, and they hearken not unto the counsel of God, for they set it aside, supposing they know of themselves, wherefore, their wisdom is foolishness and it profiteth them not. And they shall perish." (2 Nephi 9:28; see also D&C 45:29.)

Although the Lord has declared that the "glory of God is intelligence," and has consistently commanded the Saints to seek learning, there is a danger of "intellectual apostasy" when one walks by the light of reason alone. When a person criticizes the teachings of prophets by pitting intellect against inspiration, he is engaging in inappropriate intellectualism that will ultimately lead to apostasy if the intellective quest for truth is not guided by the Spirit of the Lord. (See Dallin H. Oaks in Conference Report, April 1989, pp. 34–39, also in *The Lord's Way* [Salt Lake

City: Deseret Book Co., 1991], pp. 45–75; see also Glenn L. Pace, in Conference Report, April 1989, p. 33.) President Stephen L Richards warned of the "propaganda" that comes from the "intellectual apostate":

> A part of the propaganda is that there is no warrant for official interpretation of the doctrines and standards of the Church, that everyone may read and interpret for himself, and adopt only so much of the doctrine as he chooses, and that he may classify the revelations as essential and non-essential. These propagandists are either ignorant of or ignore the Lord's declaration that "no prophecy of the scripture is of any private interpretation." (2 Peter 1:20.) They disparage orthodoxy as such and pride themselves on liberal thinking. Many of them maintain their loyalty to the Church, and some may honestly believe they are doing the Church a favor and a service in advocating their so-called broad-minded concepts.
>
> Unfortunately, some people within the Church subscribing to these views do not realize that they are falling into a trap themselves. They are giving aid and comfort to the foe; they are undermining their own testimonies and those of others. I warn the Church against them, and I warn them against themselves; and I plead with them to desist, to abandon their agnostic discussions, and to join with the faithful in promoting the cause which in their hearts they once loved, and I think they still love. (In Conference Report, October 1951, pp. 116–17.)

The Prophets have counseled us to guard against intellectual apostasy by judging the learning of the world against the measuring stick of the restored gospel and the Lord's anointed rather than by the words and works of professional or academic training and the wisdom of the world. Elder Boyd K. Packer warned against the latter tendency as he admonished students and faculty at Brigham Young University. His words are relevant and applicable to all members of the Church.

> There is almost a universal tendency for men and women who are specialists in an academic discipline to judge the

Church against the principles of their profession. There is a great need in my mind for us, as students and as teachers, to consciously and continually subjugate this tendency and relegate our professional training to a position secondary to the principles of the gospel of Jesus Christ.

In other words, rather than judge the Church and its program against the principles of our profession, we would do well to set the Church and its accepted program [and teachings] as the rule, then judge our academic training against this rule. This posture is remarkably difficult to achieve and sometimes even more difficult to maintain. ("A Dedication—To Faith," p. 6.)

To undermine, discredit, or dismiss the words of living prophets, even in the name of academic freedom or of free intellectual inquiry, is to cross the protective parameters lovingly established by the Lord that keep us from a cunning snare of the devil—intellectual apostasy. The Lord does not expect us to surrender our intellect in order to live the gospel faithfully, but neither does he want us to distance ourselves from the prophets nor surrender loyalty to the Brethren in our quest for truth. The Lord requires both intellect and inspiration—listening as well as learning.

A Voice of Warning

No matter what shape apostasy takes, from seemingly harmless murmuring to openly hateful rebellion, it always stems from some sort of pride and always ends in some kind of pain. Voices from the past—in the scriptures and the history of the restored Church—sound the clarion warning of the consequences of rejecting the living prophets. The graphic, physical examples recorded in the Old Testament are but a type and a shadow of the spiritual devastation that invariably accompanies apostasy.

Thomas B. Marsh, a voice from the early history of the Church, bore witness of this spiritual misery. During the persecutions in Missouri, Thomas B. Marsh, then the President of the Quorum of the Twelve, apostatized and became an enemy of Joseph Smith and the Church. His apostasy began over a trivial matter, but by taking offense and criticizing the Prophet he caused the small spiritual wound to fester until his soul was completely infected (see *HC* 3:166–67). After years of misery, Thomas B. Marsh came before the Saints in Salt Lake City in 1857 and asked to be rebaptized. "I have not come here to seek for any office," he declared, "except it be to be a door-keeper or a deacon; no, I am neither worthy nor fit; but I want a place among you as a humble servant of the Lord" (in *Journal of Discourses* 5:208). Brother Marsh's account of his apostasy and his own testimony serve us today as a voice of warning.

If there are any among this people who should ever apostatize and do as I have done, prepare your backs for a good whipping, if you are such as the Lord loves. But if you will take my advice, you will stand by the authorities; but if you go away and the Lord loves you as much as he did me, he will whip you back again.

Many have said to me, "How is it that a man like you, who understood so much of the revelations of God as recorded in the Book of Doctrine and Covenants, should fall away?" I told them not to feel too secure, but to take heed lest they should fall. . . . Let no one feel too secure; for, before you think of it, your steps will slide. You will not then think nor feel for a moment as you did before you lost the Spirit of Christ; for when men apostatize, they are left to grovel in the dark.

I have sought diligently to know the Spirit of Christ since I turned my face Zionward, and I believe I have obtained it. I have frequently wanted to know how my apostacy began, and I have come to the conclusion that I must have lost the Spirit of the Lord out of my heart.

The next question is, "How and when did you lose the Spirit?" I became jealous of the Prophet, and then I saw double, and overlooked everything that was right, and spent all my time looking for the evil; and then, when the Devil began to lead me, it was easy for the carnal mind to rise up, which is anger, jealousy, and wrath. I could feel it within me; I felt angry and wrathful; and the Spirit of the Lord being gone, as the Scriptures say, I was blinded, and I thought I saw a beam in Brother Joseph's eye, but it was nothing but a mote, and my own eye was filled with the beam; but I thought I saw a beam in his, and I wanted to get it out; and, as Brother Heber [C. Kimball] says, I got mad, and I wanted everybody else to be mad. I talked with Brother Brigham and Brother Heber, and I wanted them to be mad like myself; and I saw they were not mad, and I got madder still because they were not. Brother Brigham, with a cautious look, said, "Are you the leader of the Church, brother Thomas?" I answered, "No." "Well then," said he, "Why do you not let that alone?"

Well, this is about the amount of my hypocrisy—I meddled with that which was not my business. But let me tell you, my brethren and friends, if you do not want to suffer in body and mind, as I have done, if there are any of you that have the seeds of apostasy in you, do not let them make their appearance, but nip that spirit in the bud; for it is misery and affliction in this world, and destruction in the world to come. (In *Journal of Discourses* 5:206–7.)

Your safety and ours depends upon whether or not we follow the ones whom the Lord has placed to preside over his Church.

—Harold B. Lee, general conference, October 1970

CHAPTER 10

Our Future Safety

During the latter part of the nineteenth century many Saints were called to move their families and establish settlements throughout the Great Basin region. So great was their faith in the living prophet that they were willing to sacrifice virtually all they possessed to respond to his inspired call. Such sacrifices included not only the conveniences and comforts of homes; also they often laid on the altar, figuratively speaking, family security and personal safety in order to be true to their covenants—including the covenant to sustain, uphold, and hearken to the Lord's anointed.

The colonization of some parts of southern Utah and northern Arizona included a journey through one of the most dangerous canyons in the intermountain area, which was known as Hole-in-the-Rock. Latter-day Saint pioneers were, of necessity, required to build their own road down this treacherous canyon. It was a hazardous descent down the "Hole" to the river, often requiring that, in an effort to slow the descent, as many men as could find footing hang also on to ropes that were tied to the back of the wagon. Some would also tie cut cedar trees, horses, or mules to their wagons to help slow them in this perilous trek.

The account of one family who journeyed down Hole-in-the-Rock on January 26, 1880, not only stands as a powerful witness of the faith of these pioneers but can also serve as a parable for us today. In a symbolic way this true story teaches us that our safety today depends largely upon our "hanging on" to the words of the living prophets.

"Joseph Stanford Smith . . . had been one of the most active leaders in helping build the road through the Hole and on January 26 was kept busy most of the day working inside the notch lending necessary assistance to each wagon as it made the difficult journey to the river."

At last the word came that all the wagons were down, and the crossing on the ferry began. Stanford looked around for his family and wagon, but they were nowhere in sight. He dropped his shovel and climbed to the top of the crevice.

There, huddled in a heap of tattered quilts on packed dirty snow he found his wife, her baby swathed in blankets in her arms.

"Stanford, I thought you'd never come," she exclaimed.

"But where are the other children, and the wagon?" he asked.

"They're over there. They moved the wagon back while they took the others down." She pointed to a rusty stovepipe showing above a huge sandstone boulder.

For a moment Stanford's face flushed with rage. He threw his hat on the ground and stomped it—as was his habit when he was angry.

"With me down there helping get their wagons on the raft, I thought some one would bring my wagon down. Drat 'em!"

"I've got the horses harnessed and things all packed," Belle breathlessly assured him as they ran toward the wagon. Stanford hooked up the team, two at the tongue, and old Nig tied to the rear axle. The fourth horse, a cripple, had died at 50-Mile spring.

The children woke up, tumbled from their bed in the wagon, and wanted to help. Stanford climbed in and unlocked the brakes—and paused long enough to give each of the youngsters a bear hug.

Arabella climbed in and laid the baby on the bed and Stanford started the team toward the crevice through which the wagon must be lowered to the river.

"I'll cross-lock the wheels. Please throw me the chains, Belle."

She did as he asked, and then jumped down to help. Stanford took her arm and they walked to the top of the crevice, where hand in hand they looked down—10 feet of loose sand, then a rocky pitch as steep as the roof of a house and barely as wide as the wagon—below that a dizzy chute down to the landing place, once fairly level but now ploughed up with wheels and hoofs. Below that, they could not see, but Stanford knew what was down there—boulders, washouts, dugways, like narrow shelves. But it was the first drop of 150 feet that frightened him.

"I am afraid we can't make it," he exclaimed.

"But we've got to make it," she answered calmly.

They went back to the wagon where Stanford checked the harness, the axles, the tires, the brakes. He looked at Belle, and felt a surge of admiration for this brave beautiful girl. They had been called to go to San Juan, and they would go. With such a wife, no man could retreat.

"If we only had a few men to hold the wagon back we might make it, Belle."

"I'll do the holding back," said Belle, "on old Nig's lines. Isn't that what he's tied back there for?"

"Any man with sense in his head wouldn't let a woman do that," he cried.

"What else is there to do?" she countered.

"But, Belle, the children?"

"They will have to stay up here. We'll come back for them."

"And if we don't come back?"

"We'll come back. We've got to!" answered Belle.

Carefully she set three-year-old Roy on a folded quilt back from the crevice. Between his short legs she put the baby and told him: "Hold little brother 'til papa comes for you."

She told Ada to sit in front of her brothers and say a little prayer. She kissed each one and tucked quilts snugly around them. "Don't move, dears. Don't even stand up. As soon as we get the wagon down papa will come back for you!"

Ada turned to Stanford, "Will you come back, papa?" He could only nod a yes and turn away with tears. "Then I am not afraid. We'll stay here with God 'til you and mama get the wagon down." And Ada began her little prayer: "Father in heaven bless me and Roy and baby until our father comes back."

To take Belle's mind off the children, Stanford told her to test Nig's lines. "Pull back as hard as you can. I bet you couldn't pull the legs off a flea." Arabella wrapped the lines around her strong supple hands. Stanford got aboard. "Here we go. Hold tight to your lines." Arabella smiled at her little brood. "We'll be right back," she called.

Stanford braced his legs against the dashboard and they started down through the Hole-in-the-Rock. The first lurch nearly pulled Belle off her feet. She dug her heels in to hold her balance. Old Nig was thrown to his haunches. Arabella raced after him and the wagon holding to the lines with desperate strength. Nig rolled to his side and gave a shrill neigh of terror. "His dead weight will be as good as a live one," she thought.

Just then her foot caught between two rocks. She kicked it free but lost her balance and went sprawling after old Nig. She was blinded by the sand which streamed after her. She gritted her teeth and hung on to the lines. A jagged rock tore her flesh and hot pain ran up her leg from heel to hip. The wagon struck a huge boulder. The impact jerked her to her feet and flung her against the side of the cliff.

The wagon stopped with the team wedged under the tongue and Stanford leaped to the ground and loosened the tugs to free the team then turned to Arabella. There she stood, her face white against the red sandstone.

He used to tell us she was the most gallant thing he had ever seen as she stood there defiant, blood-smeared, dirt-begrimed, and with her eyes flashing dared him to sympathize.

In a shaky voice he asked, "How did you make it, Belle?"

"Oh I crow-hopped right along!" she answered. He looked away.

He walked to the apparently lifeless form of Nig, felt his flank. It quivered under his hand and Nig tried to raise his bruised and battered head.

Stanford then looked back up the crack. Up there on the sharp rocks a hundred feet above him waved a piece of white cloth, a piece of her garment. Why she had been dragged all that way!

"Looks like you lost your handkerchief, Belle." He tried to force a laugh, instead he choked and grabbed her to him, his eyes going swiftly over her. A trickle of blood ran down her leg making a pool on the rocks. "Belle, you're hurt! And we're alone here."

"Old Nig dragged me all the way down," she admitted.

"Is your leg broken?" he faltered.

She wouldn't have his sympathy; not just yet anyway. "Does that feel like it's broken?" she fairly screamed, and kicked his shin with fury.

He felt like shaking her, but her chin began quivering and he had to grin, knowing by her temper she wasn't too badly hurt. He put his arms around her and both began crying, then laughing with relief.

They had done it! Had taken the last wagon down—alone. Stanford put Belle on the bed in the wagon, found the medicine kit and cleaned the long gash in her leg.

"Darling, will you be all right?"

"Of course I will. Just leave me here and go as fast as you can for the children."

"I'll hurry," he flung over his shoulder and began the steep climb up the incline they had just come down.

He passed old Nig, who was trying to regain his feet. He climbed too fast and became dizzy. He slowed down, and looked around. He had driven a wagon down that fearful crevice, and dragged his wife behind. Her clothes and flesh torn, she had gamely said she'd "crow-hopped right along." God bless her gallant heart! He kicked the rocks at his feet and with tears streaming down his face lifted his hat in salute to Arabella, his wife. (As told by a grandson, Raymond Smith Jones, in *Hole-in-the-Rock* by David E. Miller [Salt Lake City: University Utah Press, 1966], pp. 111–14.)

Arabella Smith could represent each of us as we face the challenges of the last days, as depicted in the dangerous descent through Hole-in-the-Rock. As we journey through life we may not have to encounter the same type of physical hardships and sacrifices as did the Mormon pioneers. Perhaps our challenges are more spiritual than physical, but the perils and potential pitfalls are just as real. "We have some tight places to go," observed President Harold B. Lee, "before the Lord is through with this church and the world in this dispensation, which is the last dispensation, which shall usher in the coming of the Lord. The gospel was restored to prepare a people ready to receive him. The power of Satan will increase; we see it in evidence on every hand. There will be inroads within the Church. There will be, as President [N. Eldon] Tanner has said, 'Hypocrites, those professing, but secretly are full of dead men's bones.' We will see those who profess membership but secretly are plotting and trying to lead people not to follow the leadership that the Lord has set up to preside in this church." (In Conference Report, October 1970, pp. 152–53.)

To his chosen twelve the Savior prophesied of the false Christs and false prophets that would seek to deceive and destroy people in the last days. These assaults on the kingdom of God are only some of the "tight places" that we as a Church, both individually and as an institution, will be called to faithfully pass through. So intense will be the trials and tempests of the last days that "if possible, they shall deceive the very elect, who are the elect according to the covenant" (Joseph Smith—Matthew 1:22). In our generation, the prophets continue to warn of the dangers that lie ahead. Church members in general may not yet perceive those threats to our safety, but the watchmen on the walls do and always will be able to foresee and help forfend any hazards. After speaking about the many trials that the early Church faced, Elder Bruce R. McConkie declared during the sesquicentennial conference of the Church:

Nor are the days of our greatest sorrows and our deepest sufferings all behind us. They too lie ahead. We shall yet face greater perils, we shall yet be tested with more severe trials, and we shall yet weep more tears of sorrow than we have ever known before. . . .

We tremble because of the sorrows and wars and plagues that shall cover the earth. We weep for those in the true church who are weak and wayward and worldly and who fall by the wayside as the caravan of the kingdom rolls forward. . . .

The vision of the future is not all sweetness and light and peace. All that is yet to be shall go forward in the midst of greater evils and perils and desolations than have been known on earth at any time. (In *Ensign,* May 1980, pp. 71, 72.)

During that same conference which celebrated the growth of the Church and its contributions through one hundred and fifty years, linking the past with the present and looking forward to a glorious future, President Howard W. Hunter asked: "What makes us imagine that we may be immune from the same experiences that refined the lives of former-day Saints?" He then observed, "We must remember that the same forces of resistance which prevent our progress afford us also opportunities to overcome. God will have a tried people!" (In *Ensign,* May 1980, p. 26.)

As we live in the present and look to the future, by learning from the past we can prepare ourselves for whatever "tight places"—whether physical or spiritual—we may face. From those who have gone before we see that blessings of peace and safety are always linked with faithful obedience to the restored gospel and the words of the Lord's anointed. President Wilford Woodruff taught:

We have been favored, as no other people have, with wise counsels. Their extent and variety are immeasurable. They cover every department of human life. So far as we have observed them, prosperity and happiness have been the results. Whatever difficulties we may have to contend with today are due, if not wholly, at least in great part, to our disregard of them. Is not this the experience and testimony of all the faithful Saints who have watched the progress of events among us? Had we observed these counsels, how many of the evils from which we now suffer would never have been known among us! Our neglect of them has brought its punishment and the faithful can see it. But shall we not profit by the experience of the past and act more wisely in the future? (In pamphlet, Church Historian's Office, October 1888, p. 7.)

After prophesying of the trials and treachery that would face the Lord's people in the last days, the Savior pointed the way to safety and the means whereby deception can be averted: "And whoso treasureth up my word, shall not be deceived" (Joseph Smith—Matthew 1:37). Arabella Smith held steadfastly to the rope attached to the wagon, an act which, we might say, symbolized her commitment to follow through on the family's agreement to follow prophetic counsel. Similarly, as we steadfastly cling to the "iron rod," the "word of God," we are protected from the "mists of darkness . . . the temptations of the devil, which blindeth the eyes, and hardeneth the hearts of the children of men, and leadeth them away" (see 1 Nephi 8:2–28; 11:25; 12:17). Part of our tenaciously gripping that rod to ensure our spiritual safety is to "treasure up" the protective words of the living prophets (see D&C 1:38; 68:3–4), for President Spencer W. Kimball promised that "if we will live the gospel and follow the counsel of the leaders of the Church, we will be blessed to avoid many of the problems that plague the world. . . . We will be entitled to the wisdom and blessings of heaven in solving them." (In *Ensign*, May 1980, p. 92.)

The path to safety in the last days, as it was in times past, is found in being loyal to the Brethren and obedient to their counsels. "The great test that confronts us, as in every age when the Lord has a people on earth," Elder Bruce R. McConkie said, "is whether we will give heed to the words of his living oracles and follow the counsel and direction they give for our day and time" (in *Ensign*, May 1974, pp. 71–72). Later he said: "The day is coming, more than ever has been the case in the past, when we will be under the obligation of making a choice, of standing up for the Church, of adhering to its precepts and teachings and principles, of taking the counsel that comes from the apostles and prophets whom God has placed to teach the doctrine and bear witness to the world" (in *Ensign*, November 1974, p. 35).

Thus the safety of the Saints both today and in the future will be as dependent (if not more so) upon their following the living prophets as it was in Noah's day or in Joseph Smith's time, though the threats to the Church and the challenges to its members may be much different. While we do not have the prescience to know precisely what we will encounter and how the prophets will counsel us, we can be sure that they will continue to counsel, exhort, and warn—we will never be without the protective guidance of the Lord through his servants. The only real question is whether or not we will possess a listening ear. President Harold B. Lee so testified.

> Now the only safety we have as members of this church is to do exactly what the Lord said to the Church in that day when the Church was organized. We must learn to give heed to the words and commandments that the Lord shall give through his prophet, "as he receiveth them, walking in all holiness before me; . . . as if from mine own mouth, in all patience and faith." (D&C 21:4–5.) There will be some things that take patience and faith. You may not like what comes from the authority of the Church. It may contradict your political views. It may contradict your social views. It may interfere with some of your social life. But if you listen to these things, as if from the mouth of the Lord himself, with patience and faith, the promise is that "the gates of hell shall not prevail against you; yea, and the Lord God will disperse the powers of darkness from before you, and cause the heavens to shake for your good, and his name's glory" (D&C 21:6).
>
> . . . Your safety and ours depends on whether or not we follow the ones whom the Lord has placed to preside over his church. He knows whom he wants to preside over this church, and he will make no mistake. The Lord doesn't do things by accident. He has never done anything accidentally.
> . . .
> Let's keep our eye on the President of the Church and uphold his hands. (In Conference Report, October 1970, pp. 152–53.)

Daniel's prophecy of the stone cut out of the mountain without hands is being fulfilled. There is yet much to do in order for the Church to fill the earth and fully attain its prophesied stature. Zion will someday be established and the pure in heart will be prepared to meet the Savior. To abide the "great and dreadful day of the Lord" requires a chastened Church (see D&C 112:25), a purified people. President John Taylor taught that the ultimate establishment of a Zion society among the people of God requires two things: "The first thing necessary to the establishment of his kingdom . . . is to raise up a prophet and have him declare the will of God; the next is to have people yield obedience to the word of God through that prophet" (*The Gospel Kingdom,* p. 214).

Not only is our safety dependent upon hearing and hearkening to the words of the Lord's chosen, inspired, and authorized servants but so also is our future success, both as a Church and as individuals. The destiny of the Church is directly and inextricably linked to the faithfulness of its members in heeding the counsel of the Lord's anointed. President Stephen L Richards testified:

> I give you also my firm conviction that if we will but follow the teachings and the counsels of our President and his associates, all of which are in conformity with the pronouncements and principles given in this sacred Tabernacle for nearly a century of time, there will be fulfilled every prophecy and glorious promise ever made to Zion (in Conference Report, April 1952, p. 49).

May each Church member seek to possess the inner spiritual strength which flows from faithfully heeding the words of the living prophets. Such loyalty and obedience will clothe us with the protective armor of God. As we carefully cling to those teachings and testimonies we will neither be moved by modern anti-Christs nor deceived by the sophistries of the adversary. Just as Arabella Smith would not abandon her duty and let go of the rope, despite personal pain and hardship, we too must never "let go" of the living prophets. They will not abandon us; let us not abandon them. "We have been promised that the President of the Church will receive guidance for all of us as the revelator for the Church," taught Elder James E. Faust. "Our safety lies in paying heed to that which he says and following his counsel." (In Conference Report, October 1989, p. 11.)

Whatever the future holds for us, as individuals and as an institution, we need not fear and tremble so long as we continue to cling to the iron rod, treasuring up the words of the Lord—those in the standard works *and* those of modern prophets. Exaltation, with its accompanying "thrones, kingdoms, principalities, and powers" (see D&C 132:19–20), is reserved for those who have accepted and followed the Lord, which encompasses following his authorized servants (see D&C 84:36–38). In this promise our eternal safety is secured.

> For he that receiveth my servants receiveth me;
> And he that receiveth me receiveth my Father;
> And he that receiveth my Father receiveth my Father's kingdom;
> Therefore all that my Father hath shall be given unto him.

The Place of the Living Prophet, Seer, and Revelator

Harold B. Lee

Brother Berrett has asked me to talk to a particular subject. . . . The subject he gave me was "The Place of the Living Prophet." The interesting thing, and I suppose you as teachers have experienced it many times, is that as I began to study this I found that I needed more than one period. I would have to talk to you for six weeks to exhaust what I think would be a complete perusal of a subject such as he has assigned. So of necessity I must limit what I say to a few specifics, or generalities, as you may think of them.

In the first place, in order to limit it, I shall extend that subject somewhat, because the word "prophet," as you well know, could be defined more broadly than I am sure Brother Berrett intended my discussion to be. And I have suggested a title, "The Place of the Living Prophet, Seer, and Revelator," and I shall explain in a few moments just what I mean by that.

As I thought about this matter of "living prophet" (why did not Brother Berrett say, "The place of the prophet, seer, and revelator," instead of saying "living prophet, seer, and revelator"), I began to discover that Brother Berrett was but following what the scriptures had said. Peter, in his great testimony concerning the Master, said, "Thou art the Christ, the Son of the Living God." We have references that are made to "believe in the living prophet"—you can find it in the Book of Mormon; and in the Doctrine and Covenants, "living oracles" are referred to. Now the plain inference is that when a living prophet is

---

Address delivered at Brigham Young University to Seminary and Institute personnel, 8 July 1964.

specified, we must assume that there is such a thing as a dead prophet that the people believe in, or a dead oracle, or a dead God.

At the world's fair Brother McAllister, president of New York Stake, told us of an experience that he had which probably defines the distinction that I am trying to make in this particular subject. He was on a plane coming back from a business assignment in St. Louis and his seat mate was a Catholic priest. As they flew towards New York and became acquainted with each other, each discovered the other's identity as to church relationships. As they talked about various things, the Catholic priest said, "Have you been out to the world's fair?" "Yes," Brother McAllister said. "I am on the committee that helped to plan our pavilion out there." "Well, have you visited our Catholic exhibit?" And again Brother McAllister said yes. And the priest said, "Well, I have been to the fair and I have visited your exhibit. At the Catholic exhibit we have the dead Christ—the Pieta. But the Mormon Pavilion has the live Christ, or the living Christ." And in that I think there is a distinguishing difference.

I have a banker friend back in New York. Years ago when I met him in company with President Jacobsen, who was then presiding over the Eastern States Mission, we had had quite a discussion. President Jacobson had given him a copy of the Book of Mormon, which he had read, and he spoke very glowingly of what he called its tremendous philosophies. Near the close of the business hour he invited us to ride up to the mission home in his limousine, which we accepted. On the way, as he talked about the Book of Mormon and his reverence for its teachings, I said, "Well, why don't you do something about it? If you accept the Book of Mormon, what is holding you back? Why don't you join the Church? Why don't you accept Joseph Smith, then, as a prophet?" And he said, very thoughtfully and carefully, "Well, I suppose the whole reason is because Joseph Smith is too close to me. If he had lived two thousand years ago, I suppose I would believe. But because he is so close, I guess that is the reason I can't accept."

Here was a man saying, "I believe in the dead prophets that lived a thousand-plus years ago, but I have great difficulty believing in a living prophet." That attitude is also taken toward God. To say that the heavens are sealed and there is no revelation today is saying we do not believe in a living Christ today, or a living God today—we believe in one long-since dead and gone. So this term "living prophet" has real significance.

To lay a bit of foundation as to what the kingdom is, let me read you something that appeared in the *Millennial Star* back in 1845. It was called a "Proclamation" by Parley P. Pratt. I shall read you two excerpts from this rather lengthy perusal, but first will give you a point of view as to what this is. We sometimes hear people who talk about the

Church as a democracy. Well, it isn't any such thing. Democracy means a government where the sole authority is vested in the people— the right to nominate, the right to release, to change. The Church is not a democracy. It is more like a kingdom than a democracy—and yet it is not wholly like a kingdom, except that we accept the Lord as the king, who has under his direction an earthly head who operates and becomes his mouthpiece. It is an organization that is defined more accurately as a theocracy, which means that it is something like a kingdom as the world would define it, and yet something like a democracy. The nature of this theocracy is spoken of in the "Proclamation" in one or two places.

I think before I read to you from Parley P. Pratt I should read you a statement from the Prophet Joseph Smith. You will find it, if some of you want to read the whole treatise, in *Teachings of the Prophet Joseph Smith* on pages 322–23. I will read only two sentences:

> The Melchizedek Priesthood . . . is a perfect law of theocracy, and stands as God to give laws to the people, administering endless lives to the sons and daughters of Adam. . . . The Holy Ghost is God's messenger to administer in all those priesthoods.

Now there you have him saying the same thing—the priesthood is the perfect law of theocracy. Now listen to this "Proclamation."

> The legislative, judicial, and executive power is vested in Him [the Lord]. He reveals the laws, and he elects, chooses, or appoints the officers; and holds the right to reprove, to correct, or even to remove them at pleasure. Hence the necessity of a constant intercourse by direct revelation between him and his Church. As a precedent for the foregoing facts, we refer to the examples of all ages as recorded in the Scriptures.
>
> This order of government began in Eden—God appointed Adam to govern the earth, and gave him laws.
>
> It was perpetuated in a regular succession from Adam to Noah; from Noah to Melchizedek, Abraham, Isaac, Jacob, Joseph, Moses, Samuel, the prophets, John, Jesus, and his apostles. All, and each of which were chosen by the Lord, and not by the people. (*Millennial Star*, March 1845, vol. 5, p. 150.)

Even today we have some startling things that indicate how little we understand that. We had a case of a very popular bishop. (Now this is so far away and so long ago that none of you will know of whom I am speaking. And if you guess too closely, I will tell you you are mistaken, so don't pin me down too closely.) Here was a man who after ten years liked to be bishop. His was a brand-new meeting house and he liked it, and the people liked him. When word was noised around that he was going to be released and made a member of the high council, word was passed down the line. Now I would not assume that the bishop started it all—I assume it was these well-wishers who did it. But at any rate there were petitions being circulated to forbid the release of their beloved bishop. When the stake presidency heard about it, they came and asked for an audience with members of the Twelve and I was one that sat in. We said, "It is very simple. All you have to do when the people are convened in the sacrament meeting, is announce to the congregation that Bishop so-and-so has been extended an honorable release as the bishop of this ward and with the approval of the First Presidency and the Council of the Twelve his successor has been chosen and is about to be announced. All you who would like to give him a vote of thanks for his labors, may indicate it by raising the right hand." And immediately a young lawyer objected. He had gone to the Sunday School classes that morning and said, "How do you like your bishop? You don't want him released, do you? You be there tonight and vote against his release." And here they were not being given a chance to vote against the release of the bishop. Then the stake president of course made a mistake when he said, "Well, I went and talked to the General Authorities and they said this was the way to do it." And of course that lessened his own prestige in the eyes of his people. But then, to try to get even, nearly half of them voted against the man chosen as the successor.

Here Parley P. Pratt is saying a thing that is fundamental. The leaders are chosen by the Lord and not by the people. The Church is not a democracy. We must not speak of the Church as a democracy. It is true that the people have a voice in the kingdom of God. No officer is to preside over a branch or stake until he is sustained by a vote of that body over which he is to preside. They may reject, but they do not nominate and they do not release. That is done by a higher authority.

> But they do not confer the authority in the first place, nor can they take it away; for instance, the people did not elect the twelve apostles of Jesus Christ, nor could they by popular vote deprive them of their apostleship.
>
> As the government of the kingdom anciently existed, so is it now restored.
>
> The people did not choose that great modern apostle and prophet, Joseph Smith, but God chose him in the usual way that he has chosen others before him, viz., by open vision, and by his own voice from the heavens. (P. 150.)

This same "Proclamation" in another place states:

> The government of the Church and kingdom of God, in this and in all other ages, is purely a *Theocracy*; that is, a government under the direct control and superintendence of the Almighty. . . .
> This last key of the priesthood is the most sacred of all, and pertains exclusively to the first presidency of the church, without whose sanction and approval or authority, no sealing blessing shall be administered pertaining to things of the resurrection and the life to come. (Pp. 150–151.)

It is sometimes very interesting to get the reaction of people. I recall when President McKay announced to the Church that the First Council of Seventy were being ordained high priests in order to extend their usefulness and to give them authority to act when no other General Authority could be present. I went down to Phoenix, Arizona, and I found a Seventy who was very much disturbed. He said to me, "Didn't the Prophet Joseph Smith say that this was contrary to the order of heaven to name high priests as presidents of the First Council of Seventy when they were named in the beginning?" And I said, "Well, I had understood that he did, but had you ever thought that what was contrary to the order of heaven in 1840 might not be contrary to the order of heaven in 1960?" You see, he had not thought of that. He again was following a dead prophet, and he was forgetting that there was a living prophet today. Hence the importance of our stressing that word "living". . . .

Years ago as a young missionary, I was visiting Nauvoo and Carthage with my mission president, and we were holding a missionary meeting in the jail room where Joseph and Hyrum had met their deaths. The mission president had related the historical events that led up to the martyrdom, and then he closed with this very significant statement. He said, "When the Prophet Joseph Smith was martyred, there were many saints who died spiritually with Joseph." So it was with Brigham Young, so it was with John Taylor. And you have people today who are still quoting from what is alleged to have been revelations given to John Taylor. Well, suppose he did have revelations? Did they have any more authority than something that comes from President McKay today? Do you see? Some Church members died spiritually with Wilford Woodruff, with Lorenzo Snow, with Joseph F. Smith, with Heber J. Grant, with George Albert Smith. We have the same affliction today—willing to believe someone who is dead and gone and accept his as more authority than the words of a living authority today. Now I think that probably Brother Berrett, in putting that word "living" in, had more purpose than I at first thought when I started to think about this subject.

As I thought about this matter of prophecy, I added the words "seer and revelator"—that narrows the field, you see, to one man. The prophet, seer, and revelator means the President of the Church. There are sixteen who are sustained as prophets, seers, and revelators, but that does not mean all of them have equal authority. It means that in that body are those who may become seers as well as prophets and revelators. In a broad sense, a prophet is one who speaks, who is inspired of God to speak in his name.

The Prophet Joseph Smith said in answer to a query as to how this Church was different from all other churches: "We are different because we have the Holy Ghost." (*DHC* 4:42.) Every one of you has had hands laid upon your head and you were blessed to receive the gift of the Holy Ghost. That was in a sense, a command for you to so live that you could enjoy the gifts of the Holy Ghost. The Prophet Joseph Smith said, "No person can receive the gift of the Holy Ghost without receiving revelations, for the Holy Ghost is a revelator." (*Teachings*, p. 328.) Now in a broad sense, then, that word "prophet" might apply to all faithful church members. I do not mean that we have the right to receive revelations as to how this Church might be run, or that members of a stake may have revelations as to how or who should be named in a stake organization or in a ward as the bishop. But I do say that the bishop in his place, the mission president in his place, the stake president in his place, the quorum president, the auxiliary leader, the seminary teacher, the institute teacher, a father and mother in the home, a young person in his or her quest for a proper companion in marriage—each of us has the right. No body of people have a gift so widely diffused as the gift of prophecy. You recall the definition as contained in the Book of Revelation. John quoted the angelic messenger who came to him as saying, "I am thy fellow-servant, and of thy brethren that have the testimony of Jesus . . . for the testimony of Jesus is the spirit of prophecy." (Revelation 19:10.) Now Paul speaks of it to the Corinthians, "Wherefore I give you to understand, that no man speaking by the Spirit of God calleth Jesus accursed; and that no man can say [and the Prophet Joseph Smith said that should have been translated "no man can know"] that Jesus is the Lord, but by the Holy Ghost." (1 Corinthians 12:3.) In other words, anyone who enjoys the gift by which he may have God revealed, has the spirit of prophecy, the power of revelation, and in a sense, don't you see, is a prophet within the sphere of responsibility and authority given to him.

It was not in that broad sense that Brother Berrett apparently wanted me to speak. That is why I added the words "seer and revelator." And in order for you to get the distinction between a prophet and seer and a revelator, I read you again what was said of Mosiah that distinguishes the characteristics of one who holds the exalted title of seer and revelator to the Church:

> And the king said that a seer is greater than a prophet.
>
> And Ammon said that a seer is a revelator and a prophet also; and a gift which is greater can no man have, except he should possess the power of God, which no man can; yet a man may have great power given him from God.
>
> But a seer can know of things which are past, and also of things which are to come, and by them shall all things be revealed, or, rather, shall secret things be made manifest, and hidden things shall come to light, and things which are not known shall be made known by them, and also things shall be made known by them which otherwise could not be known.
>
> Thus God has provided a means that man, through faith, might work mighty miracles; therefore he becometh a great benefit to his fellow beings. (Mosiah 8:15–18.)

Now if you go back to that oft-quoted passage that all missionaries quote regarding authority, "And no man taketh this honour unto himself, but he that is called of God, as was Aaron" (Hebrews 5:4) you get this classic statement as you read the story of how Aaron was called. God said, defining the relationship that he, Moses, would have to God, and Aaron would have to Moses: "And thou shalt speak unto him, and put words in his [Aaron's] mouth: and I will be with thy mouth, . . . and will teach you what ye shall do. . . . and he shall be to thee instead of a mouth, and thou shalt be to him instead of God." (Exodus 4:15–16.)

Now that is as clear a relationship as I think you can find anywhere—the relationship of the prophet of the Lord and the President of the Church, the Prophet, Seer, and Revelator, to others of us to whom he may delegate authority. Sometimes we get brethren, even in General Authority circles, who become a little irritated because they are not consulted and are not asked their opinions on certain high-level matters. And I have said to them, rather gently—having had a few years more experience and perhaps lessons than they may have if they live as long as I have—"I choose not to be excited over things that are none of my business." And usually they say, "Well, it is our business. We are members of the Twelve, we are members of the General Authorities." And I have said, "You just think it is your business. It becomes our business when the President of the Church delegates to us some of the keys which he holds in fulness. Until he gives us the authority, it is not our business and we do not have the right to take his place."

The need for revelation has not been a matter recognized only by the people of the Church, but also by some of our great thinkers over the years. I quote the following from Ralph Waldo Emerson: "Miracles, prophecy, poetry, the ideal life, the holy life, exist as ancient history merely; they are not in the belief nor in the aspiration of society; but when suggested seem ridiculous. . . . It is the office of a true teacher to show us that God is, not was; that He speaketh, not spake. The true Christianity,—a faith like Christ's in the infinitude of man,—is lost . . . I look for the hour when that supreme Beauty which ravished the souls of those eastern men, and chiefly of those Hebrews, and through their lips spoke oracles to all time, shall speak in the West also." [I suppose he had not heard of the Book of Mormon when he wrote this.] "The Hebrew and Greek scriptures contain immortal sentences, that have been bread of life to millions. But they have no epical integrity; are fragmentary; are not shown in their order to the intellect. I look for the new Teacher that shall follow so far those shining laws that he shall see them come full circle; shall see their rounding complete grace; shall see the world to be the mirror of the soul. . . . Nor can the Bible be closed until the last great man is born. Men have come to speak of revelation as something long ago given and done, as if God were dead." [Do you get that point? As though God were dead, not speaking as one today, you see.] "The injury to faith" [because of that attitude with many religious preachers] "throttles the preacher; and the goodliest of institutions becomes an uncertain and inarticulate voice." Then he added, "The need was never greater of new revelation than now."[1]

That quotation comes from one of our greatest minds, and I have two or three others along the same line. Speaking as the prophets understood the need, President John Taylor said:

> A good many people, and those professing Christians, will sneer a good deal at the idea of present revelation. Whoever heard of true religion without communication with God? To me the thing is the most absurd that the human mind could conceive. I do not wonder, when the people generally reject the principle of present revelation, that skepticism and infidelity prevail to such an alarming extent. I do not wonder that so many men treat religion with contempt and regard it as something not worth the attention of intelligent beings, for without revelation religion is a mockery

---

1. From an address delivered before the Senior Class in Divinity College, Cambridge, Sunday evening, 15 July 1838. See *The Works of Emerson*, vol. 1 (Boston: Houghton Mifflin & Co., 1883), pp. 119–148.

and a farce. If I cannot have a religion that will lead me to God, and place me *en rapport* with him, and unfold to my mind the principles of immortality and eternal life, I want nothing to do with it. The principle of present revelation, then, is the very foundation of our religion. (*The Gospel Kingdom*, p. 35.)

Now that means today. Sometimes we get the notion that if it is written in a book, it makes it more true than if it is spoken in the last General Conference. Just because it is written in a book does not make it more of an authority to guide us. President Taylor goes on with this same idea and explains why the scriptures of the past are not sufficient for us today:

The Bible is good; and Paul told Timothy to study it, that he might be a workman that need not be ashamed, and that he might be able to conduct himself aright before the living church [there is that word "living" again], the pillar and ground of truth. The church-mark, with Paul, was the foundation, the pillar, the ground of truth, the living church, not the dead letter. The Book of Mormon is good and the Doctrine and Covenants, as land-marks. But a mariner who launches into the ocean requires a more certain criterion. He must be acquainted with heavenly bodies, and take his observations from them in order to steer his barque aright. Those books are good for example, precedent, and investigation, and for developing certain laws and principles. But they do not, they cannot, touch every case required to be adjudicated and set in order.

We require a living tree—a living fountain—living intelligence, proceeding from the living priesthood in heaven, through the living priesthood on earth. . . . And from the time that Adam first received a communication from God, to the time that John, on the Isle of Patmos, received his communication, or Joseph Smith had the heavens opened to him, it always required new revelations, adapted to the peculiar circumstances in which the churches or individuals were placed. Adam's revelation did not instruct Noah to build his ark; nor did Noah's revelation tell Lot to forsake Sodom; nor did either of these speak of the departure of the children of Israel from Egypt. These all had revelations for themselves, and so had Isaiah, Jeremiah, Ezekiel, Jesus, Peter, Paul, John, and Joseph. And so must we, or we shall make a shipwreck. (*The Gospel Kingdom*, p. 34.)

Now I do not know a stronger statement, and I have gone back enough generations to quote a prophet. I might have said the same thing myself in the same language, and you, because you have more faith and are better grounded in believing in a living oracle today, perhaps, would have believed. But I have gone back enough generations to President Taylor so that probably it has more "epical" authority than if I had said it in my own language today. But you see the point that he makes. Amos gives us that oft-quoted passage: "Behold, the days come . . . that I will send a famine in the land, not a famine of bread, nor a thirst for water, but of hearing the words of the Lord: and they shall wander from sea to sea, and from the north even to the east, they shall run to and fro to seek the word of the Lord, and shall not find it." (Amos 8:11–12.)

Well, that time has come. To quote President Taylor again: "We are living in a world in which the spirits who have dwelt in the bosom of God are coming into and leaving this state of existence at the rate of about a thousand million in every thirty-three years; and here are thousands of so-called ministers of religion with an inefficient gospel, that God never ordained, trying to ameliorate the condition of mankind, and sending what they call the gospel to the heathen, and they are continually calling for the pecuniary aid of their fellow Christians to assist them in this enterprise." (*The Gospel Kingdom*, p. 33.)

We have found even seminary people who are saying to their students, as students in turn have reported to us, "The Church ought to change its policy with respect to [this or that]." And I have said, "If you will just change one word so that the question will ask, 'How long is it going to be before the Lord [not the Church] changes his policy?' you will see how utterly silly your question is." When there is to be anything different from that which the Lord has told us already, he will give it to his prophet, not to some Tom, Dick or Harry that is thumbing his way across the country as we have had people tell the story; and not through someone, as another story relates, who swooned and came up and gave a revelation. I have said, "Do you suppose that when the Lord has his prophet on the earth, that he is going to take some round-about means of revealing things to his children? That is what he has a prophet for, and when he has something to give to this Church, he will give it to the President, and the President will see that the presidents of stakes and missions get it, along with General Authorities; and they in turn will see that the people are advised of any new change."

A man came in to see me and said that he had heard that some man appeared mysteriously to a group of temple workers and told them, "You had better hurry up and store for a year, or two, or three, because there will come a season when there won't be any production." He asked me what I thought about it, and I said, "Well, were you in the April Conference of 1936?" He replied, "No, I couldn't be there." And I said, "Well, you surely read the report of what was said by the Brethren in that Conference?" No, he hadn't. "Well," I said, "at that Conference the Lord did give a revelation about the storage of food. How in the world is the Lord going to get over to you what he wants you to do if you are not there when he says it, and you do not take the time to read it after it has been said?"

Well, that is it. It is a changing situation. The Lord is going to keep his people informed, if they will listen. As President Clark said in a classic talk that he gave, "What we need today is not more prophets. We have the prophets. But what we need is more people with listening ears. That is the great need of our generation." (Conference Report, October 2, 1948, p. 82.)

Going back to what President Taylor was saying: "The Christian world, by their unbelief, have made the heavens as brass, and wherever they go to declare what they call the gospel they make confusion worse confounded. But who shall debar God from taking care of his own creation, and saving his creatures? Yet this is the position that many men have taken." (*The Gospel Kingdom*, p. 33.)

Again quoting, the prophet Amos said, "Surely the Lord God will do nothing but he revealeth his secret unto his servants the prophets." (Amos 3:7.) Way back in the time of President Woodruff they were asking him when the world was coming to an end. Someone was prophesying it. I do not know whether they were talking about bomb shelters then, but something about the same, and someone asked him when he thought the world was coming to an end. And he said, "Well, I don't know, but I am still planting cherry trees." He was just that concerned, and he thought if the Lord wanted to tell anybody, he would be the first one to know. We must understand this.

Now listen to a statement from Napoleon, another great thinker, which gives light to this same thought. While he was in exile he wrote this, "I would believe in a religion if it existed from the beginning of time, but when I consider Socrates and Plato and Mohammed, I no longer believe." You see what he is saying? I am afraid sometimes our Article of Faith has been wrongly interpreted and, I am afraid, wrongly taught. "We believe in the same organization that existed in the primitive Church—namely: apostles, prophets, pastors, teachers, evangelists, and so forth"—which has too often been construed and fixed in the minds of our students to mean that there was no church on the face of the earth until it was established by Jesus in the Meridian of Time. Well, if that was the first time that Church was upon the earth, what are we going to do about all of those who lived before that time? Why of course the Church was upon the earth. The kingdom of God was established in the days of Adam, and Abraham, and Moses, the Judges, the Kings, and the Prophets, as well as the Meridian of Time. And in this, the Dispensation of the Fullness of Times, we have all the

essentials of every other dispensation plus things that have been revealed which have never been revealed in other dispensations. Then
we come to the question, "What is the kingdom of God?" Regarding
the kingdom of God, the Prophet Joseph Smith said: "Wherever there
is a righteous man" [and I am quoting now, so you won't think it is my
words again. Even a dead prophet said this.] He said:

> . . . whenever there has been a righteous man on earth unto whom
> God revealed His word and gave power and authority to adminis-
> ter in His name. And where there is a priest of God—a minister
> who has power and authority from God to administer in the ordi-
> nances of the gospel, and officiate in the priesthood of God—
> there is the kingdom of God. . . . Where there is a prophet, a
> priest, or a righteous man unto whom God gives His oracles, there
> is the kingdom of God; and where the oracles of God are not,
> there the kingdom of God is not. (*Teachings*, pp. 271–272.)

I heard President McKay talk about a picture of President John
Taylor that was up at the front of the chapel when he was growing up
as a boy in Huntsville. Underneath was a quotation, the identity of the
writer I am uncertain—it was either from Brigham Young or President
Taylor. But it said, "The Kingdom of God or nothing." You see, that
has meaning in light of what I have just been reading to you.

President Clark said something that startled folks years back. He
said, "It is my faith that the gospel plan has always been here, that his
priesthood has always been here, that his priesthood has been on the
earth, and that it will continue to be so until the end comes." Why,
when that conference session was over there were many who said,
"My goodness, doesn't President Clark realize that there have been
periods of apostasy following each dispensation of the gospel?" I
walked over to the Church Office Building with President Joseph
Fielding Smith and he said, "I believe there has never been a moment
of time since the creation but what there has been someone holding
the priesthood on the earth to hold Satan in check." And then I
thought of Enoch's city with perhaps thousands who were taken into
heaven and were translated. You remember. They must have been
translated for a purpose and may have had sojourn with those living
on the earth ever since that time. I have thought of Elijah, perhaps
Moses, for all we know—they were translated beings; also John the
Revelator. I have thought of the three Nephites. Why were they translated and permitted to tarry? For what purpose? An answer was suggested when I heard this man whom we have considered one of our
well-informed theologians say, "There has never been a moment of
time when there hasn't been someone holding the priesthood on the

earth with power to check Satan and to hold him within bounds." Now that doesn't mean that the kingdom of God was present, because these men did not have the authority to administer the saving ordinances of the gospel to the world. But these individuals were translated for a purpose known to the Lord. There is no question but what they were here.

Now, when does a person speak as a prophet? Do you recall that oft-repeated revelation in which the Lord said:

> Behold . . . this is an ensample unto all those who were ordained unto this priesthood [and he is talking of General Authorities], whose mission is appointed unto them to go forth—
>
> . . . they shall speak as they are moved upon by the Holy Ghost.
>
> And whatsoever they shall speak when moved upon by the Holy Ghost shall be scripture, shall be the will of the Lord, shall be the mind of the Lord, shall be the word of the Lord, shall be the voice of the Lord, and the power of God unto salvation. (D&C 68:2–4.)

This is when that Authority is speaking by the power of the Holy Ghost. I think as someone has rightly said, it is not to be thought that every word spoken by our leaders is inspired. The Prophet Joseph Smith wrote in his personal diary: "This morning I . . . visited with a brother and sister from Michigan, who thought that 'a prophet is always a prophet;' but I told them that a prophet was a prophet only when he was acting as such." (*Teachings*, p. 278.) It is not to be thought that every word spoken by the General Authorities is inspired, or that they are moved upon by the Holy Ghost in everything they read and write. Now you keep that in mind. I don't care what his position is, if he writes something or speaks something that goes beyond anything that you can find in the standard church works, unless that one be the prophet, seer, and revelator—*please note that one exception*—you may immediately say, "Well, that is his own idea." And if he says something that contradicts what is found in the standard church works (I think that is why we call them "standard"—it is the standard measure of all that men teach), you may know by that same token that it is false, regardless of the position of the man who says it. We can know, or have the assurance that they are speaking under inspiration if we so live that we can have a witness that what they are speaking is the word of the Lord. There is only one safety, and that is that we shall live to have the witness to know. President Brigham Young said something to the effect that "the greatest fear I have is that the people of this Church will accept what we say as the will of the

Lord without first praying about it and getting the witness within their own hearts that what we say is the word of the Lord."

Brigham Young said something further on this. He said, "It pleases me a little to think how anxious this people are for new revelations." I remember Brother Widtsoe used to tell us about being asked at a conference, "How long has it been since the Church received a revelation?" Brother Widtsoe stroked his chin thoughtfully and he said, "Oh, probably since last Thursday." That startled his interrogator. However, there are many written revelations that are not in the Doctrine and Covenants. To return to what Brigham Young said on revelation:

> It pleases me a little to think how anxious this people are for new revelation. I wish to ask you a question: Do this people know whether they have received any revelation since the death of Joseph, as a people? I can tell you that you receive them continually.
>
> It has been observed that the people want revelation. This is a revelation; and were it written, it would then be written revelation, as truly as the revelations which are contained in the book of Doctrine and Covenants. I could give you a revelation upon the subject of paying your tithing and building a temple in the name of the Lord; for the light is in me. I could put these revelations as straight to the line of truth in writing as any revelation you ever read. I could write the mind of the Lord, and you could put it in your pockets. But before we desire more written revelation, let us fulfil the revelations that are already written, and which we have scarcely begun to fulfil. (*Discourses of Brigham Young*, pp. 38–39.)

In other words, what he is saying is that when we are able to live to all the revelations he has given, then we may ask why we are not given more.

The gospel reveals many things to us. President John Taylor said a similar thing. He said, "I knew of the terrible things that were coming upon this nation previous to the Civil War. I know of many more afflictions that are awaiting this nation." Well, we ask about it today. And you would know, if you would sit with President McKay and if you had heard him just as he was about to depart to go over to choose the two sites for our temples in Europe. It had been discussed in council and the decision made to build some temples there. After it had been decided that we should build in England and we should build in Switzerland, we were all enjoined of course to secrecy lest our enemies, knowing about it, would put roadblocks in the way. And President McKay then said as a farewell, before departing for Europe,

"Brethren, pray for me—pray for me. And I will try to so live that the Lord can answer your prayers through me." And of course if he would tell you the story of the finding of the sites, it would be in itself a great testimony.

President George Albert Smith was about to close one of our General Conferences which happened to be at the time of the furor caused by the book, *No Man Knows My History,* one of the scurrilous things published against the Church, and there had been different speakers who had said something about these apostate writings with which the Church was being flooded. Just as President Smith was about to finish, he paused—and it was wholly unrelated to what he had been talking about—and he said: "Many have belittled Joseph Smith, but those who have will be forgotten in the remains of mother earth, and the odor of their infamy will ever be with them; but honor, majesty, and fidelity with God exemplified by Joseph Smith and attached to his name shall never die." (Conference Report, April 7, 1946, p. 181.) I never heard a more profound statement from any prophet. And he hadn't thought this out. It came just as a flash. And that is what has happened to every one of these who have written trying to tear down, but all honor and majesty to the name of the Prophet Joseph shall never die. Brigham Young and others have all said the same thing, and I sum it up now with what George Buchanan said:

> In times of danger, therefore, whatever my own feelings may be, and as those who are acquainted with me know, I have pronounced opinions generally upon every subject that is brought up; notwithstanding this characteristic, I look always and always have looked to the man whom God has placed to preside over his people. I watch for his demeanor, I know it is for him to give the signal. It is for him to direct the movement of the crew of the ship Zion. It is for him to direct how she shall be steered. So far as human power is necessary for this purpose, and when there are no indications of fear on his part, when he feels serene and confident, I know that I can do so with the utmost safety and that this entire people can trust in that God who placed his Church upon this earth. Keep your eyes on the captain of the ship, if you will.

Yes, we believe in a living prophet, seer, and revelator, and I bear you my solemn witness that we have a living prophet, seer, and revelator. We are not dependent only upon the revelations given in the past as contained in our standard works—as wonderful as they are—but here in 1964 we have a mouthpiece to whom God does and is revealing his mind and will. God will never permit him to lead us astray. As has been said, God would remove us out of our place if we should

attempt to do it. You have no concern. Let the management and government of God, then, be with the Lord. Do not try to find fault with
the management and affairs that pertain to him alone and by revelation through his prophet—his living prophet, his seer, and his revelator, I pray humbly, in the name of Jesus Christ. Amen.

Blind Obedience or Faith Obedience

Spencer W. Kimball

My beloved brothers and sisters and friends, I approach this opportunity with fear and trembling, humility, and fasting and prayer.

It was my privilege in the month of August to attend the great pageant at Palmyra, and I sat entranced with some forty thousand others at the Hill Cumorah, looking up at that dark hill as the night came on. I heard the voices of those who took the parts of many prophets, Nephi, Jacob, Alma, Amulek, Ammon, and finally the prophet Samuel the Lamanite, all prophesying as to the coming of the Savior of the world to them here on this continent.

It was inspirational as the program progressed to its conclusion, to see the beautiful picture as a Personage came above the hill. Because of the blackness under him, it appeared as though he stood in midair, with long white robes flowing in the breeze that blew from the top of the hill. I was inspired, and that inspiration has remained with me ever since. There was being portrayed the story of the coming of the Savior to this land when these thousands of people gathered at the temple, and were looking intently up toward heaven. They heard the voice, neither loud nor harsh, but a penetrating one, and it pierced their very souls. The third time they could understand, and they heard the voice say: "Behold my Beloved Son in whom I am well pleased, in whom I have glorified my name—hear ye him." (3 Nephi 11:7.)

Then came the voice of him who had appeared to these Nephite people saying: ". . . I am Jesus Christ." (11:10.) His message then and before and since always to his people has been: ". . . to obey is better than sacrifice, and to hearken than the fat of rams." (1 Samuel 15:22.)

Address delivered at general conference, October 1954.

So said the Prophet Samuel to the disobedient King Saul who lost his kingdom because of rebellion. The prophet warned Saul that he should discomfit his enemies but that he should not retain the spoils of war. But the bleating of the sheep and the lowing of the oxen revealed that Saul and his people had disobeyed the simple command of the Lord. Samuel chastised: "Hath the Lord as great delight in burnt offerings and sacrifices, as in obeying the voice of the Lord? . . . rebellion is as the sin of witchcraft, and stubbornness is as iniquity and idolatry."

Saul asked forgiveness, but the prophet replied: ". . . thou hast rejected the word of the Lord, and the Lord hath rejected thee from being king over Israel."

In his arrogant and haughty state he took things in his own hands, wholly disregarding the commandments of the Lord. Samuel scolded: ". . . When thou wast little in thine own sight, wast thou not made the head of the tribes of Israel, and the Lord anointed thee king over Israel? Wherefore then didst thou not obey the voice of the Lord, but didst fly upon the spoil, and didst evil in the sight of the Lord?" (1 Samuel 15:17, 19, 22–23, 26.)

Saul rationalized. It was easy for him to obey as to the disposition of the kings, for what use were conquered king? But why not keep the fat sheep and cattle? Was not his royal judgment superior to that of the lowly Samuel? Who was Samuel that his words should be obeyed implicitly, and who would know anyway?

How like Saul are many in Israel today. One will live some of the Lord's revelation on health except that he must have his occasional cup of coffee; she will not use tobacco nor liquor for which she has no yearning anyway but must have the comforting cup of tea.

He will serve in a Church position, for here is activity which he likes and honor which he craves, or contribute to a chapel where his donation will be known, but rationalization is easy as to tithepaying which he finds so difficult. He cannot afford it—sickness or death has laid a heavy hand—he is not sure it is always distributed as he would have it done, and who knows anyway of his failure?

Another will attend some meetings but Saul-like rationalize as to the rest of the day. Why should he not see a ball game, a show, do his necessary yard work, or carry on business as usual?

Another would religiously attend his outward Church duties but resist any suggestions as to family frictions in his home life or family prayers when the family is so hard to assemble?

Saul was like that. He could do the expedient things but could find alibis as to the things which countered his own desires.

To obey! To hearken! What a difficult requirement! Often we hear: "Nobody can tell me what clothes to wear, what I shall eat or drink.

No one can outline my Sabbaths, appropriate my earnings, nor in any way limit my personal freedoms! I do as I please! I give no *blind obedience!*"

Blind obedience! How little they understand! The Lord said through Joseph Smith: "Whatever God requires is right, no matter what it is, although we may not see the reason thereof until long after the events transpire." (*Scrapbook of Mormon Literature*, vol. 2, p. 173.)

When men obey commands of a creator, it is not blind obedience. How different is the cowering of a subject to his totalitarian monarch and the dignified, willing obedience one gives to his God. The dictator is ambitious, selfish, and has ulterior motives. God's every command is righteous, every directive purposeful, and all for the good of the governed. The first may be blind obedience, but the latter is certainly faith obedience.

The Patriarch Abraham, sorely tried, obeyed faithfully when commanded by the Lord to offer his son Isaac upon the altar. Blind obedience? No. He knew that God would require nothing of him which was not for his ultimate good. How that good could be accomplished he did not understand. He knew that he had been promised that through the seed of the miracle son Isaac should all the multitude of nations be blessed, and God having promised, it would be fulfilled. Undoubtedly questions arose in his mind as to how these things could be if Isaac were liquidated, but he knew that the Lord was just and would provide a way. Had not the Lord fulfilled the promise made wherein this very son was to be conceived when Abraham was old and Sarah far past the normal bearing period? In Hebrews, we read: "Therefore sprang there even of one, and him as good as dead, so many as the stars of the sky in multitude and as the sand which is by the sea shore innumerable." (Hebrews 11:12.)

Abraham was now called upon to sacrifice this beloved son who as yet had no posterity. But with faith supreme, Abraham ". . . offered up Isaac . . . accounting that God was able to raise him up, even from the dead." (Hebrews 11:17, 19.)

Knowing that God would make no capricious nor unnecessary demands, that the lad could be raised even from death if necessary, Abraham obeyed. A ram was provided.

Perhaps the criminal in the penitentiary obeys blindly, for here is compulsion. Most of his decisions are made for him. Somewhat comparable are dictator's subjects whose work, recreation, religion, and other activity are controlled and regimented. Here is *blind* obedience.

It was not blind faith when the patriarch Noah built an ark some forty-two centuries ago or when the prophet Nephi built a boat about twenty-five centuries ago. Each was commanded by the Lord to construct a seaworthy vessel. An unprecedented total flood was to envelop the earth in the one case and the greatest ocean to be crossed by the other. No experience of either builder could give guidance in these new adventures—no previous flood or ocean crossing had ever come in the life of either—there was nothing on which to base construction except directions from the Lord. Here was no blind obedience. Each knew the goodness of God and that he had purpose in his strange commands. And so each with eyes wide open, with absolute freedom of choice, built by faith. Noah's family was saved from physical drowning and spiritual decadence, and Nephi's people were saved likewise.

No swords nor bayonets, no famine nor pestilence drove the Lehites from the lush shores of Bountiful, but seeing obedience led them across uncharted oceans. The Lord had promised: ". . . inasmuch as ye shall keep my commandments, ye shall prosper, and shall be led to . . . a land which is choice above all other lands." (1 Nephi 2:20.)

And with compliance born of faith and confidence, the vessel was finished, loaded, and launched.

There was no compulsion in Noah's movements—no blind obedience. It was not raining when this man of God made the craft which was to save his family. After its completion, a full week of dry weather preceded the storm. Here was obedience born in testimony of the power, sureness, justice of God. And Noah's trust was justified, and a race was perpetuated.

When men speak of *all faith* and *all obedience* as blind, are they not covering their own weaknesses? Are they not seeking an alibi to justify their own failure to hearken?

A man obeys strictly the income tax law and pays fully and before due date his property taxes but justifies himself in disregarding the law of the Sabbath or the payment of tithes on time, if at all. In the one case he may suffer only deprivation of freedom or resources or lose his home or personal property, but in the other he opens doors to the loss of a soul. The spiritual as truly brings penalties as the temporal; the principal difference is the swiftness of punishment, the Lord being so longsuffering.

One would hardly call the first blind obedience, yet he sometimes regards the spiritual commands as such.

Is it blind obedience when the student pays his tuition, reads his text assignments, attends classes, and thus qualifies for his eventual degrees? Perhaps he himself might set different and easier standards for graduation, but he obeys every requirement of the catalog whether or not he understands its total implication.

Is it blind obedience when one regards the sign "High Voltage—Keep Away," or is it the obedience of faith in the judgment of experts who know the hazard?

Is it blind obedience when the air traveler fastens his seat belt as that sign flashes or is it confidence in the experience and wisdom of those who know more of hazards and dangers?

Is it blind obedience when the little child gleefully jumps from the table into the strong arms of its smiling father, or is this implicit trust in a loving parent who feels sure of his catch and who loves the child better than life itself?

Is it blind obedience when an afflicted one takes vile-tasting medicine prescribed by his physician or yields his own precious body to the scalpel of the surgeon or is this the obedience of faith in one in whom confidence may safely be imposed?

Is it blind obedience when the pilot guides his ship between the buoys which mark the reefs and thus keeps his vessel in deep water or is it confidence in the integrity of those who have set up protective devices?

Is it then blind obedience when we, with our limited vision, elementary knowledge, selfish desires, ulterior motives, and carnal urges, accept and follow the guidance and obey the commands of our loving Father who begot us, created a world for us, loves us, and has planned a constructive program for us, wholly without ulterior motive, whose greatest joy and glory is to "bring to pass the immortality and eternal life" of all his children?

Blind obedience it might be when no agency exists, when there is regimentation, but in all of the commands of the Lord given through his servants, there is total agency free of compulsion. Some remonstrate that agency is lacking where penalties are imposed and condemnations threatened—to be damned for rejecting the gospel seems harsh to some and to take away free agency. This is not true, for the decision is ours—we may accept or reject, comply or ignore.

In all of our life activities it is the same—we may attend college or stay away from campus; we may apply ourselves to our studies or waste our time; we may fulfill all requirements or ignore them. The decision is ours; the agency is free.

We may take the medicine or secretly pour it down the drain; we may yield our bodies to the surgeon's knife or refuse his service; we may follow paths or get lost in the jungle; but we cannot avoid the penalties of disobedience to law.

We may speed one hundred miles an hour, park our car against fireplugs, drive on the wrong side of the road, resist arrest, rob a bank, but we will pay penalties sooner or later, even the utmost farthing. No soul is clever enough to evade penalties indefinitely or to counter this extensive and basic law of retribution. Without free agency men would be lifeless, limp weaklings, and worthless to themselves and to the world.

Our Heavenly Father, knowing all things, gave us this fundamental law of free agency. He could force our obedience, compel our goodness, regiment our acts, but that would make of us spineless creatures without will or purpose, or destiny.

Our Lord wept bitterly when he saw his creatures breaking his commandments in the predeluge days, but he refrained from force. They must have their agency: "The Lord said unto Enoch: Behold these thy brethren; they are the workmanship of mine own hands, and I gave unto them their knowledge, in the day I created them; and in the Garden of Eden, gave I unto man his agency." (Moses 7:32.)

They were permitted to ignore the warnings of the prophets till their cup of iniquity was full, ran over, and flooded the world and drowned its inhabitants.

Rewards for faithfulness and penalties for disobedience are certain. God is longsuffering, patient, and kind, whereas men and natural laws are often swift and cruel.

Our righteous and wise parents, Adam and Eve, were exemplary in the matter of obedience born of childlike faith: "And Adam was obedient unto the commandments of the Lord. And after many days an angel of the Lord appeared unto Adam saying: Why dost thou offer sacrifices unto the Lord? And Adam said unto him: I know not, save the Lord commanded me. And then the angel spake, saying: This thing is a similitude of the sacrifice of the Only Begotten of the Father, which is full of grace and truth." (Moses 5:5-7.)

Blind obedience? Assuredly not. They had known Jehovah, heard his voice, walked with him in the Garden of Eden, and knew of his goodness, justice, and understanding. And so for "many days" they killed the blemishless lambs and offered them without knowing why, but in total confidence that there was righteous purpose in the law and that the reason would unfold later after compliance.

Obedience was paramount in the healing of the lepers. They cried: "Jesus, Master, have mercy on us. And when he saw them, he said unto them, Go shew yourselves unto the priests. And it came to pass, that, as they went, they were cleansed." (Luke 17:13-14.)

It is certain that the priests made no contribution to the healing. The ten had probably lived all their lives in the jurisdiction of the priests who are not known ever to have healed lepers. The miracle happened when, but not until, they obeyed in every detail. No blind obedience here. These lepers knew Christ would not fail them. They had faith not only in his power but also in his goodness and integrity.

So also did the man born blind move toward wholeness of sight, yet he obeyed the voice of authority. Questioned by the skeptical Pharisees as to his unparalleled sight recovery, he stoutly maintained, "He put clay upon mine eyes, and I washed, and do see. . . . He is a

prophet. . . . One thing I know, that, whereas I was blind, now I see."
(John 9:15, 17, 25.)

A simple little formula it was. A little spittle, a little clay, a simple
anointing, a simple command, and an act of faith obedience; and darkness was replaced with light. "Lord, I believe," he said as he worshiped
in gratitude. Blind obedience, would you say? It was a blind man, but a
seeing obedience. The Savior had ". . . spat on the ground, and made
clay of the spittle, and he anointed the eyes of the blind man with the
clay. And said unto him, Go, wash in the pool of Siloam. . . . He went
his way therefore, and washed, and came seeing." (John 9:6–7.)

How simple the process! How gentle the command! How faithful
the obedience! How glorious the reward!

Strange—we provide pure, sterile tissue for spittle and forbid ex-
pectorating even on sidewalks.

We bathe with soap, scrub with disinfectants, and scald dishes,
pots, and pans with boiling water to kill the germs from the filth of
clay.

We use for culinary purposes and especially in hospitals and sick-
rooms only water purified by chemical processes.

But here the Master disregarded all our rules of sanitation and
prescribed spittle, germ-ridden clay, and impure water from the con-
taminated pool of Siloam which bathed the sweaty bodies of laborers
and the sore bodies of the sick and diseased.

Is there healing in mere clay to make eyes see? Is there medicinal
value in the spittle to cure infirmities? Are there curative properties in
the waters of Siloam to open eyes of congenital blind? The answer is
obvious. The miracle was conceived in the womb of faith and born and
matured in the act of obedience.

Had the command involved oil instead of spittle, herbs instead of
clay, and waters of a pure bubbling spring instead of filthy Siloam, the
result would have been the same. But some would have said that oil
and herbs and pure water had healed the eyes, but even the untrained
must know that these could not cure one. Consequently, only one conclusion could be drawn: The unparalleled miracle was positively the result of faith obedience. But had the sightless one disobeyed any of the
phases of the command, he would indubitably have suffered till death
with continued blindness.

Though there is no compulsion, the spiritual laws of today must
also be obeyed if blessings are to be realized, for as the Lord has said:

I, the Lord, am bound when ye do what I say; but when ye do
not what I say, ye have no promise. (D&C 82:10.)

And:

Mine anger is kindled against the rebellious. (D&C 56:1.)

And:

And the rebellious shall be pierced with much sorrow; for their iniquities shall be spoken upon the housetops, and their secret acts shall be revealed. (D&C 1:3.)

And:

Behold, I, the Lord, utter my voice, and it shall be obeyed. Wherefore, verily I say, let the wicked take heed, and let the rebellious fear and tremble; and let the unbelieving hold their lips, for the day of wrath shall come upon them as a whirlwind, and all flesh shall know that I am God. (D&C 63:5–6.)

And my people must needs be chastened until they learn obedience, if it must needs be, by the things which they suffer. (D&C 105:6.)

And when we obtain any blessing from God, it is by obedience to that law upon which it is predicated. (D&C 130:21.)

And so we render intelligent, constructive obedience when we voluntarily, humbly, and happily obey the commands of our Lord:

1. Be ye clean who bear the vessels of the Lord.
2. Thou shalt go to the house of prayer upon my holy day.
3. Bring all the tithes into the storehouse.
4. Honor the Sabbath Day to keep it holy.
5. Ye are the temple of God—defile it not with liquor, tobacco, tea, and coffee.
6. Repent or suffer.
7. Bow down upon thy knees before the Lord.
8. Judge not that ye be not judged.
9. Except a man be born of the water and of the Spirit, he cannot enter into the kingdom of God.
10. A man must enter into the new and everlasting covenant to be exalted.
11. Woe unto those who come not unto this priesthood.

May God bless all of us, members of his Church, and all others, in the great world which he has created and peopled to live and obey his commandments, I pray in the name of Jesus Christ. Amen.

When Are Church Leaders' Words Entitled to Claim of Scripture?

J. Reuben Clark, Jr.

. . . We may leave here our discussion of the first subject assigned to us and pass to the last: When Are the Writings and Sermons of Church Leaders Entitled to the Claim of Being Scripture?

I assume the scripture behind this question is the declaration of the Lord in a revelation given through Joseph primarily to Orson Hyde, Luke S. Johnson, Lyman E. Johnson, and William E. McLellin, who were to engage in missionary work. After addressing a word first to Orson Hyde, the Lord continued:

> And, behold, and lo, this is an ensample unto all those who were ordained unto this priesthood, whose mission is appointed unto them to go forth—
>
> And this is the ensample unto them, that they shall speak as they are moved upon by the Holy Ghost.
>
> And whatsoever they shall speak when moved upon by the Holy Ghost shall be scripture, shall be the will of the Lord, shall be the mind of the Lord, shall be the word of the Lord, shall be the voice of the Lord, and the power of God unto salvation. (D&C 68:2–4.)

The very words of the revelation recognize that the Brethren may speak when they are not "moved upon by the Holy Ghost," yet only when they do so speak, as so "moved upon," is what they say Scripture. No exceptions are given to this rule or principle. It is universal in its application.

Address delivered at Brigham Young University to Seminary and Institute teachers, 7 July 1954.

The question is, how shall we know when the things they have spoken were said as they were "moved upon by the Holy Ghost?"

I have given some thought to this question, and the answer thereto so far as I can determine, is We can tell when the speakers are "moved upon by the Holy Ghost" only when we, ourselves, are "moved upon by the Holy Ghost."

In a way, this completely shifts the responsibility from them to us to determine when they so speak.

We might here profitably repeat what Brother Brigham preached. He said:

> Were your faith concentrated upon the proper object, your confidence unshaken, your lives pure and holy, every one fulfilling the duties of his or her calling according to the Priesthood and capacity bestowed upon you, you would be filled with the Holy Ghost, and it would be as impossible for any man to deceive and lead you to destruction as for a feather to remain unconsumed in the midst of intense heat. (*Journal of Discourses*, vol. 7, p. 277.)

On another occasion he said:

> I am more afraid that this people have so much confidence in their leaders that they will not inquire for themselves of God whether they are led by Him. I am fearful they settle down in a state of blind self-security, trusting their eternal destiny in the hands of their leaders with a reckless confidence that in itself would thwart the purposes of God in their salvation, and weaken that influence they could give to their leaders, did they know for themselves, by the revelations of Jesus, that they are led in the right way. Let every man and woman know, by the whisperings of the Spirit of God to themselves, whether their leaders are walking in the path the Lord dictates, or not. (*Journal of Discourses*, vol. 9, p. 150.)

So, we might leave this whole discussion here except that there are some collateral matters involved in the problem that it may not be entirely amiss to consider.

From the earliest days of the Church the Lord has given commandments and bestowed blessings that involved the operation of the principle behind our main question—the determination of whether our brethren, when they speak, are "moved upon by the Holy Ghost."

Guidance by the Written Word

Speaking to the Prophet, Oliver Cowdery, and David Whitmer (at Fayette) as early as June, 1829, the Lord said to Oliver Cowdery regarding the written word: "Behold, I have manifested unto you, by my Spirit in many instances, that the things which you have written are true; wherefore you know that they are true. And if you know that they are true, behold, I give unto you a commandment, that you rely upon the things which are written; for in them are all things written concerning the foundation of my church, my gospel, and my rock." (D&C 18:2–4.)

Thus early did the Lord seem to make clear to Oliver Cowdery that he must be guided by the written word; he was not to rely upon his own ideas and concepts.

Two years later (June 7, 1831), the Lord stressed again the importance of following the written word. Speaking to the Prophet, Sidney Rigdon, Lyman Wight, John Corrill, John Murdock, Hyrum Smith, and several others, the Lord said: "And let them journey from thence preaching the word by the way, saying none other things than that which the prophets and apostles have written, and that which is taught them by the Comforter through the prayer of faith." (D&C 52:9; and see D&C 18:32–33.)

Time and again the Lord told these early Brethren of their duty to spread the Gospel, and in spreading the Gospel, they were to speak with the voice of a trump. (See D&C 19:27; 24:12; 27:16; 28:8, 16; 29:4; 30:5, 9; 32:1; 33:2; 34:5; 35:17, 23; 36:1, 5–6; 37:2; 39:11; 42:6, 11–12; 49:1–4; 52:9–10; 58:46–47, 63–64; 66:5–13; 68:4–5; 71:1–11; 88:77 passim; 93:51; 101:39; 106:2; 107:25–35.)

Not to Teach Sectarianism

In a commandment given to Leman Copley (March, 1831), as he went into missionary work among the Shakers, the Lord gave this significant commandment, which has in it a message for all amongst us who teach sectarianism: "And my servant Leman shall be ordained unto this work, that he may reason with them, not according to that which he has received of them, but according to that which shall be taught him by you my servants; and by so doing I will bless him, otherwise he shall not prosper." (D&C 49:4.)

Evil Spirits Not to Be Listened To

To a group of elders (in May, 1831), who had been confused by the manifestations of different spirits, the Lord, answering a special request made of him by the Prophet, gave these instructions and commandments:

> Wherefore, I the Lord ask you this question—unto what were ye ordained?
> To preach my gospel by the Spirit, even the Comforter which was sent forth to teach the truth.
> And then received ye spirits which ye could not understand, and received them to be of God; and in this are ye justified?
> Behold, ye shall answer this question yourselves; nevertheless, I will be merciful unto you; he that is weak among you hereafter shall be made strong.
> Verily I say unto you, he that is ordained of me and sent forth to preach the word of truth by the Comforter, in the Spirit of truth, doth he preach it by the Spirit of truth or some other way?
> And if it be by some other way it is not of God.
> And again, he that receiveth the word of truth, doth he receive it by the Spirit of truth or some other way?
> If it be some other way it is not of God.
> Therefore, why is it that ye cannot understand and know, that he that receiveth the word by the Spirit of truth receiveth it as it is preached by the Spirit of truth?
> Wherefore, he that preacheth and he that receiveth, understand one another, and both are edified and rejoice together.
> And that which doth not edify is not of God, and is darkness.
> That which is of God is light; and he that receiveth light, and continueth in God, receiveth more light; and that light groweth brighter and brighter until the perfect day. (D&C 50:13–24.)

This whole revelation (D&C 50) should be read with great care. There is much instruction given in it. But I wish particularly to call your attention to verses 21 and 22, just quoted:

> Therefore, why is it that ye cannot understand and know, that he that receiveth the word by the Spirit of truth receiveth it as it is preached by the Spirit of truth?
> Wherefore, he that preacheth, and he that receiveth, understand one another, and both are edified and rejoice together.

Both are "moved upon by the Holy Ghost."

Scope of the Lord's Instructions

I recur to the declaration of the Lord made (November, 1831) through the Prophet Joseph to Orson Hyde, Luke S. Johnson, Lyman

E. Johnson, and William E. McLellin, as concerned their duties to preach the Gospel as missionaries. I will re-read the passages pertinent to our discussion:

> And, behold, and lo, this is an ensample unto all those who were ordained unto this priesthood, whose mission is appointed unto them to go forth—
>
> And this is the ensample unto them, that they shall speak as they are moved upon by the Holy Ghost.
>
> And whatsoever they shall speak when moved upon by the Holy Ghost shall be scripture, shall be the will of the Lord, shall be the mind of the Lord, shall be the word of the Lord, shall be the voice of the Lord, and the power of God unto salvation.
>
> Behold, this is the promise of the Lord unto you, O ye my servants. (D&C 68:2–5.)

Perhaps we should note that these promises relate, in their terms, to missionary work.

What Missionaries Should Teach

As to missionary work, we will wish to remember that in April of 1829, the Lord, speaking to Joseph and Oliver, said: "Say nothing but repentance unto this generation; keep my commandments, and assist to bring forth my work, according to my commandments, and you shall be blessed." (D&C 6:9.)

The same instruction was given to Joseph and Hyrum a little later (May, 1829) in the same words. (D&C 11:9.)

The instruction was repeated a third time (about a year later, March, 1830), now to Martin Harris (through a revelation given to him through the Prophet Joseph). In this revelation, the Lord added, after instructing Martin as to his missionary work which was to be prosecuted diligently and "with all humility, trusting in me, reviling not against revilers. And of tenets thou shalt not talk, but thou shalt declare repentance and faith on the Savior, and remission of sins by baptism, and by fire, yea, even the Holy Ghost." (D&C 19:30–31.)

This is repeating some essentials of what the Lord had commanded twice before. Then the Lord said: "Behold, this is a great and the last commandment which I shall give unto you concerning this matter; for this shall suffice for thy daily walk, even unto the end of thy life." (D&C 19:32.)

The Lord seems just a little impatient here. It may be the Brethren had been talking about tenets, about which at that time they were scantily informed. The Church had not yet been organized.

Assuming that the revelation regarding the scriptural character and status of the words of the Brethren when "moved upon by the Holy Ghost" referred, at the time, to missionary work, and reminding ourselves of our question—how shall we know when the Brethren so speak?—we should recall the quotation we have just made from an earlier revelation when the Lord said: "Wherefore, he that preacheth and he that receiveth, understand one another, and both are edified and rejoice together"—that is, both are led and inspired by the Comforter, the Spirit of Truth. (D&C 50:22.) Both are "moved upon by the Holy Ghost."

Again considering missionary work, this mutual understanding between preacher and investigator is surely that which brings conversion, one of the prime purposes of missionary work. It would not be easy to preach false doctrines, undetected, on the first principles of the Gospel. So we need say no more about that.

Principle Goes Beyond Missionary Work

However, over the years, a broader interpretation has been given to this passage: "And whatsoever they shall speak when moved upon by the Holy Ghost shall be scripture, shall be the will of the Lord, shall be the mind of the Lord, shall be the word of the Lord, shall be the voice of the Lord, and the power of God unto salvation." (D&C 68:4.)

In considering the problem involved here, it should be in mind that some of the General Authorities have had assigned to them a special calling; they possess a special gift; they are sustained as prophets, seers, and revelators, which gives them a special spiritual endowment in connection with their teaching of the people. They have the right, the power, and authority to declare the mind and will of God to his people, subject to the over-all power and authority of the President of the Church. Others of the General Authorities are not given this special spiritual endowment and authority covering their teaching; they have a resulting limitation, and the resulting limitation upon their power and authority in teaching applies to every other officer and member of the Church, for none of them is spiritually endowed as a prophet, seer, and revelator. Furthermore, as just indicated, the President of the Church has a further and special spiritual endowment in this respect, for he is the Prophet, Seer, and Revelator for the whole Church.

Position of the President of the Church

Here we must have in mind—must know—that only the President of the Church, the Presiding High Priest, is sustained as Prophet, Seer, and Revelator for the Church, and he alone has the right to receive revelations for the Church, either new or amendatory, or to give authoritative interpretations of scriptures that shall be binding on the Church, or change in any way the existing doctrines of the Church. He is God's sole mouthpiece on earth for The Church of Jesus Christ of Latter-day Saints, the only true Church. He alone may declare the mind and will of God to his people. No officer of any other church in the world has this high right and lofty prerogative.

So when any other person, irrespective of who he is, undertakes to do any of these things, you may know he is not "moved upon by the Holy Ghost," in so speaking, unless he has special authorization from the President of the Church. (D&C 90:1–4, 9, 12–16; 107:8, 65–66, 91–92; 115:19; 124:125; DHC 2:477; 6:363.)

Thus far it is clear.

Interpretations of Scriptures

But there are many places where the scriptures are not too clear, and where different interpretations may be given to them; there are many doctrines, tenets as the Lord called them, that have not been officially defined and declared. It is in the consideration and discussion of these scriptures and doctrines that opportunities arise for differences of views as to meanings and extent. In view of the fundamental principle just announced as to the position of the President of the Church, other bearers of the Priesthood, those with the special spiritual endowment and those without it, should be cautious in their expressions about and interpretations of scriptures and doctrines. They must act and teach subject to the over-all power and authority of the President of the Church. It would be most unfortunate were this not always strictly observed by the bearers of this special spiritual endowment, other than the President. Sometimes in the past they have spoken "out of turn," so to speak. Furthermore, at times even those not members of the General Authorities are said to have been heard to declare their own views on various matters concerning which no official view or declaration has been made by the mouthpiece of the Lord, sometimes with an assured certainty that might deceive the uninformed and unwary. The experience of Pelatiah Brown in the days of the Prophet is an illustration of this general principle. (DHC, vol. V, pp. 339–45.)

There have been rare occasions when even the President of the Church in his preaching and teaching has not been "moved upon by the Holy Ghost." You will recall the Prophet Joseph declared that a prophet is not always a prophet.

To this point runs a simple story my father told me as a boy, I do not know on what authority, but it illustrates the point. His story was that during the excitement incident to the coming of Johnston's Army, Brother Brigham preached to the people in a morning meeting a sermon vibrant with defiance to the approaching army, and declaring an intention to oppose and drive them back. In the afternoon meeting he arose and said that Brigham Young had been talking in the morning, but the Lord was going to talk now. He then delivered an address, the tempo of which was the opposite from the morning talk.

I do not know if this ever happened, but I say it illustrates a principle—that even the President of the Church, himself, may not always be "moved upon by the Holy Ghost," when he addresses the people. This has happened about matters of doctrine (usually of a highly speculative character) where a subsequent President of the Church and the people themselves have felt that in declaring the doctrine, the announcer was not "moved upon by the Holy Ghost."

How shall the Church know when these adventurous expeditions of the brethren into these highly speculative principles and doctrines meet the requirements of the statutes that the announcers thereof have been "moved upon by the Holy Ghost"? The Church will know by the testimony of the Holy Ghost in the body of the members, whether the brethren in voicing their views are "moved upon by the Holy Ghost"; and in due time that knowledge will be made manifest. I refer again to the observations of Brother Brigham on this general question.

Differences of View

But this matter of disagreements over doctrine, and the announcement by high authority of incorrect doctrines, is not new.

It will be recalled that disagreements among brethren in high places about doctrines made clear appeared in the early days of the Apostolic Church. Indeed, at the Last Supper, "there was also a strife among them, which of them should be accounted the greatest"; this was in the presence of the Savior himself. (Luke 22:24.)

The disciples had earlier had the same dispute when they were at Capernaum. (Mark 9:33; Luke 9:46.) And not long after that, James and John, of their own volition or at the instance of their mother, apparently the latter, asked Jesus that one of them might sit on his right hand and the other on his left. (Matthew 20:20ff; Mark 10:35ff.)

This matter of precedence seems to have troubled the disciples.

There were disputes over doctrine. You will recall that Paul and Barnabas had differences (not over doctrine, however), and says the record, "the contention was so sharp between them, that they departed asunder one from the other." (Acts 15:36ff.)

Paul had an apparently unseemly dispute with Peter about circumcision. Paul boasted to the Galatians, "I said unto Peter before them all . . ." (Galatians 2:14).

Peter, replying more or less in kind, wrote: ". . . even as our beloved brother Paul also according to the wisdom given unto him hath written unto you; as also in all his epistles, speaking in them of these things; in which are some things hard to be understood, which they that are unlearned and unstable wrest, as they do also the other scriptures, unto their own destruction." (2 Peter 3:15–16.)

This same question regarding circumcision became so disturbing to the Church that "the apostles and elders came together for to consider of this matter," in Jerusalem. Paul, Barnabas, and Peter were there and participated in the discussion. The Pharisee disciples stood for circumcision of Gentiles. James delivered the decision against the necessity of circumcising the Gentile converts. (Acts 15:1ff.)

Conditions After the Passing of the Apostles

So it was with the Apostolic Church. After the passing of the Apostles, bickerings, contentions, strife, rebellion grew apace and ripened in a few generations into the Great Apostasy. I should like to quote here three paragraphs from a work by Dr. Islay Burns (at one time a Professor of Church History, Free Church College, Glasgow). He writes:

> It is the year 101 of the Christian era. The last of the apostles is just dead. The rich evening radiance which in his solitary ministry had for 30 years lingered on the earth when all his companions were gone, has at last passed away, and the dark night settles down again. The age of inspiration is over—that peerless century which began with the birth of Christ, and closed with the death of John—and the course of the ages descends once more to the ordinary level of common time.
>
> It was with the Church now as with the disciples at Bethany, when the last gleam of the Savior's ascending train had passed from their sight, and they turned their faces, reluctant and sad, to

the dark world again. The termination of the age of inspiration was in truth the very complement and consummation of the ascension of the Lord. The sun can then only be said to have fairly set, when his departing glory has died away from the horizon, and the chill stars shine out sharp and clear on the dun and naked sky.

That time has now fully come. The last gleam of inspired wisdom and truth vanished from the earth with the beloved apostle's gentle farewell, and we pass at once across the mysterious line which separates the sacred from the secular annals of the world— the history of the apostolic age from the history of the Christian Church. (Islay Burns, *The First Three Christian Centuries* [London: T. Nelson and Sons, 1884], p. 49.)

So spoke Burns.

This tragic sunset rapidly deepened into twilight of not too long life, and then came the spiritual darkness of an Apostate night. For the better part of two millenniums men groped about, spiritually stumbling one over the other, vainly seeking even a spark of spiritual light, until, on that beautiful spring morning, a century and a third ago, a pillar of light above the brightness of the noonday sun, gradually fell from the heavens till it enveloped a young boy in the woods praying mightily for spiritual light. As he looked up he saw two persons standing in the light above him, the Father and the Son. The morning of the Dispensation of the Fullness of Times had come, breaking the darkness of the long generations of spiritual night. As in the creation, light was to replace darkness, day was to follow night.

The Church in the Last Dispensation

The Church was organized, named by direct command of the Lord, "The Church of Jesus Christ of Latter-day Saints."

You know its history—the trials, tribulations, hardships, persecutions, mobbings, murders, and final expulsion of its members into the western wilderness. You know the loyalty to death itself of some; the disloyalty almost to the point of murder of others. You know the dissensions, the bickerings, the false witnessing, the disputes, the jealousies, the ambitions, the treachery, that tore at the very vitals of the young Church. You know the apostasies, the excommunications of men in the very highest places, because they did not recognize when men in high places were not "moved upon by the Holy Ghost," in their teachings. These malcontents followed those who had not the guidance of the Holy Ghost. Finally, the machinations of evil men, inside and outside the Church, brought Joseph and Hyrum to a martyr's death. But God's work moved on.

How Revelation and Inspiration Are Given

Preliminary to a little further consideration of the principle involved in being "moved upon by the Holy Ghost," we might call attention to the difficulties some have in conceiving how revelation comes, particularly its physiological and psychological characteristics. Some have very fixed and definite ideas on these matters and set up standards by which they test the genuineness or non-genuineness of revelations which Church members generally and the Church itself accept as revelations.

On that point I would like to call your attention to the experience of Naaman the leper, captain of the host of the King of Syria. A captive Jewish maiden, servant in the house of Naaman, told Naaman's wife there was a prophet in Samaria who could cure Naaman's leprosy. Hearing of this report, the Syrian King ordered Naaman to go to Samaria, and gave him a letter to be delivered to the King of Israel. Naaman went to Samaria with presents, to the great distress and fear of Jehoram, who feared a trick.

Elisha learning the situation and the King's distress, had Naaman sent to him. When Naaman reached Elisha's home, Elisha did not go to see Naaman, but sent a servant to tell him to wash seven times in the waters of Jordan and he would be healed.

"Naaman was wroth," says the record, and went away, saying he thought Elisha "will surely come out to me, and stand, and call on the name of the Lord his God, and strike his hand over the place, and recover the leper." Humiliated, for he carried a royal commission, Naaman "turned and went away in a rage." But his servants pointed out that if Elisha had asked him to do some great thing, he would have done it, then why not do the simple thing of washing in the Jordan. Mollified at least, perhaps half believing, he went and bathed seven times in the waters of the Jordan, "and his flesh came again like unto the flesh of a little child, and he was clean." (2 Kings 5:1ff.)

Read the whole story again; it is interesting and has valuable lessons.

One lesson is—We do not tell the Lord how to do things. He frames his own plans, draws his own blueprints, shapes his own course, conceives his own strategy, moves and acts as in his infinite knowledge and wisdom he determines. When lack-faiths and doubters and skeptics begin to map out the plans, methods, and procedures they would demand that God follow, they would do well to remember God's power, wisdom, knowledge, and authority.

The First Vision

Before noting a few ways in which the inspiration of the Lord and the revelations of his mind and will have come to men, I want to refer to one aspect of the First Vision, that part (on which is hung a charge of epilepsy to discredit and destroy Joseph's inspiration and mission) which relates that as he came out of the vision he found himself lying on his back, looking up into heaven, without strength, though he soon recovered. You might find it interesting to compare this with the account of the condition of Moses after his great theophany (Moses 1:9–10), and of Daniel (Daniel 8:27), also of the incidents connected with the transfiguration on the mount. (Matthew 17:1ff.; Mark 9:1ff.; Luke 9:28ff.)

I wish to make here one observation about the First Vision.

No man or woman is a true member of the Church who does not fully accept the First Vision, just as no man is a Christian who does not accept, first, the Fall of Adam, and second, the Atonement of Jesus Christ. Any titular Church member who does not accept the First Vision but who continues to pose as a Church member, lacks not only moral courage but intellectual integrity and honor if he does not avow himself an apostate and discontinue going about the Church, and among the youth particularly, as a Churchman, teaching not only lack-faith but faith-destroying doctrines. He is a true wolf in sheep's clothing.

Language of a Revelation

There are those who insist that unless the Prophet of the Lord declares, "Thus saith the Lord," the message may not be taken as a revelation. This is a false testing standard. For while many of our modern revelations as contained in the Doctrine and Covenants do contain these words, there are many that do not. Nor is it necessary that an actual voice be heard in order that a message from our Heavenly Father shall be a true revelation, as shown by revelations given in former dispensations, as well as in our own.

For example: Enos records that while struggling in prayer for forgiveness of his sins, first "there came a voice unto me, saying: . . ." then, as he continued his struggling in the spirit, he declares, "the voice of the Lord came into my mind again saying . . ." It is not clear whether the voice was the same on both occasions, or a real voice first and then a voice in the mind. But it does not matter, the message came from the Lord each time. (Enos 1:5, 10.)

In that great revelation, designated by the Prophet as the Olive

Leaf, the opening sentence is, "Verily, thus saith the Lord unto you who have assembled yourselves together to receive his will concerning you . . ." yet further in the revelation, the Lord says: "Behold, that which you hear is as the voice of one crying in the wilderness—in the wilderness, because you cannot see him—my voice, because my voice is Spirit; my Spirit is truth; truth abideth and hath no end; and if it be in you it shall abound." (D&C 88:1, 66.)

In that glorious vision and revelation recorded as Section 76 of the Doctrine and Covenants, the Prophet Joseph records:

> By the power of the Spirit our eyes were opened and our understandings were enlightened, so as to see and understand the things of God. . . .
>
> And while we mediated upon these things, the Lord touched the eyes of our understandings and they were opened, and the glory of the Lord shone round about.
>
> And we beheld the glory of the Son, on the right hand of the Father, and received of his fulness.

And later, telling of the works of Lucifer and the sufferings of those upon whom he made war and overcame, the record says: ". . . thus came the voice of the Lord unto us: Thus saith the Lord concerning all those who know my power, and have been made partakers thereof" . . . and then are overcome by Satan. (D&C 76:12, 19–20, 30–31.)

In another revelation, the record reads: "Verily I say unto you my friends, I speak unto you with my voice, even the voice of my Spirit." (D&C 97:1.)

Very early in Church history (April, 1829), giving assurance to Oliver Cowdery, the Lord said: "Yea, behold, I will tell you in your mind and in your heart, by the Holy Ghost, which shall come upon you and which shall dwell in your heart. Now, behold, this is the spirit of revelation; behold, this is the spirit by which Moses brought the children of Israel through the Red Sea on dry ground." (D&C 8:2–3.)

A little later, the Lord gave to Oliver the sign of the burning in his bosom when his translations were right, and a stupor of thought when the translations were wrong. (D&C 9:8–9.)

On other occasions, in ancient times and in modern days, the records leave no question but that a real voice was heard, as when the Lord spoke, time and again, to the boy Samuel, a servant to the High Priest Eli, from whose family the Lord took the high office belonging to it, because of the wickedness of his sons, Hophni and Phinehas. (1 Samuel 3:1ff.)

And in modern days (April 3, 1836), in the great vision of Joseph and Oliver in the Temple at Kirtland, the record reads:

The veil was taken from our minds, and the eyes of our understanding were opened.

We saw the Lord standing upon the breastwork of the pulpit, before us; and under his feet was a paved work of pure gold, in color like amber.

His eyes were as a flame of fire; the hair of his head was white like the pure snow; his countenance shone above the brightness of the sun; and his voice was as the sound of the rushing of great waters, even the voice of Jehovah, saying:

I am the first and the last; I am he who liveth, I am he who was slain; I am your advocate with the Father. (D&C 110:1–4.)

Joseph's Work in Revelation and Vision

To close this phase of our talk, I would like to read to you descriptions of how the Prophet received revelations, and how he looked on such occasions. You are probably all familiar with the record.

Elder Parley P. Pratt (speaking of the revelation now printed as Section 50 of the Doctrine and Covenants, given in May, 1831) describes how the Prophet worked when receiving revelations. He says:

> After we had joined in prayer in his translating room, he dictated in our presence the following revelation:—(Each sentence was uttered slowly and very distinctly, and with a pause between each, sufficiently long for it to be recorded, by an ordinary writer, in long hand.
>
> This was the manner in which all his written revelations were dictated and written. There was never any hesitation, reviewing, or reading back, in order to keep the run of the subject; neither did any of these communications undergo revisions, interlinings, or corrections. As he dictated them so they stood, so far as I have witnessed; and I was present to witness the dictation of several communications of several pages each. . . .) (*Autobiography of Parley Parker Pratt*, Parley P. Pratt (fils) ed. [Salt Lake City: Deseret Book Company, 1938], p. 62.)

It seems clear that on this occasion there was no audible voice, though the opening sentence of the revelation reads: "Hearken unto me, saith the Lord your God . . ."

However, President B. H. Roberts points out that when some of the early revelations were published in the Book of Commandments in 1833, they "were revised by the Prophet himself in the way of correcting errors made by the scribes and publishers; and some additional clauses were inserted to throw increased light upon the subjects treated in the revelations, and paragraphs added, to make the principles for instructions apply to officers not in the Church at the time some of the earlier revelations were given. The addition of verses 65, 66, and 67 in sec. XX of the Doctrine and Covenants is an example." (DHC, vol. 1, p. 173, note.)

At Montrose, Iowa, in August, 1842 (there is some uncertainty as to the exact date), the Prophet, attending a Masonic ceremony, prophesied that the Saints would be driven to the Rocky Mountains, and declared events incident to the move. Brother Anson Call describes this scene as quoted in his biography by Tullidge, as follows:

> . . . Joseph, as he was tasting the cold water, warned the brethren not to be too free with it. With the tumbler still in his hand he prophesied that the Saints would yet go to the Rocky Mountains; and, said he, this water tastes much like that of the crystal streams that are running from the snow-capped mountains. We will let Mr. Call describe this prophetic scene:
>
> I had before seen him in a vision, and now saw while he was talking his countenance change to white; not the deadly white of bloodless face, but a living brilliant white. He seemed absorbed in gazing at something at a great distance, and said: "I am gazing upon the valleys of those mountains." This was followed by a vivid description of the scenery of these mountains, as I have since become acquainted with it. Pointing to Shadrach Roundy and others, he said: "There are some men here who shall do a great work in that land." Pointing to me, he said, "There is Anson, he shall go and shall assist in building up cities from one end of the country to the other, and you, rather extending the idea to all those he had spoken of, shall perform as great a work as has been done by man, so that the nations of the earth shall be astonished, and many of them will be gathered in that land and assist in building cities and temples, and Israel shall be made to rejoice."
>
> It is impossible to represent in words this scene which is still vivid in my mind, of the grandeur of Joseph's appearance, his beautiful descriptions of this land, and his wonderful prophetic utterances as they emanated from the glorious inspirations that overshadowed him. There was a force and power in his exclamations of which the following is but a faint echo: "Oh the beauty of those snow-capped mountains! The cool refreshing streams that are running down through those mountain gorges!" Then gazing in another direction, as if there was a change of locality: "Oh the scenes that this people will pass through! The dead that will lay between here and there." Then turning in another direction as if the

scene had again changed: "Oh the apostasy that will take place before my brethren reach that land!" "But," he continued, "The priesthood shall prevail over its enemies, triumph over the devil and be established upon the earth, never more to be thrown down!" He then charged us with great force and power, to be faithful to those things that had been and should be committed to our charge, with the promise of all the blessings that the Priesthood could bestow. "Remember these things and treasure them up. Amen." (Tullidge's Histories, vol. I. History of Northern Utah, and Southern Idaho.—Biographical Supplement, p. 271 et seq.) (DHC, vol. V, p. 86, note.)

Brother Pratt affirms he had frequently witnessed the Prophet receiving revelations always in the way he described, and Brother Call says he had before seen the Prophet in a vision.

Stirring records of a glorious event!

One can partly understand how the early Saints clung to Joseph and why the early brethren followed and protected him even to death itself. Faith and knowledge and love rose to loftiest heights in those early days of tribulation and martyrdom, and jealousy and hate and the spirit of murder, inspired by Satan, sank to the depths of lowest degree, working for the defeat of God's work.

Supremely great is the calling of a Prophet of God to declare the mind and the will of God touching the trials, the vicissitudes, the grievous persecutions that follow the righteous of the children of men, and then to proclaim the glories of the infinite goodness of God, his mercy and love, his forgiveness, his unbounded helpfulness, his divine purposes, his final destiny of man.

Yet we must not forget that prophets are mortal men, with men's infirmities.

Asked if a prophet was always a prophet, Brother Joseph quickly affirmed that "a prophet was a prophet only when he was acting as such." (DHC, vol. V, p. 265.)

He pointed out that James declared "that Elias was a man subject to like passions as we are, yet he had such power with God, that He, in answer to his prayers, shut the heavens that they gave no rain for the space of three years and six months; and again, in answer to his prayer, the heavens gave forth rain, and the earth gave forth fruit." (James 5:17–18; DHC, vol. II, p. 302.)

On another occasion Joseph quoted the saying of John that "the testimony of Jesus is the spirit of prophecy" (Revelation 19:10) and declared: ". . . if I profess to be a witness or teacher, and have not the spirit of prophecy, which is the testimony of Jesus, I must be a false witness; but if I be a true teacher and witness, I must possess the spirit of prophecy, and that constitutes a prophet." (DHC, vol. V, pp. 215–16.)

There is not time to say more on this occasion.

I have tried to suggest the meaning of the scripture which says that what the Priesthood says when "moved upon by the Holy Ghost," is itself scripture. I have tried to indicate my own thoughts as to some of the limitations which attend the exercise of this principle, both as to those who are entitled to have their words taken as scripture, and also as to the doctrines that might fall from the lips of those not possessing the special gift and endowment. I have shown that even the President of the Church has not always spoken under the direction of the Holy Ghost, for a prophet is not always a prophet. I noted that the Apostles of the Primitive Church had their differences, that in our own Church, leaders have differed in view from the first.

I have observed that the Lord has his own ways of communicating his mind and will to his prophets, uninfluenced by the thoughts or views of men as to his proper procedure; that sometimes he evidently speaks with an audible voice, but that at other times he speaks inaudibly to the ear but clearly to the mind of the prophet. I quoted how the Prophet Joseph worked as he received revelations and how his countenance changed in appearance at such times. I have tried to explain briefly how, as Joseph said, a prophet is not always a prophet, but is a prophet only when acting as such, and that this means that not always may the words of a prophet be taken as a prophecy or revelation, but only when he, too, is speaking as "moved upon by the Holy Ghost."

I repeat here some of the elemental rules that, as to certain matters, will enable us always to know when others than the Presiding High Priest, the Prophet, Seer and Revelator, the President of the Church, will not be speaking as "moved upon by the Holy Ghost."

When any one except the President of the Church undertakes to proclaim a revelation from God for the guidance of the Church, we may know he is not "moved upon by the Holy Ghost."

When any one except the President of the Church undertakes to proclaim that any scripture of the Church has been modified, changed, or abrogated, we may know he is not "moved upon by the Holy Ghost," unless he is acting under the direct authority and direction of the President.

When any one except the President of the Church undertakes to proclaim a new doctrine of the Church, we may know that he is not "moved upon by the Holy Ghost," unless he is acting under the direct authority and direction of the President.

When any one except the President of the Church undertakes to proclaim that any doctrine of the Church has been modified, changed, or abrogated, we may know that he is not "moved upon by the Holy

Ghost," unless he is acting under the direction and by the authority of the President.

When any man except the President of the Church undertakes to proclaim one unsettled doctrine, as among two or more doctrines in dispute, as the settled doctrine of the Church, we may know that he is not "moved upon by the Holy Ghost," unless he is acting under the direction and by the authority of the President.

Of these things we may have a confident assurance without chance for doubt or quibbling.

God grant us the power so to live that always we may be "moved upon by the Holy Ghost," to the end that we may always detect false teachings and so be preserved in the faith that shall lead us into immortality and eternal life, I humbly pray, in the name of him through whom, only, we approach the Father. Even so. Amen.

Loyalty

Marion G. Romney

I desire to call your attention to the principle of loyalty, loyalty to the truth and loyalty to the men whom God has chosen to lead the cause of truth. I speak of "the truth" and these "men" jointly, because it is impossible fully to accept the one and partly reject the other.

I raise my voice on this matter to warn and counsel you to be on your guard against criticism. I have heard some myself and have been told about more. It comes, in part, from those who hold, or have held, prominent positions. Ostensibly, they are in good standing in the Church. In expressing their feelings, they frequently say, "We are members of the Church, too, you know, and our feelings should be considered."

They assume that one can be in full harmony with the spirit of the gospel, enjoy full fellowship in the Church, and at the same time be out of harmony with the leaders of the Church and the counsel and directions they give. Such a position is wholly inconsistent, because the guidance of this Church comes, not alone from the written word, but also from continuous revelation, and the Lord gives that revelation to the Church through His chosen leaders and none else. It follows, therefore, that those who profess to accept the gospel and who at the same time criticize and refuse to follow the counsel of the leaders, are assuming an indefensible position.

Such a spirit leads to apostasy. It is not new. It was prevalent in the days of Jesus. Some who boasted of being Abraham's children, said of the Son of God: "Behold a man gluttonous, and a winebibber, a friend of publicans and sinners." (Matthew 11:19.) But those who

Address delivered at general conference, April 1942.

stood by Him enjoying the spirit of truth knew Him, as did Peter, who said "Thou art the Christ, the Son of the living God."

In the days of the Prophet Joseph, there was criticism against him and the counsel he gave. Some of the leading brethren of the Church charged him with being a fallen prophet. They did not deny the gospel, but they contended that the Prophet had fallen.

Those were critical times for the Church. They have now long since passed into history, but the records remain. The issues are now clear. Joseph Smith was the Lord's prophet, and so continued, notwithstanding all the abuse directed at him. He now sits enthroned in yonder heavens, and those who criticized him apostatized and left the Church. Thomas B. Marsh, who left the Church in 1839 because he became jealous of the Prophet, found his way in 1857 to Salt Lake City, and in addressing the Saints, said: "If there are any among this people who should ever apostatize and do as I have done, prepare your backs for a good whipping if you are such as the Lord loves. *But if you will take my advice, you will stand by the authorities.*"

As we look back upon these important events, it seems that the issues were always so clearly drawn that anyone could have seen the truth. And yet, there seem always to have been great intellects on the side of error. This is one of life's tragedies. Surely there can be nothing of more importance than to be always and everlastingly on the side with truth as we meet the complex problems of our lives. It is comforting to know that that is where we may be if we will but hearken to the spirit of truth. For the Lord has said that "the Spirit giveth light to every man that cometh into the world; and the Spirit enlighteneth every man through the world, *that hearkeneth to the voice of the Spirit.*" (D&C 84:46.) That this is no idle promise is shown by the fact that on nearly all occasions there have stood with God's spokesmen those who were loyal to the truth and to the men whom God had chosen to lead the cause of truth. At the time of the attack on the Prophet in Kirtland, Brigham Young was present, and when the criticism was expressed he arose and in plain and forceful language said that Joseph was a Prophet and he knew it, "and that they might rail and slander him as much as they pleased, they could but destroy their own authority and cut the thread that bound them to the Prophet of God and sink themselves to hell." Later he said:

> Some of the leading men at Kirtland were much opposed to the Prophet meddling with temporal affairs, thinking that his duty embraced spiritual things alone and that the people should be left to attend to their temporal affairs without any interference whatever from prophets and apostles. In a public meeting, I said: "Ye elders of Israel: Now, will some of you draw the line of demarca-

tion between the spiritual and temporal within the Kingdom of God, so that I may understand it!" Not one of them could do it. When I saw a man standing in the path before the Prophet, I felt like hurling him out of the way and branding him as a fool.

Here was loyalty, loyalty both to the truth and to the man whom God had called to represent it.

Why was it that the vision of Brigham Young was clear and that of Thomas B. Marsh was cloudy; that Brigham Young remained true to the Prophet, and that Thomas B. Marsh criticized him? It was because Brigham Young always hearkened to the spirit of truth, and Thomas B. Marsh did not.

Last October, I attended an outlying stake's conference. A number of the speakers had just attended for the first time a general conference. Their reports were soul stirring. One bishop wished that every member of his ward might attend just one conference in the tabernacle. Another, when he stood with the vast congregation for the first time, was so moved that tears ran down his cheeks, and his voice so choked that he could not join in the singing. A third was impressed with President Grant's closing remarks. He said as he finished his talk: "Three times the President said 'I bless you, I bless you, I bless you.'"

In another outlying stake, an ex-bishop said to me that the conference was nothing but a political convention. In another a man said that whether he would follow the counsel of the leaders depended upon what subject they discussed.

How are these different responses accounted for? I will tell you. The members of the one group were observing and keeping the commandments of God, and the others were not; one group was walking in the light of truth, and the other was in the dark; one group enjoyed the *Spirit of the Lord,* and the others did not.

If we are to be on the side of truth, we must have the Spirit of the Lord. To the obtaining of that spirit, prayer is an indispensable prerequisite. Praying will keep one's vision clear on this question of loyalty as on all other questions. By praying I do not mean, however, just saying prayers. Prayers may be said in a perfunctory manner. Access to the Spirit of God, which is a directing power, cannot be so obtained. The divine injunction to pray is not to be satisfied in a casual manner nor by an effort to obtain divine approval of a predetermined course. A firm resolve to comply with the will of God must accompany the petition for knowledge as to what His will is. When one brings himself to the position that he will pursue the truth wherever it may lead, even though it may require a reversal of his former position, he can, without hypocrisy, go before the Lord in prayer. Then, when he prays with all the energy of his soul, he is entitled to and he will receive guidance.

The mind and will of the Lord as to the course he should take will be made known unto him.

I assure you, however, that the Spirit of the Lord will never direct a person to take a position in opposition to the counsel of the Presidency of His Church. Such could not be, and I'll tell you why. The Spirit of the Lord is "truth." The Prophet Joseph Smith says that "The glory of God is intelligence, or, in other words, *light and truth.*"

The Presidency, in directing the Church and its affairs and in counseling the people, do so under the directing power of this *"light and truth."* When a man and the Presidency are both directed on the same subject by "light and truth," there can be no conflict. And so, my brethren, all who are out of harmony in any degree with the Presidency have need to repent and to seek the Lord for forgiveness and to put themselves in full harmony.

In response to a contention that to follow such a course is tantamount to surrendering one's "moral agency," suppose a person were in a forest with his vision limited by the denseness of the growth about him. Would he be surrendering his agency in following directions of one who stands on a lookout tower, commanding an unobstructed view? To me, our leaders are true watchmen on the towers of Zion, and those who follow their counsel are exercising their agency just as freely as would be the man in the forest. For I accept as a fact, without any reservation, that this Church is headed by the Lord Jesus Christ, and that He, through the men whom He chooses and appoints to lead His people, gives it active direction. I believe that He communicates to them His will, and that they, enjoying His spirit, counsel us.

The Savior Himself gave us the great example on this point. As He labored and suffered under the weight of the sins of this world in the accomplishment of the great atonement, He cried out in the agony of His soul, "O my Father, if it be possible, let this cup pass from me: Nevertheless not as I will, but as thou wilt." (Matthew 26:39.) And so saying, he subjected Himself to the will of His Father in consummation of His supreme mission. Who will say that in so doing He surrendered His free agency?

That we may all have the vision and the courage to be loyal to the truth and loyal to the men whom God has chosen to lead in the cause of truth, I humbly pray, in the name of Jesus Christ. Amen.

Follow the Brethren

Boyd K. Packer

This is a devotional assembly. This is the one assembly for the entire student body of the University which is called for devotional or inspirational purposes. As we come here to speak to you, representing the General Authorities of the Church, we are under much more of an obligation than to merely be informative. I sense that many of you come here with the expectation that you may draw forth from us answers to some questions that you may have.

Since this is a devotional assembly, you have the right to expect some inspiration from your attendance here. But I think that it is important that you know this: the inspiration you may draw from the General Authorities as they come here to speak to you depends only partly on the effort they have expended in the preparation *of* their sermons; it depends much more considerably on what preparation you have made *for* their message. In this I make no differentiation between the members of the faculty and the student body.

There is a tendency always for us to be a little resistant to instruction. We hear a stirring sermon and we are always wont to say, "I wish Brother Jones were here. He surely needed that instruction." Or we may even hear a sermon and consent to the truth of the words and yet be unwilling to change.

A poet framed this:

> The sermon was ended,
> The priest had descended.
> Much delighted were they,
> But preferred the old way.

Address delivered at Brigham Young University devotional assembly, 23 March 1965.

With that much said by way of introduction, the whole burden of my message today can be said in three simple words: *Follow the Brethren.* Though I may elaborate and attempt to illustrate and emphasize, there is the fact, the disarmingly simple fact, that in the three words *Follow the Brethren* rests the most important counsel that I could give to you.

There is a lesson to be drawn from the twenty-sixth chapter of Matthew. The occasion, the Last Supper. Quoting from the twenty-first verse: "And as they did eat, he said, Verily I say unto you, that one of you shall betray me."

I remind you that these men were apostles. They were of apostolic stature. It has always been interesting to me that they did not on that occasion nudge one another and say, "I'll bet that is old Judas. He has surely been acting queer lately." It reflects something of their stature. Rather it is recorded: "They were exceedingly sorrowful, and began every one of them to say unto him, Lord, is it I?" (Matthew 26:22.)

Would you, I plead, overrule the tendency to disregard counsel and assume for just a moment something apostolic in attitude at least, and ask yourself these questions: Do I need to improve myself? Should I take this counsel to heart and act upon it? If there is one weak or failing, unwilling to follow the Brethren, Lord, is it I?

In The Church of Jesus Christ of Latter-day Saints there is no paid ministry, no professional clergy, as is common in other churches. More significant even than this is that there is no laity, no lay membership as such; men are eligible to hold the priesthood and to carry on the ministry of the Church, and both men and women serve in many auxiliary capacities. This responsibility comes to men in all walks of life, and with this responsibility also comes the authority. There are many who would deny, and others who would disregard it; nevertheless, the measure of that authority does not depend on whether men sustain that authority, but rather depends on whether God will recognize and honor that authority.

The fifth article of faith reads: "We believe that a man must be called of God, by prophecy, and by the laying on of hands, by those who are in authority, to preach the Gospel and administer in the ordinances thereof."

In this article of faith lies a significant evidence of the truth of the gospel. I am interested in the word *must*: "We believe that a man *must* be called of God." You know, we do not ordinarily use that word in the Church. I question whether there has ever been a stake president receive a directive from the Brethren saying, "You are hereby ordered and directed that you must do such and such." Rather, I think the spirit of the communication would be, "After consideration it is suggested that . . ."

Unfortunately many of us will read it as it is written, but we act as though it read something like this: "We believe in some circumstances, not usually, inadvertently perhaps, there may have been some inspiration with reference to the call of some men to office, possibly maybe to the higher offices of the Church, but ordinarily it is the natural thought process leading to the appointment of the officials of the Church."

This position seems to be supported in the minds of those who are looking for weaknesses when they see the humanity in the leadership of the Church—bishops, stake presidents, and General Authorities. They sometimes notice haphazard and occasionally inadequate demonstrations of leadership and seize upon these as evidence that the human element predominates.

Others among us are willing to sustain part of the leadership of the Church and question and criticize others of us.

Some of us suppose that if we were called to a high office in the Church immediately we would be loyal, and would show the dedication necessary. We would step forward and valiantly commit ourselves to this service.

But, you can put it down in your little black book that if you will not be loyal in the small things you will not be loyal in the large things. If you will not respond to the so-called insignificant or menial tasks which need to be performed in the Church and kingdom, there will be no opportunity for service in the so-called greater challenges.

A man who says he will sustain the President of the Church or the General Authorities but cannot sustain his own bishop is deceiving himself. The man who will not sustain the bishop of his ward and the president of his stake will not sustain the President of the Church.

I have learned from experience that those people who come to us for counsel saying they cannot go to their bishops are unwilling to accept counsel from their bishops. They are unwilling or unable to accept counsel from the General Authorities. Actually, the inspiration of the Lord will come to their bishop and he can counsel them correctly.

Oh, how frustrating it is, my brethren and sisters, when some members of the Church come to us for counsel. One may receive an impression—an inspiration, if you will—as to what they should do. They listen, and then we see them turn aside from that counsel in favor of some desire of their own that will certainly lead them astray.

Some of us are very jealous of our prerogatives and feel that obedience to priesthood authority is to forfeit one's agency. If we only knew, my brethren and sisters, that it is through obedience that we gain freedom.

No one loves freedom more than the holder of the priesthood. President John Taylor spoke very vigorously on this subject:

I was not born a slave! I cannot, will not be a slave. I would not be a slave to God! I would be His servant, friend, His son. I would go at His behest; but would not be His slave. I would rather be extinct than be a slave. His friend I feel I am, and He is mine:—a slave! The manacles would pierce my very bones—the clanking chains would grate against my soul—a poor, lost, servile, crawling wretch, to lick the dust and fawn and smile upon the thing who gave the lash! . . . But stop! I am God's free man; I will not, cannot be a slave! ("Oil for Their Lamps," p. 73.)

The Lord said: "If ye continue in my word, then are ye my disciples indeed; and ye shall know the truth, and the truth shall make you free." (John 8:31–32.)

It is not an easy thing to be amenable always to priesthood authority. I recite the experience of the founder of this University, Dr. Karl G. Maeser. He had been the headmaster of a school in Dresden—a man of distinction, a man of high station. In 1856, Brother Maeser and his wife and small son, together with a Brother Schoenfeld and several other converts, left Germany bound for Zion.

When they arrived in England Brother Maeser was surprised to be called on a mission in England. Much to their disappointment the families were separated and the Schoenfelds continued on to America. While the Maesers remained in England to fill the call from the Church authorities, the proud professor was often required to perform menial tasks to which in his former station he had never stooped.

It was customary among the higher German people that a man of Brother Maeser's standing never should be seen on the street carrying packages, but when the elders were going to the train they told him to bring their carpet bags. Brother Maeser paced the floor of his room, his pride deeply hurt. The idea of carrying the suitcases was almost more than he could stand, and his wife was also deeply hurt and upset to think that he had to do so.

Finally he said, "Well, they hold the priesthood; they have told me to go, and I will go." He surrendered his pride and carried the bags.

While the men who preside over you in the wards and stakes of the Church may seem like very ordinary men, there is something extraordinary about them. It is the mantle of priesthood authority and the inspiration of the call which they have answered.

I wish you could accompany the General Authorities some time on an assignment to reorganize a stake. It has been my experience on a number of occasions to assist in these reorganizations. It never fails to be a remarkable experience. Some time ago, late one Sunday night, returning with Elder Marion G. Romney after the reorganization of a stake, we were riding along silently, too weary I suppose to be interested in conversation, when he said, "Boyd, this gospel is true!" (An interesting statement from a member of the Twelve.) And then he added, "You couldn't go through what we have been through in the last forty-eight hours without knowing that for sure."

I then rehearsed in my mind the events of the previous hours; the interviews we had held, the decisions made. We had interviewed the priesthood leadership of the stake and invited each of them to make suggestions with reference to a new stake president. Virtually all of them mentioned the same man. They indicated him to be an ideal man for a stake president with appropriate experience, a fine family, sensible and sound, worthy in every way. Near the end of our interviewing, with just two or three left, we interviewed this man and we found him equal to all of the estimates that had been made of him during the day. As he left the room at the conclusion of the interview, Brother Romney said, "Well, what do you think?"

I answered that it was my feeling that we had not seen the new president yet.

This confirmed the feelings of Brother Romney, who then said, "Perhaps we should get some more men in here. It may be that the new president is not among the present priesthood leadership of the stake." Then he said, "But suppose we interview the remaining few before we take that course."

There was another interview held, as ordinary as all of the others had been during the day—the same questions, same answers—but at the conclusion of this interview, Brother Romney said, "Well, now how do you feel?"

"As far as I am concerned," I said, "we can quit interviewing." Again this confirmed Brother Romney, for the feeling had come that this was the man that the Lord had set His hand upon to preside over that stake.

How did we know? Because we knew, both of us—together, at once, without any doubt. In reality our assignment was not to *choose* a stake president, but rather to *find* the man that the Lord had chosen. The Lord speaks in an unmistakable way. *Men are called by prophecy.*

It is in the way we answer the call that we show the measure of our devotion.

The faith of the members of the Church in the earlier days was tested many, many times. In a conference report for 1856, we find the following. Heber C. Kimball, a counselor in the First Presidency, is speaking: "I will present to this congregation the names of those whom we have selected to go on missions. Some are appointed to go to Europe, Australia, and the East Indies. And several will be sent to Las Vegas, to the north, and to Fort Supply, to strengthen the settlements there."

Such announcements often came as a complete surprise to members of the Church sitting in the audience. Because of their faith, I suppose the only question they had on their minds in response to such a call was "When?" "When shall we go?" I am not so sure but that a similar call made today would call forth the response from many among us, not "When?" but "Why?" "Why should *I* go?"

On one occasion I was in the office of President Henry D. Moyle when a phone call he had placed earlier in the day came through. After greeting the caller, he said, "I wonder if your business affairs would bring you into Salt Lake City sometime in the near future? I would like to meet with you and your wife, for I have a matter of some importance that I would like to discuss with you."

Well, though it was many miles away, that man all of a sudden discovered that his business would bring him to Salt Lake City the very next morning. I was in the same office the following day when President Moyle announced to this man that he had been called to preside over one of the missions of the Church. "Now," he said, "we don't want to rush you into this decision. Would you call me in a day or two, as soon as you are able to make a determination as to your feelings concerning this call?"

The man looked at his wife and she looked at him, and without saying a word there was that silent conversation between husband and wife, and that gentle, almost imperceptible nod. He turned back to President Moyle and said, "Well, President, what is there to say. What could we tell you in a few days that we couldn't tell you now? We have been called. What answer is there? Of course we will respond to the call."

Then President Moyle said rather gently, "Well, if you feel that way about it, actually there is some urgency about this matter. I wonder if you could be prepared to leave by ship from the West Coast on the thirteenth of March."

The man gulped, for that was just eleven days away. He glanced at his wife. There was another silent conversation, and he said, "Yes, President, we can meet that appointment."

"What about your business?" said the President. "What about your grain elevator? What about your livestock? What about your other holdings?"

"I don't know," said the man, "but we will make arrangements somehow. All of those things will be all right."

Such is the great miracle that we see repeated over and over, day after day, among the faithful. And yet there are many among us who have not the faith to respond to the call or to sustain those who have been so called.

There are some specific things that you can do. Search your soul. How do you regard the leadership of the Church? Do you sustain your bishop? Do you sustain your stake president and the General Authorities of the Church? Or are you among those who are neutral, or critical, who speak evilly, or who refuse calls? Better ask, "Lord, is it I?"

Avoid being critical of those serving in responsible priesthood callings. Show yourself to be loyal. Cultivate the disposition to sustain and to bless. Pray. Pray continually for your leaders.

Never say no to an opportunity to serve in the Church. If you are called to an assignment by one who has authority, there is but one answer. It is, of course, expected that you set forth clearly what your circumstances are, but any assignment that comes under call from your bishop or your stake president is a call that comes from the Lord. An article of our faith defines it so, and I bear witness that it is so.

Once called to such positions, do not presume to set your own date of release. A release is in effect another call. Men do not call themselves to offices in the Church. Why must we presume that we have the authority to release ourselves? A release should come by the same authority from whence came the call.

Act in the office to which you are called with all diligence. Do not be a slothful servant. Be punctual and dependable and faithful.

You have the right to *know* concerning calls that come to you. Be humble and reverent and prayerful concerning responsibilities that are placed upon your shoulders. Keep those standards of worthiness so that the Lord can communicate with you concerning the responsibilities that are yours in the call that you have answered.

The Lord said:

Wherefore, lift up your hearts and rejoice, and gird up your loins, and take upon you my whole armor, that ye may be able to withstand the evil day, having done all, that ye may be able to stand.

Stand, therefore, having your loins girt about with truth, having on the breastplate of righteousness, and your feet shod with the preparation of the gospel of peace, which I have sent mine angels to commit unto you;

Taking the shield of faith wherewith ye shall be able to quench all the fiery darts of the wicked;

And take the helmet of salvation, and the sword of my Spirit, which I will pour out upon you, and my word which I reveal unto you, and be agreed as touching all things whatsoever ye ask of me, and be faithful until I come, and ye shall be caught up, that where I am ye shall be also. (D&C 27:15–18.)

In closing, I say again, *Follow the Brethren*. In a few days there opens another general conference of the Church. The servants of the Lord will counsel us. You may listen with anxious ears and hearts, or you may turn that counsel aside. As in these devotionals, what you shall gain will depend not so much upon their preparation *of* the messages as upon your preparation *for* them.

Remember the verses from the Doctrine and Covenants:

> What I the Lord have spoken, I have spoken, and I excuse not myself; and though the heavens and the earth pass away, my word shall not pass away, but shall all be fulfilled, whether by mine own voice or by the voice of my servants, it is the same.
>
> For behold, and lo, the Lord is God, and the Spirit beareth record, and the record is true, and the truth abideth forever and ever. (D&C 1:38–39.)

Returning again to Karl G. Maeser, on one occasion he was leading a party of young missionaries across the Alps. As they slowly ascended the steep slope, he looked back and saw a row of sticks thrust into the glacial snow to mark the one safe path across the otherwise treacherous mountains.

Something about those sticks impressed him, and halting the company of missionaries he gestured toward them and said, "Brethren, there stands the priesthood. They are just common sticks like the rest of us—some of them may even seem to be a little crooked, but the position they hold makes them what they are. If we step aside from the path they mark, we are lost."

I bear witness, my brethren and sisters, fellow students, that in this Church men are as they indeed must be—called of God by prophecy. May we learn in our youth this lesson; it will see us faithful through all of the challenges of our lives. May we learn to follow the Brethren, I pray, in the name of Jesus Christ. Amen.

The Church Is on Course

Gordon B. Hinckley

A few weeks ago, while returning from a regional conference, we had an experience that remains vivid in my mind. As we approached the airport, the captain came on the public address system and spoke in crisp and authoritative tones: "We have an emergency! Please give me your attention. We have an emergency, and the cabin crew will give you instructions. For your own safety, please do what they ask you to do."

The crew sprang into action. This was the moment for which their training had prepared them. Every one of them knew precisely what to do. All utensils were quickly secured in locked containers.

Passengers were shifted to put strong men at each emergency exit.

We were told to remove our glasses, lower our heads, and firmly grasp our ankles.

A woman with a baby seated immediately behind me was crying. Others could be heard sobbing. Everyone knew that this was not just an exercise, but that it was for real and that it was serious.

A man emerged from the flight deck door. He recognized me and stooped down to say, "I am an off-duty pilot. The primary control system has failed, but I think we are going to be all right. They have managed to get the landing gear down and the flaps down."

Strangely, I felt no fear. In many years of flying, I have had experiences when I *have* known fear. But on this occasion, I felt calm. I knew that a redundancy system had been built into the plane to handle just such an emergency and that the crew had been well trained.

I also knew that the effectiveness of that redundancy system would be known in a minute or two when the rubber hit the runway.

Address delivered at general conference, October 1992.

That moment came quickly. To the relief of everyone, the plane touched down smoothly, the landing gear held in place, the engines were reversed, and the aircraft was brought to a stop.

Fire engines were standing nearby. We were towed to the gate. The crew were appropriately applauded, and some of us expressed to the Lord our gratitude.

I have reflected on this experience in terms of the Church of which we are members. The head of the Church is the Lord Jesus Christ. It is His Church. But the earthly head is our prophet. Prophets are men who are endowed with a divine calling. Notwithstanding the divinity of that calling, they are human. They are subject to the problems of mortality.

We love and respect and honor and look to the prophet of this day, President Ezra Taft Benson. He has been a great and gifted leader, a man whose voice has rung out in testimony of this work across the world. He holds all the keys of the priesthood on the earth in this day. But he has reached an age where he cannot do many of the things he once did. This does not detract from his calling as a prophet. But it places limitations upon his physical activities.

We have seen comparable situations in times past. President Wilford Woodruff grew old in office. So did Presidents Heber J. Grant, David O. McKay, Joseph Fielding Smith, and, more recently, Spencer W. Kimball.

Some people, evidently not knowing the system, worry that because of the President's age, the Church faces a crisis. They seem not to realize that there is a backup system. In the very nature of this system, there is always on board a trained crew, if I may so speak of them. They have been thoroughly schooled in Church procedures. More importantly, they also hold the keys of the eternal priesthood of God. They, too, have been put in place by the Lord.

I hope I will not sound presumptuous in reminding you of the unique and tremendous system of redundancy and backup which the Lord has structured into His kingdom so that without interruption it may go forward, meeting any emergency that might arise and handling every contingency with which it is faced. To me, it is a wondrous and constantly renewing miracle.

Yesterday afternoon, we sustained Ezra Taft Benson as prophet, seer, and revelator, and President of The Church of Jesus Christ of Latter-day Saints.

We next sustained his Counselors and then the members of the Council of the Twelve Apostles as prophets, seers, and revelators. With fifteen men so described, endowed, and sustained, one not familiar with the Church might feel that there would be great confusion.

But the Lord's kingdom is one of order. There is no confusion in its leadership.

When a man is ordained to the apostleship and set apart as a member of the Council of the Twelve, he is given the keys of the priesthood of God. Each of the fifteen living men so ordained holds these keys. However, only the President of the Church has the right to exercise them in their fulness. He may delegate the exercise of various of them to one or more of his Brethren. Each has the keys but is authorized to use them only to the degree granted him by the prophet of the Lord.

Such agency has been given by President Benson to his Counselors and to the Twelve according to various responsibilities delegated to them.

According to the revelation of the Lord, "of the Melchizedek Priesthood, three Presiding High Priests, chosen by the body, appointed and ordained to that office, and upheld by the confidence, faith, and prayer of the church, form a quorum of the Presidency of the Church." (D&C 107:22.)

This "Presidency of the High Priesthood, after the order of Melchizedek, have a right to officiate in all the offices in the church." (D&C 107:9.)

Further pertaining to this principle, "it is according to the dignity of his office that he [the president] should preside over the council of the church; and it is his privilege to be assisted by two other presidents, appointed after the same manner that he himself was appointed. And in case of the absence of one or both of those who are appointed to assist him, he has power to preside over the council without an assistant; and in case he himself is absent, the other presidents have power to preside in his stead, both or either of them." (D&C 102:10–11.)

We who serve as Counselors recognize and know the parameters of our authority and our responsibility. Our only desire is to assist and help our leader with the tremendous burdens of his office. The Church is growing large, with more than eight million members now. It is moving across the world. Its program is extensive, complex, and deals with a host of elements. The responsibilities are many and varied.

But I can say that regardless of the circumstances, the work goes forward in an orderly and wonderful way. As it was during the time when President Kimball was ill, we have moved without hesitation when there is well-established policy. Where there is not firmly established policy, we have talked with the President and received his approval before taking action. Let it never be said that there has been any disposition to assume authority or to do anything or say anything or teach anything which might be at variance with the wishes of him who has been put in his place by the Lord. We wish to be his loyal servants. We ask no honor for ourselves. We simply desire to do that which needs to be done, when it needs to be done, and according to policies on which the President has expressed himself.

Now, as I have indicated, there are twelve others on whom have been conferred the keys of the apostleship. They are, as the revelation describes them, "the twelve traveling councilors . . . called to be the Twelve Apostles, or special witnesses of the name of Christ in all the world—thus differing from other officers in the church in the duties of their calling. And they form a quorum, equal in authority and power to the three presidents previously mentioned." (D&C 107:23–24.)

You ask, can there be two separate bodies with equal authority, without confusion? Yes. The Lord has given the answer to this. He has said, "The Twelve are a Traveling Presiding High Council, to officiate in the name of the Lord, under the direction of the Presidency of the Church." (D&C 107:33.)

Concerning this matter, President Joseph F. Smith said:

> The duty of the Twelve Apostles of the Church is to preach the gospel to the world, to send it to the inhabitants of the earth and to bear testimony of Jesus Christ the Son of God, as living witnesses of his divine mission. That is their special calling and they are always under the direction of the Presidency of The Church of Jesus Christ of Latter-day Saints when that presidency is intact, and there is never at the same time two equal heads in the Church—never. The Lord never ordained any such thing, nor designed it. There is always a head in the Church, and if the Presidency of the Church are removed by death or other cause, then the next head of the Church is the Twelve Apostles, until a presidency is again organized of three presiding high priests who have the right to hold the office of First Presidency over the Church. (*Gospel Doctrine,* pp. 177–78.)

Here then, my brothers and sisters, is the remarkable plan of the Lord for the governance of His earthly kingdom. The authority to conduct its affairs was received in this dispensation under the hands of Peter, James, and John, who were ordained by the Lord when He was on the earth. And, as we have seen, there is order in the exercise of that authority.

I wish now to say a few words about the men who are members of the Quorum of the First Presidency and the Quorum of the Twelve Apostles. I know all of those presently serving. I have known all who have filled these chairs in the last sixty years. I am confident that no one of them ever aspired to office. No one campaigned for it. I think none ever thought himself worthy of it. This is a singular and remarkable thing.

In the United States we presently are in a campaign to elect men and women to public office. Millions upon millions of dollars are being spent in the process, with hundreds of thousands working to promote the interests of their favorite candidates.

How different it is with the work of the Lord. No faithful member of this Church would think of applying for ecclesiastical office. Rather, "we believe that a man must be called of God, by prophecy, and by the laying on of hands by those who are in authority, to preach the Gospel and administer in the ordinances thereof." (Articles of Faith 1:5.)

The Lord Himself said of the Twelve whom He selected: "Ye have not chosen me, but I have chosen you, and ordained you." (John 15:16.)

I am confident that no man was ever called as a General Authority of this Church, certainly none I have known, who did not get on his knees, confessing his weaknesses and pleading with the Lord to safeguard him against temptation and any wrongdoing, and asking for the strength and the wisdom and the inspiration to perform well that which he is called upon to do.

I feel that I know my Brethren. I know my leader, President Benson. I have knelt with him in prayer and heard his petitions. I know his heart, and I can testify of its goodness. I know his love and I can testify of its reality. I know his prophetic pleading, and I can testify of its sincerity.

I know my associate in the Presidency, Thomas S. Monson. I know of his strength and desire to advance our Father's kingdom.

I know each of the Twelve in seniority, from President Howard W. Hunter to Elder Richard G. Scott.

These are my associates in this the work of the Almighty. As I said before, none sought this sacred office. Each was called, and in some instances made serious sacrifice in accepting the call. We pray together. We meet in solemn assembly in the house of the Lord. Periodically, we partake together the sacrament of the Lord's Supper and renew our covenants with Him who is our God, taking upon ourselves anew the name of the Lord of whom we are called to testify.

As Brethren, we discuss various problems that come before us. Each man is different. We speak from various backgrounds and experiences. We discuss ways to improve and strengthen the work. At the outset of these discussions, there may be various points of view. But before the discussion is ended, there is total unanimity, else no action is taken. The Lord Himself has declared that such unity is an absolute necessity.

Is this a different kind of government? It is the government of the kingdom of God in the earth. It is unique in its organization. It is a system under which, if one man is unable to function, the work does not stumble or falter. To revert to my earlier illustration, there is a crew aboard with long in-depth training. There is a system, a divinely mandated system, under which there is backup and redundancy to move the work and govern the Church in all the world, regardless of difficulties that may befall any of its leaders.

My Brethren of whom I have spoken are Apostles of the Lord Jesus Christ. I bear witness of their integrity. I bear witness of their faith. I bear witness of the voice of inspiration and revelation in their calls. Every one is a man of tested strength. But the greatest of these strengths lies in the acknowledgment that he must have divinely given direction and blessing if he is to perform acceptably.

Now, in conclusion, do you believe this body of men would ever lead this church astray? Remember whose church this is. It carries the name of the Lord Jesus Christ, who stands as its head. His is the power to remove any found remiss in his duty or in teaching that which is not in harmony with His divine will.

I say for each and all that we have no personal agenda. We have only the Lord's agenda. There are those who criticize when we issue a statement of counsel or warning. Please know that our pleadings are not motivated by any selfish desire. Please know that our warnings are not without substance and reason. Please know that the decisions to speak out on various matters are not reached without deliberation, discussion, and prayer. Please know that our only ambition is to help each of you with your problems, your struggles, your families, your lives.

May I say, by way of personal testimony, that for more than a third of a century I have served as a General Authority of this Church. For twenty of those years, I sat in the circle of the Council of the Twelve. For eleven-plus years, I have served as a Counselor in the First Presidency. I know how the system works. I know that it is divine in its plan and in its authority. I know that there is no desire to teach anything other than what the Lord would have taught. He has said that "the decisions of these quorums, or either of them, are to be made in all righteousness, in holiness, and lowliness of heart, meekness and long suffering, and in faith, and virtue, and knowledge, temperance, patience, godliness, brotherly kindness and charity." (D&C 107:30.) It is in this spirit that we seek to serve.

He further said, concerning that which is taught by His servants, that "those who receive it in faith, and work righteousness, shall receive a crown of eternal life; but those who harden their hearts in unbelief, and reject it, it shall turn to their own condemnation." (D&C 20:14–15.)

When we plead with our people to observe the Sabbath day, to refrain from making it a day of merchandising, we are only repeating that which the Lord declared anciently and which He has confirmed through modern revelation. When we decry gambling, we are only reiterating what has been said by prophets who have gone before. When we urge the strengthening of the foundations of our homes, we are only doing that which will bless the lives of our families. When we urge our people to live the law of tithing, we are only repeating that which the Lord spoke of anciently and confirmed anew in this dispensation for the blessing of His people. When we warn against pornography, immorality, drugs, and such, we are doing only that which prophets have always done.

Ours is the responsibility outlined by Ezekiel: "Son of man, I have made thee a watchman unto the House of Israel: therefore hear the word at my mouth, and give them warning from me." (Ezekiel 3:17.)

We have no selfish desire in any of this, other than the wish that our brethren and sisters will be happy, that peace and love will be found in their homes, that they will be blessed by the power of the Almighty in their various undertakings in righteousness.

I thank all who with uplifted hands and generous hearts sustain us and uphold us in these responsibilities.

May the Almighty bless you, my beloved brethren and sisters. This is the work of God our Eternal Father, who lives and rules in the universe. It is the work of the Lord Jesus Christ, our Savior and our Redeemer, the Living Son of the Living God. It has been established upon the earth with divine authority, with a prophet and other leaders called through the voice of revelation and trained through long years of service. It will never fail. It will continue to succeed.

I make a promise to all who uphold and sustain it, and who strive with faith and prayer to live its principles, that they will be blessed with happiness and accomplishment in this life and joy and eternal life in the world to come. In the name of Jesus Christ, amen.

Bibliography

Aune, David E. *Prophecy in Early Christianity and the Ancient Mediterranean World*. Grand Rapids, MI: William B. Eerdmans Publishing Co., 1983.

Benson, Ezra Taft. "150th Year for Twelve: 'Witnesses to All World.'" *Church News*. January 27, 1985.

_____. *The Teachings of Ezra Taft Benson*. Salt Lake City: Bookcraft, 1988.

Cannon, George Q. *Gospel Truth*. Edited by Jerreld L. Newquist. 2 vols. 1957. Reprint (2 vols. in 1). Salt Lake City: Deseret Book Co., 1987.

_____. "What Is Apostasy?" *Deseret News*. November 3, 1869.

Clark, J. Reuben, Jr. "When Are Church Leaders' Words Entitled to Claim of Scripture?" *Church News*, 31 July 1954.

Doxey, Roy W. *Latter-day Prophets and the Doctrine and Covenants*. 4 vols. Salt Lake City: Deseret Book Co., 1978.

Encyclopedia of Mormonism. Edited by Daniel H. Ludlow. 5 vols. New York: Macmillan Publishing Co., 1992.

Fyans, J. Thomas. "Seventies Began 150 Years Ago." *Church News*. 27 January 1985.

Gentry, Leland H. "A History of the Latter-day Saints in Northern Missouri from 1836 to 1839." Unpublished doctoral dissertation. Brigham Young University, 1965.

Groberg, John H. "There Is the Light." *New Era*. March 1977, pp. 45–46.

Hanks, Richard K. "Eph Hanks, Pioneer Scout." Unpublished master's thesis. Brigham Young University, 1973.

Hill, Gordon Orvill. "A History of Kirtland Camp: Its Initial Purpose and Notable Accomplishments." Unpublished master's thesis. Brigham Young University, 1975.

Hinckley, Gordon B. "In . . . Counsellors There Is Safety." *Ensign*. November 1990.

Journal of Discourses. 26 vols. Liverpool: F. D. Richards and Sons, 1851–86.

Kimball, Spencer W. "In the World, but Not of It." *Speeches of the Year*. Provo: BYU, 14 May 1968.

———. *The Teachings of Spencer W. Kimball*. Edited by Edward L. Kimball. Salt Lake City: Bookcraft, 1982.

———. "That You May Not Be Deceived." *Speeches of the Year*. Provo: BYU, 11 November 1959.

Lee, Harold B. "Be Loyal to the Royal Within You." *Speeches of the Year*. Provo: BYU, 11 September 1973.

———. "Be Secure in the Gospel of Jesus Christ." *Speeches of the Year*. Provo: BYU, 11 February 1958.

———. *Stand Ye in Holy Places*. Salt Lake City: Deseret Book Co., 1974.

Maxwell, Neal A. *All These Things Shall Give Thee Experience*. Salt Lake City: Deseret Book Co., 1979.

———. *Things As They Really Are*. Salt Lake City: Deseret Book Co., 1978.

Miller, David E. *Hole-in-the-Rock*. Salt Lake City: University of Utah Press, 1966.

McConkie, Bruce R. *A New Witness for the Articles of Faith*. Salt Lake City: Deseret Book Co., 1985.

———. "Are the General Authorities Human?" Typescript of unpublished address given at the Institute Forum at the University of Utah Institute of Religion, 28 October 1966.

———. *Mormon Doctrine*. 2nd ed. Salt Lake City: Bookcraft, 1966.

———. "Succession in the Presidency." *Speeches of the Year*. Provo: BYU, 8 January 1974.

———. "The Keys of the Kingdom." *Ensign*. May 1983.

———. *The Mortal Messiah*. 4 vols. Salt Lake City: Deseret Book Co., 1979–81.

———. "This Generation Shall Have My Word Through You." *Ensign*. June 1980.

Moyle, Henry D. "Beware of Temptation." *Speeches of the Year*. Provo: BYU, 6 January 1963.

Napier, B. N. "Prophet, Prophetism." *Interpreter's Dictionary of the Bible*. 5 vols. Nashville: Abingdon Press, 1962.

Nelson, Russell M. "Listen to Learn." *Ensign*. May 1991.

Oaks, Dallin H. "Criticism." *Ensign*. February 1987.

———. "Our Strengths Can Become Our Downfall." Fireside Address delivered at Brigham Young University, Provo, 7 June 1992.

_____. *The Lord's Way*. Salt Lake City: Deseret Book Co., 1991.

Packer, Boyd K. "A Dedication—To Faith." *Speeches of the Year*. Provo: BYU, 29 April 1969.

_____. "Follow the Brethren." *That All May Be Edified*. Salt Lake City: Bookcraft, 1982.

_____. "I Say Unto You, Be One." *Speeches of the Year*. Provo: BYU, 12 February 1991.

_____. "It Is the Position That Counts." *New Era*. June 1977.

Petersen, Mark E. *Why the Religious Life*. Salt Lake City: Deseret Book Co., 1966.

Smith, Joseph. *History of the Church*. 7 vols. 2nd ed. Edited by B. H. Roberts. Salt Lake City: The Church of Jesus Christ of Latter-day Saints, 1932–51.

_____. *Teachings of the Prophet Joseph Smith*. Selected by Joseph Fielding Smith. Salt Lake City: Deseret Book Co., 1938.

Smith, Joseph F. *Gospel Doctrine*. Salt Lake City: Deseret Book Co., 1939.

Smith, Joseph Fielding. *Church History and Modern Revelation*. 2 vols. Salt Lake City: Deseret Book Co., 1953.

_____. *Doctrines of Salvation*. 3 vols. Compiled by Bruce R. McConkie. Salt Lake City: Bookcraft, 1954–56.

_____. "The First Presidency and the Council of the Twelve." *Improvement Era*. November 1966.

Taylor, John. *The Gospel Kingdom*. Selected by G. Homer Durham. Salt Lake City: Bookcraft, 1943.

Tanner, N. Eldon. "We Thank Thee, O God, for a Prophet to Guide Us in These Latter Days." *Ensign*. March 1975.

Whitney, Orson F. *Saturday Night Thoughts*. Salt Lake City: Deseret Book Co., 1921.

Widtsoe, John A. *Evidences and Reconciliations*. (3 vols. in 1). Arranged by G. Homer Durham. Salt Lake City: Bookcraft, 1960.

Woodruff, Wilford. *Discourses of Wilford Woodruff*. Selected by G. Homer Durham. Salt Lake City: Bookcraft, 1946.

_____. *Pamphlet*. 1888. In LDS Church Historian's Archives.

Young, Brigham. *Manuscript History*, 3 May 1846. In LDS Church Historian's Archives.

Index